Gay Men in Modern Southern Literature

PETER LANG
New York • Washington, D.C./Baltimore • Bern
Frankfurt am Main • Berlin • Brussels • Vienna • Oxford

William Mark Poteet

Gay Men in Modern Southern Literature

Ritual, Initiation, & the Construction of Masculinity

PETER LANG
New York • Washington, D.C./Baltimore • Bern
Frankfurt am Main • Berlin • Brussels • Vienna • Oxford

Library of Congress Cataloging-in-Publication Data

Poteet, William Mark.
Gay men in modern southern literature: ritual, initiation, and the construction of masculinity / William Mark Poteet.
p. cm.
Includes bibliographical references.
1. American literature—Southern States—History and criticism.
2. Homosexuality and literature—Southern States—History—20th century.
3. Williams, Tennessee, 1911–1983—Criticism and interpretation.
4. Nelson, Charles, 1942– —Criticism and interpretation.
5. Price, Reynolds, 1933– —Criticism and interpretation. 6. Gay men in literature. 7. Masculinity in literature. 8. Initiation rites in literature.
9. Literature and society—Southern States—History—20th century.
10. Southern States—Social life and customs—1865– I. Title.
PS261.P68 810.9'3538—dc22 2006022447
ISBN 0-8204-8691-4

Bibliographic information published by **Die Deutsche Bibliothek.**
Die Deutsche Bibliothek lists this publication in the "Deutsche Nationalbibliografie"; detailed bibliographic data is available on the Internet at http://dnb.ddb.de/.

29 Broadway, New York, NY 10006
www.peterlang.com

to Keith E. Donnelly

Table of Contents

⁂ Acknowledgments

I would like to thank several people for making this book possible. I am particularly grateful to Dr. Ronald Emerick, whose assistance and encouragement, from beginning to end, was invaluable. The following individuals also gave me guidance and advice: Dr. Martha Bower, Dr. Mike Sell, John Van Kirk, and Dr. Nancy Lang.

I would also like to thank my family for their unwavering support during all of my endeavors.

⁂ Introduction

The modern American South and its literature, to current audiences, probably seems an unusual and unlikely location for an examination of homosexuality, masculinity, and ritual initiation. The post–Civil War South has always suffered from a tragic, and often comic, misunderstanding by other parts of the country. The South is: prejudiced, poor, ignorant, overly religious, sexist, homophobic, etc. Of course, as with any sweeping generalizations, all of the above are not true, not in any inclusive, essentialist way. And because this book is a study of homosexuality and masculinity in Southern literature, it stands to reason that just *how* the South perceives the two is a paramount question to be answered. Literature, in a large part, can help answer this question. Homosexuality is no more or less common in the South than in other parts of the country; the major difference is how Southerners deal with homosexuality. The South has an ambivalent penchant for both celebrating and reproving difference, as opposed to hiding it away. A cursory reading of the last century of Southern literature reveals a plethora of "different" characters, usually a family member who is always considered as much and important a part of the family as the "normal" members. Just read Eudora Welty or Carson McCullers or Flannery O'Connor or William Faulkner. It is basically this simple—in the South you don't put your "touched" great aunt in a home somewhere; you put her out on the front porch, give her a pretty hat, and ask her advice, which usually comes from an unexpected angle and turns out to be pretty good. Not to equate homosexuality with being "touched," just to equate it with being "different" and recognized, if not particularly socially acceptable. Everybody in the South has a gay uncle—everybody. Why is this Southern attitude toward homosexuality important? The importance lies in the fact that the societal attitudes toward homosexuality in the South have, without doubt, highly influenced its literature.

The South's cultural ambivalence toward difference, demonstrated in the tension and anxiety between acceptance and denial, has had a profound effect on its gay literature. Southern gay authors have had to form strategies of cultural approach to their writing and create alternate modes of representation for a subject as socially provocative as homosexuality. A different masculinity, a gay masculinity, uses the concept of ritual to express itself for the various writers considered here, and ritual is created and represented by complexly disparate methods: the subtleties of memory and staging, the boldness of forced initiation, and the invocation of metaphysics.

This book is a study of how traditional American Southern cultural traits inform the concepts of masculinity, initiation, and homosexuality in modern literature written by three very different Southern writers: Tennessee Williams, Charles Nelson, and Reynolds Price. Why the modern South? Why masculinity and initiation? Why these three writers? Williams and Nelson are both "out" gay writers; whereas, Price has never discussed his sexual orientation publically, though his fiction contains some of the most well-developed and provocative gay characters in recent Southern writing. It is interesting, and somewhat puzzling, that several gay (and some straight) men writing in the modern South have been so willing to write about homosexuality as a topic, often putting themselves at literary odds with the rest of the country. One thinks of post–World War II writers such as Tennessee Williams, Truman Capote, and Reynolds Price, writers whose gay-themed works span the genres—from plays to short stories and poetry, essays to novels. Of course recent literary critics have considered this point also, albeit somewhat briefly and oftentimes perfunctorily. As little as twenty-five years ago, many critics of gay Southern literature were still couching their opinions in mostly subtle, yet sometimes bold, homophobic discourse.

In a 1977 essay on Brick Pollitt's emotional detachment in Tennessee Williams' play *Cat on a Hot Tin Roof*, Charles E. May refuses to connect

Brick's inertia with confusion and anxiety over his sexual orientation. Rather, May believes that Brick's difficulties stem from metaphysical, and thus loftier, confusion, and that his problem is, "a more basic and pervasive one for which his sexual dilemma is merely a symbolic objectification."[1] While Brick's emotional turmoil may, in fact, be part of a greater metaphysical dilemma, his homosexuality is hardly symbolic, and to consider it so is a critical attempt to elide it and resist acknowledging its existence. A more recent example of this type of resistant critical approach to gay Southern literature appears in a 1997 essay by Michael Hogan. In a study of five of Reynolds Price's short stories, Hogan argues that the texts should be read from a purely homosocial, as opposed to homosexual, theoretical standpoint. He states, "it seems rather unproductive to argue for some quasi-queer' status for these stories." And just as Charles E. May managed to do with Williams' gay characters twenty years prior, Hogan asserts, "while each of these stories centers upon male relationships, to read them as fraught with homoerotic frenzy is to misread them."[2] The stories that Hogan refers to can, indeed, be read in a simple homosocial context, as a way of mitigating their gay themes, but they can also easily be read from a gay perspective, one that moves beyond the homosocial toward a more positive light. A masculinity theoretical approach to the study of modern gay-written Southern literature can help achieve a way to move beyond current critical trends, which tend to be generated from two often disparate positions.

A great amount of the critical work done today on modern Southern writing, though highly influenced by poststructuralist dynamics, still seems to be preoccupied with the sometimes facile concept of "Southerness"—the same concept that fueled much of the New Critical and Agrarian schools of thought begun in the 1930s. One thinks of critics such as Allen Tate and Cleanth Brooks; one thinks of authors such as Robert Penn Warren and William Faulkner. In the introduction to *Southern Literature and Literary Theory*, editor Jefferson Humphries constructs a powerful argument for evolving contemporary Southern literary criticism into a new "amalgam" with more recent European models of critical inquiry. Humphries states, "for me, the fusion of Southern studies with European modes of close reading represents the final stage of escape from the organic nationalism of the Old South."[3] Because modern gay and lesbian studies can be viewed as extensions of those "European modes of close reading," it would seem to follow logically that those gender/sexual-orientation approaches to modern Southern writing would help, in a large part, to create the "fusion" that Humphries posits. However, these critical stances seem to be prone to exclusivity; that is, they often examine the gender/sexuality issues in a text, while ignoring its "Southerness"—hardly aiming toward the direction of the "fusion" that Humphries envisions for the future of modern Southern literary theory. Masculinity theory can, in part, help bridge this intellectual "gap" between traditional Southern literary criticism and gay criticism by bringing both dynamics into play and observing how they work together; perhaps a type of theoretical symbiosis is a more reachable and appropriate goal than fusion.

Since its inception, primarily in the fields of sociology and psychology in the 1970s, masculinity studies has had an apologetic tone. The most common cause for this need to mitigate is often found in the introductions of books or opening paragraphs of essays. A prime example can be found in Peter Middleton's *The Inward Gaze: Masculinity and Subjectivity in Modern Culture*, when he states, "any man writing about men and masculinity quickly realizes that this is a most self-conscious project, an almost self-consuming process in which the discourse he uses constantly asks itself if its productions are yet more versions of masculine self-promotion."[4] The persistent, nagging question in masculinity theory almost always comes down to this: Isn't it just another way to reassert and extend the existing patriarchy through cleverly masked masculine hegemonic discourse? Middleton addresses this concern when he argues:

> We need to recognize that it may sometimes be possible to read men's texts as transfigurative proposals as well as exposures of ideology, because at times men's texts are trying to initiate processes which require further development. Such a project would

> include the rereading of gay writers and their placement at the centre of new literary histories.[5]

This book represents the beginning of just such a project, and a part of its regional approach, its Southern slant, to literature and masculinity theory is meant to be, to a certain degree, protective, to maintain a focus in an effort to avoid grossly essentializing experience and identity. Masculinity theorist Michael S. Kimmel makes a point that further supports my purposes: "The challenge to the hegemonic definition of masculinity came from men whose masculinity was cast as deviant: men of color, gay men, and ethnic men. We understand now that we cannot speak of masculinity' as a singular term, but must examine *masculinities*: the ways in which different men construct different versions of masculinity."[6] Since texts are fundamentally imbued with culture, Southern writers are obsessed with writing about their culture and various societies, primarily as a way to preserve them, and gay male southern writers are, and have been in the past, bold and prolific in their production of gay-themed works for the very same reason.

The South's obsession with the past and history and with the family and generations makes it a location where the concepts of ritual and initiation are still important and recognized elements of everyday life. There is a decided observance of traditional rituals in the South that can be seen to this day. It is not unusual to be driving in some rural Tennessee county and see a group of people congregated on a river bank, while in the river a preacher and a member of the congregation, both dressed in long white robes, participate in the ancient ritual of baptism, metaphorically, as the old Baptist hymn states, being "washed in the blood." Male initiation rituals are also common, as evidenced by the rather brutal and barbaric deer hunting traditions of the rural South, which remains today a hunting and gun culture. When a young man kills his first deer, the older male members of the hunting party "blood" him, that is, they drain blood from the newly killed deer and rub it on the young man's face, arms, and hands. It is not uncommon or unusual for the young hunter to also drink a small cup of the deer's blood—in 2006. Even high school and college sports, with their secretive and usually localized male initiation rituals, also figure into the mix. All of the above-mentioned rituals of male initiation are not, of course, particular to the South; however, they are practiced more commonly and are imbued with much more reverence and tradition there than in other parts of the United States. Interestingly, ritual and initiation, especially coming-of-age initiation for males, is common in all three of the primary "oral culture" groups in the United States, groups that have maintained a storytelling tradition that has also translated to their literatures. The rural South, urban Jewish communities, and Native American tribes all still practice very old and respected rituals, with a high emphasis, perhaps sexist, on male initiation into the groups. The connection among these groups, from oral tradition to ritual male initiation, is fertile ground for further sociological study.

In this examination of modern Southern literature written by gay men I utilize, in part, Michael Moon's theory of redundant gay initiation (discussed in detail here in chapter one), outlined in his book, *A Small Boy and Others: Imitation and Initiation in American Culture from Henry James to Andy Warhol* (1998). Moon's theory posits that many gay men have the need to witness repeated sexual acts performed by strangers, and that this need is a result of their lack of traditional heterosexual sexual initiation, what he refers to as "common rites of passage," usually found in such masculine spheres as sports and the military.[7] And while there is no doubt that institutions such as organized sports and the military have a high percentage of gay men in their respective ranks, these men, most often "closeted," either do not or grudgingly participate in heterosexual male initiation rituals. By their very hidden identities, gay men in these spheres cannot conduct their own such rituals, so Moon argues that they replace these organized, recognized, and more respected heterosexual rituals with one of their own creation, the repeated witnessing of homosexual acts performed by other men. As with all rituals, there is a literal and figurative meaning here, so in the works of literature considered in this study, I have identified several foms of "witnessing," including specular witnessing by both the audience and the characters on stage in the plays of

Tennessee Williams, literal witnessing of male sexual acts in the bawdy and picaresque military fiction of Charles Nelson, and a much more subtle "witnessing" of homosexual male sexuality in the concept of a closed community of desire among men in the works of Reynolds Price.

Oddly, for the vast quantity of critical writing on Tennessee Williams, there is somewhat of a dearth of serious consideration of homosexuality in his plays, and until recently what did exist was mostly vitriolic in tone. A brief, but nonetheless important, case in point is *Tennessee Williams: A Tribute* (1977), edited by Jac Tharpe, a voluminous collection of the "standard" Williams critical essays written over a twenty-five-year period. Of the fifty-three included essays, written mostly by prominent Williams scholars, only one deals primarily with homosexuality in the plays. Of course, since the advent of gay studies, scholars have reread Williams from a different critical viewpoint, but even these rereadings can prove problematic. The most common of these critical problems is the fact that many critics, even gay and queer theorists, oftentimes try to divorce the plays and their writer from historical context, thus creating examinations that become primarily concerned with the homosocial and homophobic on stage and in Williams' own life. This critical standpoint is beginning to change, as evidenced by such writers as Dean Shackelford writing about two contemporary Williams critics, John Clum and Nicholas deJongh: "no American writer who wished to establish a reputation with a widespread audience could come out' in public without facing censure or even rejection as an artist, a fact which critics John Clum and Nicholas deJongh seem to ignore when considering the elements of the closet in Williams' plays."[8] Masculinity theory, with its awareness of gender/identity construction dynamics, serves as one method of effectively addressing this conflict in Tennessee Williams gay scholarship.

Reynolds Price is, according to many important literary critics, probably the finest living Southern writer today; however, Price remains surprisingly under criticized. The only major works of criticism dedicated solely to Reynolds Price are common academic venues for critical studies of little known authors. This point alone generates enough speculation about Price's writing to make him a major part of the subject of a new scholarly work. Price's oeuvre not only represents the highest literary merit; he is also incredibly prolific in all genres. Among the few Price critics, there has been conjecture about this academic discrepancy. Constance Rooke attributes Price's lack of critical and popular notice to his unique writing style:

> His style is highly pronounced, unusual, and quite often difficult. The language generally is highly charged, and the sentences are elaborate, the metaphors are often startling, and the precise description of all action (whether physical or emotional) often slows us down.[9]

Price does write with what could be called a "profound" literary voice, greatly influenced by Biblical narratives and Milton. He is, in his own right, one of the most well respected Milton scholars in the country, having taught Milton and Renaissance literature at Duke University for over forty years. James A. Schiff, one of the other major Price critics, agrees with Constance Rooke's views about lack of critical studies of Price, but he elaborates:

> Price's career has spanned an era in American literature in which academia has been generally more receptive to writing which is clever, bleak, and postmodern—the antithesis of Price's work.…Though his work is often bold and original, Price is a traditionalist in regard to narrative technique, theme, and subject matter.[10]

Broadly speaking, both Rooke and Schiff are correct in their assertions; Price can be read as a traditionalist in current American letters. However, several aspects of his style and subjects speak to a more subtle type of modern complexity in his prose. In most of his fiction, Price elegantly blends genres, creating a narrative of chronological action punctuated with vivid dreams, long poems, and narrative letters. Price's rather bold, frequent, and unusual treatment of homosexuality in his fiction is particularly intriguing, hardly the type of subject matter or theme that would produce the term "traditionalist." Indeed, Price, a highly spiritual man who has translated several biblical texts and written numerous religious themed books and articles, is often considered one of America's most important Christian writers, creating an interesting paradox. Generally, Price's literary critics do deal with homosexuality in his fiction, because it is almost always such an important and intricately woven element to the story, but like Tennessee Williams' critics, they tend to be more concerned with his "Southerness" and stylistic techniques. Recent, newer approaches to gay subjectivity and masculinity, tools that were not available to the early Price critics such as Rooke, can go a long way in helping better explicate the homosexuality "conundrum" Price's work seems always to present to critics. Though the final installment in *A Great Circle*, Price's family saga trilogy, *The Promise of Rest* (1995), deals primarily with gay relationships, it nevertheless generates numerous questions best dealt with by inquiry predicated not just in gay theory, but also in new concepts about the nature of masculine subjectivity.

The mysterious Charles Nelson, something of a gay version of Thomas Pynchon or J.D. Salinger, has only two novels to his credit: *The Boy Who Picked the Bullets Up* (1981) and *Panthers in the Skins of Men* (1989). Both novels, the latter a sequel, concern the adventures of Kurt Strom, a gay navy medic and ex-professional baseball player. The first is set mainly in Vietnam from 1966 to 1967, and the second is set in the United States in 1968, after Kurt returns home from military duty. *The Boy Who Picked the Bullets Up* (both novels' titles are lines from Rimbaud poems) is considered an underground classic of American gay literature. It often appears, rather dichotomously, on bibliographies for both gay fiction and Vietnam War fiction. One of the most vexing problems, when writing about Nelson, is the utter lack of information about him. He is a Southern writer, having grown up in Louisiana, and there is an unmistakable Southern "flavor" to his prose, from the language to the comedy. Also, *The Boy Who Picked the Bullets Up* is written in epistolary form—all letters written by Kurt, no answers. Though not necessarily distinct to Southern writing, letters almost always seem to play an important or pivotal role in the narrative structure of Southern fiction, reflecting the inbred Southern penchant for letter writing and story telling. Nelson's protagonist, Kurt Strom, is obsessed with two things, gay sexual conquest and masculinity. The works are both patently written in the picaresque tradition, with a ribald main character and several episodic adventures; however, they can also be read as a psychologically complex modern version of Choderlos de Laclos's eighteenth-century French classic, *Les Liasions Dangereuses.* As with de Laclos's dissolute courtiers, Nelson's characters are playing very sophisticated erotic games here, and most of them are predicated on the sexual pursuit of some avatar of traditional masculinity. These games, and their players, present numerous theoretical and literary complexities.

Another element that makes Charles Nelson's fiction interesting and important as a topic of examination is the fact that there is *no* literary criticism on his writing. Nelson's prose style is sophisticated and lively, his subject matter complex, and his themes important, so the lack of critical writing on his work is not reflected by any lack of literary merit on the writer's part. There are two major reasons for the absence of Nelson from academic writing. First, the blatant sexual content of the novels—they are raw and graphic, one of the primary dynamics that seems always to blur that imaginary line between pornography and erotica, or what critic Maurice Charney more properly terms "sexual fiction." Second, Nelson's lack of literary production and coyness about his identity have probably presented problems that previous writers were just not willing to address.

There are, of course, other prominent gay male Southern writers who merit further study in the future. One who comes directly to mind is Truman Capote. Tennessee Williams, world-renowned playwright, represents the mainstream of modern Southern literature, while Reynolds Price, though highly respected, represents a more insular, literary figure. Charles Nelson, with his raucous style and subject matter, represents the fringe of Southern letters. Capote falls somewhere in the middle of all of these designations. With Capote's most "gay" work, *Answered Prayers* (1988), there are numerous bibliographical problems. The book was published posthumously, edited haphazardly, shows signs of being highly abridged, and stands as a flawed, perhaps not completely original, text. Its provenance as a manuscript has always been in question. However, Capote, much like Price, also exists in a position of fruitful potential examination.

The theoretical approach used in this study of modern gay-written Southern literature, masculinity theory, though still in the developmental stage when related to literary texts, is quickly gaining a foothold in the academy. Its usage in film theory and cultural studies is common and standard, but masculinity theory is also beginning to have more of an impact on literary criticism than it has in the past. This fact is evidenced by such books as Peter Middleton's *The Inward Gaze: Masculinity and Subjectivity in Modern Culture* (1992), which addresses several literary texts, and Robert Vorlicky's *Act Like a Man: Challenging Masculinities in American Drama* (1995). One of the most interesting aspects of masculinity theory is how it has influenced both popular and trade publications for the past decade. Michelangelo Signorile's in-depth social study of masculinity and gay men, *Life Outside: The Signorile Report on Gay Men: Sex, Drugs, and the Passages of Life* (1997), makes a surprisingly everyday usage of complex theoretical concepts to help gay men understand the many elements of its title better. Steven Zeeland's series of books on gay men, masculinity, and the military are anecdotal, theoretical, and carefully crafted, so much so that Zeeland's books are praised and recommended by such influential gender theorists, queer theorists, and masculinity theorists as Judith Butler, Frank Browning, and Susan Faludi. Brian Pronger, a physical education professor at the University of Toronto, has to his credit an insightful book entitled *The Arena of Masculinity: Sports, Homosexuality, and the Meaning of Sex* (1990), which manages to balance a well-written and approachable text with complex cultural theories, from Heidegger to Foucault.

Masculinity theory and gay criticism represent a more appropriate focus of examination of Southern-ness and culture as initiation than a more deconstructive, queer approach to the subject. The terms "masculine" and "gay" constitute a more stable theoretical position, which better lends itself to a study of regional identity. Though this concept at first appears "essentialist" and limiting, current poststructuralist theory allows for a type of "strategic" essentialism specifically geared to a limited, local, political, or historic topic. Gay criticism involves an inherent resistance to homophobia and heterosexism, and both of these concepts, because of the South's rigid and unrelenting social rules of masculinity, inform a critical look at Southern-ness and homosexuality. Queer theory, predicated in a large part on deconstructing stable identities and redefining subjectivities, must always be vigilant of and face the risk of "playing back" into the hands of traditional masculine, patriarchal, and heteronormative dynamics. Because of these theoretical pitfalls of a queer theory approach to regional masculinity and homosexuality, gay criticism, tempered by "strategic" essentialism, becomes a more logical theoretical model.

The primary purpose of a work based on masculinity theory and addressing such a select group as modern gay male Southern authors represents an ongoing process of "pushing" gay and lesbian studies past some of the primary locations in which they seem to have been "stuck" for a very long time, particularly that of the oftentimes facile, analogous comparisons to race and class. Not that critical/theoretical work in that field was not important at one time—it was, but it has been done. Hopefully, this critical examination can be part of the ongoing project of modernizing Southern literary criticism, to create what Middleton referred to above as a "transfigurative proposal," to help align it with more current theoretical trends, and to *move* it also—beyond the oppressive shadows of monumental authors such as William Faulkner and canonical critics such as Louis D. Rubin, Jr. and Lewis P. Simpson. Many gay Southern men have bravely written about what it is like to be homosexual, different, the outsider, in a culture that thrives on tradition and masculinity, the very concepts that homosexuality seems to rub against. In all that literary and cultural friction there exists great meaning.

❋ CHAPTER 1

The Cell That Burns the Hardest: Masculinity, Initiation, and Memory in the Plays of Tennessee Williams

> "Many Americans would die naked in the middle of the road before they'd tell you what's hurt them most. But a born Southerner will show you the cell in their heart that burns the hardest. They'll hold it out to you in their bare right hand."
> — Reynolds Price, *The Tongues of Angels*

A cursory reading of the above quotation, from North Carolina writer Reynolds Price, might suggest that Southerners feel a constant need to confess, to share personal troubles both in their lives and their literature. Many contemporary historians and sociologists of Southern culture recognize this supposed need for confession, and usually attribute it to a collective, cultural sense of guilt. In *The Burden of Southern History*, noted historian C. Vann Woodward argues, rather broadly and bluntly, that after the Civil War, "the South's preoccupation was with guilt."[1] As far as Southern literature is concerned, many modern critics feel that "the predominant mode of Southern fiction is *apologia*, [which] acknowledges the collective guilt of Southern writers over the subjugation of blacks in antebellum society."[2] But as Price's quotation indicates, this type of confession has less to do with an admission of misdeeds and faults or a hope for absolution, and more to do with sharing, the seemingly plaintive yet inviting offer of the "bare right hand." That bare right hand does not simply display the burdens, the troubles, the inter-workings of a single human heart, it also begs to be taken and clasped. Confession extends beyond an admission of guilt, which may well be justified, to its more complex and layered meaning, an acknowledgment of a belief or a creed. The act of sharing becomes more important than the act of confessing, and the acknowledgment of a belief or a creed speaks to the ritual involved in becoming part of something—an initiation.

Though Price's quotation is not gender specific, it is generated from his position as a male Southern writer, and it relates to not only a Southern disposition for constant confession and sharing but also to what Michael Moon explains as a type of gay initiation predicated on repetition. In *A Small Boy and Others: Imitation and Initiation in American Culture from Henry James to Andy Warhol*, Moon outlines a theory of gay and queer representations based on a combination of mimetic disorientation and repetitive acts of initiation. In this work, Moon refers to gay S-M writer John Preston's article, "The Theatre of Sexual Initiation," as the basis for his ideas on how and why gay men's identities are, in a large part, created by ritual and redundant initiation. Preston's article details the activities of gay men in a 1970s New York City sex club, *The Mineshaft*.[3] He maintains that the need gay men have to witness repeated sexual acts performed by strangers is a result of their lack of traditional heterosexual sexual initiation, what he refers to as "common rites of passage," usually found in such masculine spheres as sports and the military. As Moon points out:

> Iterability is, of course, a crucial feature of imitation, but it is not ordinarily thought of as a primary feature of initiation. Seeing repetition as a feature of "the theater of initiation" may help one begin to see how imitation and initiation are more closely related than they are more ordinarily considered to be. Many narratives of queer desire suggest that this may be the case.[4]

A theory of redundant initiation runs counter to most mythological and symbolic beliefs in which these rites are viewed as a teleological process wherein the initiate ultimately and successfully *becomes*. Judith J. Thompson demonstrates that in the plays of Tennessee Williams these "rituals of initiation" almost always fail or lack proper completion.[5] They must be constantly reenacted. This concept of a theater of initiation predicated on repetition suggests that seeing and imitating are its prime dynamics; however, there are more subtle and implied methods of representing and depicting gay desire through redundancy and initiation on the stage of Tennessee Williams.

When people think of dramatic representations of the twentieth-century American South, they almost automatically bring to mind Tennessee Williams, but as Kimball King points out, "although many consider Tennessee Williams to be this century's foremost playwright, surprisingly little has been said about his debt to Southern literary conventions or his regional bias."[6] In fact, much more has been said, and written, by literary critics about Williams' treatment of homosexuality in his plays. King fails to consider that complicated and intricate representations of male homosexuality might just qualify as "Southern literary conventions" and "regional bias," especially in Williams' case. A high probability exists that most modern American audiences' (of the baby boomer generation, at least) first exposure to homosexuality as a literary topic (and trope) came from seeing either a stage production or a film version of a Tennessee Williams play. Whether it was *A Streetcar Named Desire* (1947), *Cat on a Hot Tin Roof* (1955), or *Suddenly Last Summer* (1958), and whether or not the viewer wanted to see them, gay characters were always present, even if they existed just as a memory. Few literary critics have noted this obvious absence, and when they do it is often read as reluctance on Williams' part as a playwright. In a 1968 essay entitled "What Tennessee Williams Didn't Write," about absent/missing gay characters in the plays, James T. Nardin speculates that, "perhaps Mr. Williams himself is sufficiently Puritan to be unable to put the most repulsive of his people and scenes before us."[7] As recently as 1985, in an American literature anthology used by college students, the introduction to Williams' classic play, *The Glass Menagerie*, (1945) lists a litany of "depravities" that the playwright first brought to the American stage: "murder, rape, castration, drug addiction, homosexuality, alcoholism, fetishism, nymphomania, even cannibalism."[8] It is hardly surprising that Williams chose to relegate his gay characters to dramatic memory. As Dean Shackelford points out when contextualizing Williams with the historical period of his greatest success, the late 1940s through the early 1960s, "no American writer who wished to establish a reputation with a widespread audience could come out' in public without facing censure or even rejection as an artist...."[9] If Williams had written his gay characters actually to appear on stage, he would have, in essence, "come out," especially if they were represented in any type of positive or normal manner. Therefore, Williams devised a method, either consciously or unconsciously, of incorporating gay characters into his major works of the period; he has on stage characters reconstruct the absent gay men from memory, and they become intrinsically important to the dramatic action of the plays.

In Tennessee Williams' first successful work, *The Glass Menagerie* (1945), the character Tom Wingfield steps onto the stage, and in his introductory monologue tells the audience that "the play is memory."[10] In the three plays considered here, Williams creates a fusion between his concept of the theater of memory and the theater of initiation. Characters in each play are haunted by relentless memories of the missing gay characters, and these unforgiving recollections are of initiatory and ritualistic homosexual acts.

With his psychologically probing dialog and complexly informative stage directions, Tennessee Williams offers the viewer/reader a way into the subjective natures of both female and male characters; however, a close critical reading of these three plays illustrates a tension between male and female memory and character reconstruction. This tension is generated, in part, by the order in which the plays were written, an order that is telling and inextricably linked to the notions of gay masculinity, memory, and initiation. In the first play, *A Streetcar Named Desire,* Allan, Blanche DuBois's dead gay husband, is recreated from memory by female characters alone, Blanche and her sister Stella. No man in the play remembers Allan. *Cat on a Hot Tin Roof,* the second of the plays, presents three characters reconstructing the dead gay friend; Maggie, Brick, and Big Daddy all have varying memories of Skipper. In the third play, *Suddenly Last Summer,* the dead gay character, Sebastian, is recreated from memory, once again, by female characters alone, his cousin

Catharine and his mother Violet; no men in the play remember Sebastian. In all of these plays certain characters are actively competing for the memory reconstruction of an absent gay man, but only in *Cat on a Hot Tin Roof* do men compete in this process. Why? In *A Streetcar Named Desire*, Tennessee Williams originally determined this method of presenting gay characters on the stage, his fused theaters of initiation and memory. This technique proved to be dramatically effective, so he repeated it in *Cat on a Hot Tin Roof*, only to be confronted with the daunting, powerful, and conflicting masculine subjectivities of Brick and Big Daddy, one of the primary reasons that the play constantly causes problems and questions for literary critics. With *Suddenly Last Summer*, Williams returned to missing gay men reconstructed entirely by female memory, as if in *Cat on a Hot Tin Roof* he had walked a little too close to the fire of his own perceptions of homosexuality, masculinity, and memory. When fused, the theaters of memory and initiation produce a revelatory stage for characters, author, and viewer.

A Streetcar Named Desire

> "All stories comprise within themselves the ghosts of the alternative stories they are trying to suppress."
>
> —Alan Sinfield, *Cultural Politics—Queer Readings*

"I have always depended on the kindness of strangers." Blanche DuBois's emblematic words from *A Streetcar Named Desire* have become ubiquitous in American culture.[11] Whether in one of the many film versions or stage productions of the play, most people are familiar with the story of Blanche, the faded Southern belle, displaced from her family's Mississippi plantation and forced to travel to New Orleans' French Quarter and live with her sister Stella and brother-in-law Stanley Kowalski. Considered by many to be one of the greatest works of American drama, the play is most often examined as a clashing of individuals and worlds: Blanche represents the effete, Romantic antebellum South, while her brother-in-law Stanley, the Polish American worker, represents the new middle-class South—coarse and modern, practical and brutal. However, as Bert Cardullo astutely notes:

> Blanche's struggle throughout *Streetcar* is surely more with herself than with Stanley. Her *conflict* with him may be inevitable from the moment she enters his home, given their opposing views of life and each's claim to Stella. The inevitability of her doom, however, springs not from the character of this conflict but from her rejection of Allan Grey on the dance floor of Moon Lake Casino many years before.[12]

Blanche's rejection of Allan, her young husband, stems from her accidentally seeing him involved in a sexual act with an older man, and their confrontation on the dance floor leads to Allan committing suicide.

Of course, as a female character Blanche is not an active participant in the theater of homosexual male initiation; however, she is the source of the theater of memory which enables the scene to be ritualistically repeated and reinforced. She becomes a fictive conduit through which the playwright can transmit the subtextual gay theatrical rite. Williams juxtaposes Blanche's recall of the gay sex scene with her viewing of the hypermasculine and homosocial interaction of Stanley and his macho poker-playing friends. This is evidenced by the fact that both tableaux, Allan's sexual encounter and its consequences and Stanley's poker game(s), are remembered/enacted twice in the play. In her study of memory in *Streetcar,* Judith J. Thompson states that

> although the entire pattern of the story—from its initially romantic expectations to its subsequent disillusionment and ultimately destructive consequences—reoccurs again and again, it is particularly that one act of the cruel exposure, humiliation, and fatal rejection of her idealized young husband for his sexual transgression that haunts the guilt-ridden Blanche; thus, it is reenacted in a retributive version, not once, but twice in the course of the play.[13]

Traditionally, many critics have observed that "Williams had called the short play from which *Streetcar* evolved *The Poker Night*, and in the final version two of the most crucial scenes are presented within the framework of poker games played onstage."[14] But nowhere are parallels drawn between these two homosexual/homosocial male performance tableaux contained within the play, Allan's gay sex encounter and Stanley's poker games, and their double portrayals. According to Joseph N. Riddel, Stanley's quotidian existence, including his regular poker games, indicates that "realistically viewed, Stanley's world is a dreadfully boring repetition of acts, but symbolically, it fulfills a timeless, ritualistic cycle."[15] So critics do find both redundancy and ritual in *Streetcar*, although in Blanche's case they are only perceived as "retributive" and in Stanley's as "boring" and symbolically necessary and fulfilling. In Williams' fused theaters of memory and initiation they remain this—and become much more.

The persistence of memory is introduced as a major theme early in the play. After Blanche first arrives in the Elysian Fields section of New Orleans, and she must explain to her sister Stella how and why she lost the family plantation Belle Reve, she tells of all the recent family deaths. Blanche says of the dying, "and sometimes they even cry out to you, Don't let me go!' Even the old, sometimes, say, Don't let me go'" (27). In Blanche's internal theater of memory the dead also seem to chant this phrase. Williams extends this admonition of and from the past throughout the structure of the play. For Blanche, memory is not only inescapable, it is also indulgent. Williams supplies the audience with theatrical markers to signal when the theater of memory is about to begin; chief among these are consistent images and sounds from the past. "Besides the series of stories told by Blanche and others about her past,..." Thompson states that "aural and visual images that only Blanche hears and sees are expressionistically presented to reflect her present torment...." The first of the aural markers comes at the end of scene one, when Stanley asks Blanche about her dead husband. Before she can answer, the stage directions indicate that: "[*The music of the polka rises up, faint in the distance*]"(31). This music, later identified as the *Varsouviana* polka, will introduce and accompany Blanche's memory of Allan's suicide throughout the play; Thompson calls it "an aural symbol of her guilt"[16] Here Michael Moon's theory of a gay masculine "theater of initiation" based on repetition seems to become problematic when applied to Tennessee Williams' drama and combined with his "theater of memory." How can a character's guilt and torment from and with the past supply gay men with a sense of initiation and a way into understanding their own masculine subjectivities?

Blanche DuBois's constant anguish over her gay husband's death and her role in it speak to a common tradition in twentieth-century American literature. Until the advent of the gay rights movement in the late 1960s, there existed a type of tacit literary approval of depictions of fictional gay characters, with one important caveat: The character must die by the end of the text, preferably by his or her own hand. This convention extends from the very beginnings of modern American gay writing, as evidenced by the fact that "in 1899 Alfred J. Cohen's *A Marriage Below Zero* explicitly made homosexuality the central theme, though in a negative way; he also established the long lasting tradition of ending the tale with the suicide of the homosexual character."[17] The reading public at large could marginally accept gay characters in literature as long as the characters were willing ultimately to punish themselves for their sexual transgressions. This type of fictional suicide served two purposes. First, it supplied a severe and graphic reminder to heterosexual readers of the cost of aberrant sexual behavior, reinforcing existing homophobic beliefs and myths. Second, and perhaps more important, it attempted to deny gay readers any *pleasure* in a homosexual representation. In *Streetcar*, the gay viewer/reader can transcend Blanche's guilt and pain, both of which are justified. As Leonard Berkman states, "Blanche's most fundamental regret... is not that she happened to marry a homosexual...Blanche's concern is more directly that, when made aware of her husband's homosexuality, she brought on the boy's suicide by her unqualified expression of disgust."[18] Laurilyn J. Harris argues that most critics fail to contextualize the scene, when she states that "such criticisms view the past from the context of the present. What would a sixteen year old girl living in the second quarter of the twentieth century know of the psychological intricacies of the then taboo subject of homosexuality?"[19] Blanche's culturally predictable reaction simply represents another way in which Williams allows the gay viewer/reader to see beyond her guilt. Once past her self-torment, there is a tableau of two men engaged in a sexual encounter. Pleasure from the scene must be earned, and Williams provides the ability to achieve this pleasure by the reiteration of the scene from Blanche's tortured memory moderated and complexly re-sexualized by the homosocial interaction of Stanley and his card playing friends. Early in the play, Blanche demonstrates her desire to internalize and absorb Stanley's vigor and sexuality when she says to Stella, "oh, I guess he's just not the type that goes for jasmine perfume, but maybe he's what we need to mix with our blood now that we've lost Belle Reve. We trashed it out" (44). Her plural pronoun use indicates that both she and Stella need Stanley's energy and vitality; however, of the two surviving DuBois family members, Blanche alone lost Belle Reve, alone trashed it. Her use of *we* is both plural and imperially singular. Blanche (and Williams) needs Stanley's masculinity for the proper reconstruction of her dead gay husband. Allan's delicate, effete homosexuality and Stanley's brutal, animalistic heterosexuality both inform and create the theater of memory/initiation in *A Streetcar Named Desire*.

Near the end of scene one, when Stanley first enters, Williams describes his sexual energy in great detail in the stage directions:

> [*Since earliest manhood the center of his life has been pleasure with women, the giving and taking of it, not with weak indulgence, dependently, but with the power and pride of a richly feathered male bird among hens. Branching out from this complete and satisfying center are all the auxiliary channels of his life, such as heartiness with men, his appreciation of rough humor, his love of good drink and food and games, his car, his radio, everything that is his, that bears his emblem of the gaudy seed-bearer.*] (29)

Interestingly, first after the heteronormative sexual center, Williams lists "heartiness with men" as a primary "auxiliary channel" of Stanley's life. Eve Kosofsky Sedgwick defines "male homosocial desire" as social interaction(s) among men, traditional male bonding, which allow men subconsciously to express and consciously repress homoerotic attraction to one another; to resist homosexual identification, homosociality is inherently, and oftentimes rabidly so, homophobic.[20] Ironically, the playwright will use this homosocial interaction between Stanley and his friends, this "heartiness," throughout the play as a way to expose Blanche and the audience to normal male behavior—what real men do when they are together in a room. The interplay and reiteration of Blanche's memory of walking unannounced into a room to discover Allan and the older man having sex and her witnessing Stanley and his friends playing cards serve to draw attention to the repetition of masculine ritual and initiation, both homosexual and homosocial.

Another way in which Williams juxtaposes and draws parallels between Blanche's memory of Allan engaged in homosexual sex and Stanley and his poker buddies engaged in homosocial exchange is by the intensity of the two scenes. To set the scene/mood for the first poker game at the Kowalski apartment, played at the beginning of scene three, Williams describes the ambience in the stage directions: *"there is a picture of Van Gogh's of a billiard-parlor at night. The kitchen now suggests that sort of lurid nocturnal brilliance, the raw colors of childhood's spectrum"* (45). The tableau is represented as vivid and bright, to the point of gaudy.[21] About the poker players, Williams writes that they, *"wear colored shirts, solid blues, a purple, a red-and-white check, a light green, and they are men at the peak of their physical manhood, as coarse and direct and powerful as the primary colors"* (45). However, when he describes the bedroom, behind the card players and in the shadows, he writes that it is *"relatively dim with only the light that spills between the portieres and through the wide window on the street"* (45). The poker players, at the "peak of their physical manhood," are drawn starkly and in bright light, with the bold colors and intensity directly informing their collective masculinity. Out in the open, they have nothing to hide, no furtiveness, about their manhood—no unmanly secrets. The dim, shadow-hidden bedroom in the background represents not only the location of Stanley and Stella's sexual activity and where Stanley will rape Blanche at the end of scene ten; it also relates to the dark room, the private space, into which Blanche enters to find her husband and another man having sex. According to Henry I. Schvey, "it is obvious from Williams's description of The Poker Night scene that he has taken great pains over the precise visual effects down to the smallest details of colour and shape."[22] It is also obvious that Williams makes Blanche's memory theater dim and nebulous, to show it in opposition to the card game. As the character Tom Wingfield says in his introductory monologue at the beginning of *The Glass Menagerie*, "being a memory play, it is dimly lighted, it is sentimental, it is not realistic."[23]

Stanley's poker game is presented as an intense visual scene, a kind of masculine spectacle (the second poker game in scene eleven is described in the same terms: *"The atmosphere of the kitchen is now the same raw, lurid one of the disastrous poker night"* (131).) However, Blanche's mental reconstruction of Allan's gay sexual encounter strictly follows Williams' dictum of the dimness of memory theater. She first relates the entire story, in detail, in scene six to Stanley's friend Mitch. She describes her love for Allan in terms of light and dark: "It was like you suddenly turned a blinding light on something that had always been half in shadow, that's how it struck the world for me" (95). A few lines later she makes her discovery of Allan's homosexuality, and just as love was revealed to her "suddenly," making clear what had been hidden, she says:

> Then I found out. In the worst of all possible ways. By coming suddenly into a room that I thought was empty—which wasn't empty, but had two people in it...the boy I had married and an older man who had been his friend for years...(95)

Williams uses the stage direction immediately following these lines to illustrate how the theater of memory resists light, and thus attempts to resist reality:

> [*A locomotive is heard approaching outside. She claps her hands to her ears and crouches over. The headlight of the locomotive glares into the room as it thunders past. As the noise recedes she straightens slowly and continues speaking.*] (95)

Only after the harsh, garish light of the real world has been cast on and quickly removed from her telling of the story, her memory theater, can Blanche continue. For Williams, scant light can be directed on the theater of gay memory and initiation, making it appear as if its sexuality, physicality, and masculinity must be shaded, almost to the point of being elided. The gay theater of memory and initiation must borrow its light, vitality, and sexuality from the lurid and stark heteronormative and homosocial scenes of Stanley and his hypermasculine friends.

During the first poker game in the kitchen of the Kowalski apartment, Stanley and his friends—Steve, Mitch, and Pablo—engage in typical male camaraderie while Stella and Blanche are out for the night. Williams charges the scene with homosocial energy by the above examined intense visual images and by the exchange of dialogue. At the start of the game, Stanley says to Mitch: "When I'm losing you want to eat! Ante up! Openers? Openers? Get y'r ass off the table, Mitch. Nothing belongs on a poker table but cards, chips and whiskey"(46). In essence, Mitch's opener, his ante for the hand, becomes his *ass*, a primary physical (and psychic) location for male homosexual desire, offered up on the table. Stanley quickly and emphatically reminds him of his error. In Luce Irigaray's *This Sex Which Is Not One*, her examination of homosexual/homosocial cultural interaction and the commodification of women points out that

> The use of and traffic in women subtend and uphold the reign of masculine hom(m)o-sexuality, even while they maintain that hom(m)o-sexuality in speculations, mirror games, identifications, and more or less rivalrous appropriations, which defer its real practice. Reigning everywhere, although prohibited in practice, hom(m)o-sexuality is played out through the bodies of women, matter, or sign, and heterosexuality has been up to now just an alibi for the smooth workings of man's relations with himself, of relations among men.[24]

In the broader cultural/economic context of her remarks, Irigaray demonstrates how homosexuality/homosociality inform all masculine social exchanges. The poker game in *Streetcar* represents a microcosm of the male-dominated cultural/economic sphere, an appropriate heteronormative male game of speculation. A male ass, anted up, becomes a prize for other men to compete for, to win—it must be removed from the table to facilitate Irigaray's idea of "the smooth workings of man's relations with himself, of relations among men." However, the *offer* is plainly made.

The tenor of the poker players' conversation then turns to sexually suggestive jocularity. Mitch, the only bachelor in the group, wants to get the game started because he has a sick mother at home to care for. When he complains, Stanley offers to fix him a "sugar-tit," a pacifier made from soaking a cloth in sugar water, and a common, traditional Southern threat for unmanly behavior. Mitch's terse reply to Stanley is to "go rut" (46). The use of *rut*, the excited sexual state and action of goats and deer, is another way in which Williams shows the animal nature of Stanley and his friends' sexuality, so it is no surprise when this remark is immediately followed by the telling of a "dirty joke" involving animals, sex, and a man.[25] Steve tells a joke about an old farmer throwing corn to his chickens; a rooster, another sexually representative animal, is chasing a young hen but gives up his decidedly carnal pursuit when he sees the feed corn being tossed. The farmer's comment and the punch line are: "Lord God, I hopes I never gits *that* hongry!" (47).[26] According to Peter Lyman:

> The humor of male bonding relationships generally is sexual and aggressive, and frequently consists of sexist or racist jokes. As Freud observed, the jokes that individual men direct toward women are generally erotic, tend to clever forms (like the double entendre), and have a seductive purpose. The jokes that men tell about women in the presence of other men are sexual and aggressive rather than erotic and use hostile rather than clever verbal forms; and...have the creation of male group bonding as their purpose.[27]

Williams uses this "dirty joke" not only to illustrate the homosocial relationship, the "male group bonding," among the friends, he also uses it to sexualize the poker game further. He will use a similar joke for the same purpose in *Cat on a Hot Tin Roof.*

Just as Steve finishes telling the joke, Blanche and Stella return to the apartment; women intrude into the male location and the men must quickly alter the homosocial dynamics. The next lines form an intricate and telling interplay of intrusion:

> BLANCHE: Poker is so fascinating. Could I kibitz?
> STANLEY: You could not. Why don't you women go up and sit with Eunice?
> STELLA: Because it is nearly two-thirty. [*Blanche crosses into the bedroom and partially closes the portieres*] Couldn't you call it quits after one more hand?
> [*A chair scrapes. Stanley gives a loud whack of his hand on her thigh.*]
> STELLA [*sharply*]: That's not fun, Stanley.
> [*The men laugh. Stella goes into the bedroom.*] (48)

Instead of asking to watch, Blanche specifically asks if she can *kibitz*, a Yiddish word commonly meaning to be a busybody; but Blanche uses the word correctly. The proper meaning of the Yiddish word literally means to be a spectator, especially at a card game, and to give unsolicited and unwanted advice to the players. Stanley immediately refuses her request to participate, to enter the homosocial sphere, by suggesting that the women go upstairs and visit Eunice, Steve's wife, another woman sequestered from the poker game. Thus far the female characters have not been allowed to view the poker game, so Blanche's memory theater reconstruction of Allan's homosexual act, laden with romance and tragedy and physically latent, still lacks the sexuality it must borrow from the homosocial poker game to complete the theater of initiation. Williams achieves this act of borrowing by staging a complex and reciprocal scopophilic exchange for the remainder of scene three; this process begins with the above noted stage direction that indicates that when Blanche crosses to the doorless bedroom she only partially closes the curtains.

Tennessee Williams once again employs his ingenious manipulation of theatricality, stagecraft, and spectatorship. In the Wingfield apartment in *The Glass Menagerie*, he creates a theater within a theater by structuring a second proscenium arch centered in the primary proscenium arch, the large, open doorway framing the dining room. In the stage directions, he describes this doorway as framed by "*transparent faded portieres*," which Williams defines in theatrical terms as a "*second curtain*."[28] In *Streetcar* the "portieres" serve a similar function, the focus and control of spectatorship—Blanche's, the poker players', and the audience's. The curtains will appear again, for the same purpose, at the beginning of scene eleven, after Stanley has raped Blanche: "*the portieres are partially open on the poker players—Stanley, Steve, Mitch and Pablo—who sit around the table in the kitchen*" (131). Critics often note the use of this curtain effect in the play, but it is always examined in linear fashion; the audience looks through the stage curtains, sees the card game, then sees what the poker players see, Blanche through the open portieres in the bedroom. Quirino points out that after Blanche and Stella return to the apartment during the card game, "they are unwelcome intruders in the masculine game." He then affirms the traditional linear reading of the scene by maintaining that "the scene then continues in twin focus on the card game in the kitchen and on Blanche's flirtation with Mitch in the bedroom."[29] What critics fail to notice is that Blanche is also a spectator, a true kibitzer, looking back through the open curtains.

As the scene continues, Blanche blatantly exposes herself through the opened curtains in a rather obvious attempt to flirt with Mitch, Stanley's friend whom she finds interesting. In the stage directions, Williams indicates that "[*She takes off the blouse and stands in her pink silk brassiere and white skirt in the light through the portieres. The game has continued in undertones*]" (50). Blanche's sexual spectacle becomes distracting for the poker players. When Mitch stops paying attention to the game, Stanley points out that "he was looking through them drapes. [*He jumps up and jerks roughly at curtains to close them*]" (52). The scene shifts from the kitchen/poker game to the bedroom when Mitch goes through the closed curtains to talk with Blanche.

In a short section of scene three, Williams has managed to infuse all of the dramatic action with high sexual tension. Even Stella is not immune; while she stands with Blanche in the opened curtains, Stella jokingly tells her of how the upstairs couple's boisterous lovemaking cracked the ceiling plaster one night (50). When Williams opens the internal stage curtains, the audience and the characters participate in a rollicking, almost comic, display of sexuality, unlike

Blanche's sterile memory theater scene of Allan engaged in homosexual sex. That memory is more sterile, nebulous, and sexless than descriptive or titillating, like the poker game scene. One critic asserts that "throughout the play we are aware of Blanche's being ghoul haunted by the suicide of her husband...."[30] Not only is the gay sexual image in the play vague, it can also be interpreted as being generated by "ghouls," relating it to archaic, vampiric, corpse-feeding descriptions of gay sex.

Blanche's memory of her dead husband's gay sex act is purposely vague and hazy, because according to Williams all theater of memory must be "dim." When Blanche tells Mitch the story about Allan's suicide, blowing his brains out on the dance floor after Blanche's public accusation, she says, "and then the searchlight which had been turned on the world was turned off again and never for one moment since has there been any light that's stronger than this—kitchen—candle . . ." (96). This image, from the end of scene six, stands in high contrast to the bright, "lurid" homosocial atmosphere of the kitchen poker game that Blanche observes. Before Blanche's detailed description of her memory of Allan's sexual transgression, the audience and Blanche actually witness a kind of homosocial restaging of it at the disastrous end of scene three.

Blanche's numerous female intrusions into the masculine sphere of the poker game reach a climax near the end of scene three when she switches the radio, which had previously been playing the more appropriate Xavier Cugat Latin music, to a classical waltz and begins dancing with Mitch. Enraged and drunk, Stanley reopens the curtains to reveal the scene when he "*stalks fiercely through the portieres into the bedroom*" (57). He throws the radio out of the window, and (offstage) strikes his pregnant wife Stella, an amplified form of the precursory and seemingly innocent smack on the thigh he gives her earlier in the scene, the one at which the other men laugh. Blanche must once again view the masculine interactions of men in a bedroom, but as opposed to her memory theater image, this one is blatantly, if homosocially, sexual:

> BLANCHE: Lunacy, absolute lunacy!
>
> MITCH: Get him in here, men.

> [*Stanley is forced, pinioned by the two men, into the bedroom. He nearly throws them off. Then all at once he subsides and is limp in their grasp.*
> [*They speak quietly and lovingly to him and he leans his face on one of their shoulders.*] (57–58)

The homosexual implications of the scene are obvious, and while its violence preshadows Stanley's rape of Blanche in the same bedroom, the language that Williams uses in the stage directions implies a homoerotic tone, almost romantic, albeit a false romance identical to the kind Blanche attaches to her past and her memories. Directly after this episode, Mitch reinforces the card game's homosocial order and code when he announces, to no one in particular, "poker shouldn't be played in a house with women" (58). As the men take Stanley to the bathroom to put him under a cold shower, his earlier and resigned homoerotic actions are replaced by his once again heterosexual, animal self; he tells them to "let the rut go of me, you sons of bitches!" (58). As the shower runs, Mitch repeats the homosocial code: "[*sadly but firmly*] Poker should not be played in a house with women" (59). Shortly after this scene, when Stanley has been banished from the apartment, he screams his now famous reconciliation call from the street, "STELL-LAHHHHH!" (60).

Scene four, set during the morning aftermath of the poker game, further serves to draw parallels between Blanche's memory of Allan and the homosocial display of the previous night. Stella gives Blanche a short lesson in male behavior and forgiveness when she tells her, "when men are drinking and playing poker anything can happen. It's always a powder-keg. He didn't know what he was doing..." (63). Later, when Blanche reconstructs her memory of Allan killing himself on the dance floor at The Moon Lake Casino, we learn that all of the participants were also drunk and in a volatile situation, and that Allan probably didn't know what he was doing either. Stella can forgive Stanley and his poker playing buddies their veiled and homosocial behavior; however, Blanche cannot forgive Allan and his friend their homosexual act. In the same conversation, Blanche also affirms her spectatorship of the homosocial card game, and what she learns from it:

> STELLA: Blanche, you saw him [Stanley] at his worst last night.
> BLANCHE: On the contrary, I saw him at his best! What such a man has to offer is animal force and he gave a wonderful exhibition of that! But the only way to live with such a man is to—go to bed with him! And that's your job—not mine! (69)

Here Williams' theater of memory and Moon's theater of initiation begin to collide and fuse, allowing the gay reader/viewer the ability to reconstruct Allan's homosexual act. The line between Blanche's dead, idealized, and romantic gay husband and Stella's living, brutal, and hypermasculine/sexual husband actually begins to blur. It will take Blanche's detailed memory in scene six to complete this complicated process.

At the end of scene six, in a conversation with Mitch, Blanche tells the complete story of her ill fated marriage to Allan Grey, her personal, psychic theater of memory. Williams places the story at almost the exact center of *Streetcar's* eleven-scene structure, as if all dramatic action prior to it radiates backward and all after it projects forward, further emphasizing its often neglected importance. Blanche's language throughout the story connotes a sense of softness and gentility in direct opposition to the coarse and basic language used to describe Stanley. In the historically contextualized parlance of 1947 (and in Blanche s retrospective vision), Williams idiomatically makes the reader/viewer aware of Allan's homosexuality: "There was something different about the boy, a nervousness, a softness and tenderness which wasn't like a man's, although he wasn't the least bit effeminate looking—still—that thing was there...." (95).[31] Williams objectifies, almost anthropomorphizes, Allan's homosexuality into a *thing*, independent of his subjectivity; whereas, Stanley's animal like nature defines his masculine identity and subjectivity. Like Stanley, Allan is described in terms of his masculinity; he is not "effeminate looking." However, Blanche supposes that unlike Stanley's brutish sexuality, Allan's was controllable:

> He came to me for help. I didn't know that. I didn't find out anything till after our marriage when we'd run away and come back and all I knew was I'd failed him in some mysterious way and wasn't able to give the help he needed but couldn't speak of! (95)

She further explains her memories of inertia and futility when she says, "he was in the quicksands and clutching at me—but I wasn't holding him out, I was slipping in with him! I didn't know that..." (95). The very crux of Blanche's memory theater is that she realizes her misjudgment about Allan, which mitigates and excuses the gay viewer/reader from a shared guilt of reconstructing the homosexual sex scene. This is not the act of taking pleasure from Blanche's pain, which was culturally necessary in 1947 for Williams to include homosexuality in the play; it is the act of extending perception past that pain into the realm of possible male sexuality—what gay men do in a bedroom, ironically remasculinized and granted physicality by the homosocial interactions of Stanley and his friends. Recurrent memory and repetition of initiation reiterate the point to confirm it. In one sense, Tennessee Williams *sacrifices* Blanche for gay pleasure. Perhaps this is why Blanche DuBois has become an icon in the gay community.[32]

Blanche is not the only character in *Streetcar* to reconstruct the dead Allan from memory; her sister Stella also remembers—but in a very different way. In scene seven, shortly after Blanche has told the story of her marriage to Mitch and Stanley has discovered the details of Blanche's promiscuous past, Stella tells Stanley:

> But when she was young, very young, she married a boy who wrote poetry.... He was extremely good-looking. I think Blanche didn't just love him but worshipped the ground he walked on! Adored him and thought him almost too fine to be human! But then she found out—...This beautiful and talented young man was a degenerate. (102)

Stella's memory of Allan, like Blanche's, has more to do with Blanche than Allan. Her recollection of the marriage does not create a theater of memory, but serves to supply a realistic account. It also confirms Blanche's memory theater by corroboration, a necessary confirmation given Blanche's tenuous grasp on reality. Williams' linguistic signals for gay are there: "a boy who wrote poetry," "extremely good-looking," "beautiful and talented." But unlike Blanche, who tries to separate homosexuality ("that thing") from Allan in her memory theater, Stella names it and attaches it firmly by referring to him as a degenerate.

Stella's memory of Allan reflects the selective and pragmatic influence Stanley has upon her, further defining her position as "woman" in the homosocial order of the play. This is best evidenced in the final scene, scene eleven, after Stanley has raped Blanche, and she must be institutionalized. Stella says to Eunice, "I couldn't believe her story and go on living with Stanley" (133). Eunice's reply also reinforces how the female characters respond to their husbands' homosocial dominance, when she tells Stella, "don't ever believe it. Life has got to go on. No matter what happens, you've got to keep on going" (133). Williams reiterates Allan's sexual encounter by providing two varying memories of it; Blanche's romantic and nebulous theater of memory, and Stella's rather harsh and condemning account filtered by complex homosocial dynamics—the only one that Stanley can hear.

The final reenacting of Allan's homosexual transgression and his subsequent suicide occurs in scene nine, after Stanley has informed Mitch about Blanche's promiscuous past and Mitch confronts her. In this conversation with him, Blanche's growing mental instability becomes clear:

> MITCH: What music?
> BLANCHE: The "Varsouviana"! The polka tune they were playing when Allan—
> Wait!
> [*A distant revolver shot is heard. Blanche seems relieved.*]
> There now, the shot! It always stops after that.
> [*The polka music dies out again.*]
> Yes, now it's stopped.
> MITCH: Are you boxed out of your mind? (114 –115)

Here Williams pulls the reader/viewer into Blanche's internal theater of memory, allowing (or forcing) us to reconstruct the scene and draw our own conclusions—or pleasures. And, ironically, by the end of the play Blanche will become "boxed" *into* her mind.

A Streetcar Named Desire creates a nexus, a point at which Tennessee Williams' "memory theater" and Michael Moon's "theater of initiation" meet, interact, and then merge. The more traditional critical readings of the play, primarily mythological and religious influence through the use of symbols and the tension between romanticism and reality, remain valid. However, psychic theaters, infused into the play, allow gay men, especially gay men of the day, a way to derive pleasure from the homosexual representation of Allan and his friend. The reiteration of the scene is paramount to its importance, and masculine initiation must be borrowed from the homosocial, a less than ideal (but considering the time, necessary) method to sexualize gay men. Moon's concept of mimetic disorientation informs and problematizes the play, because the only models of male sexuality, Allan and Stanley, are already disoriented by the prevailing strictures of 1947. Allan must be effete, degenerate—and dead. Stanley must be brutal, hyper masculine—and cruel. Blanche, her own sad story intact, also acts as an interlocutor in what could, ostensibly, be considered a traditional Hegelian dialectic of masculinity and homosexuality, especially in the context of Hegel's assertion that "thought and reality are one and the same."[33] This approach, however, begs the obvious point that homosexuality and masculinity are mutually exclusive from one another, which would transport the viewer/reader right back to 1947. In the end, Blanche DuBois, even in her madness, must still "always depend on the kindness of strangers," though her dependency is constantly disappointed. Tennessee Williams dramatically depends on that same "kindness" from the strangers who constitute his audience, his readers; and disappointment can only be assuaged by understanding.

❋ CHAPTER 2

Cat on a Hot Tin Roof

"When a football player loses his supreme confidence in his super-masculinity, he is in deep trouble."
—Vince Lombardi

Brick Pollitt, the former college and professional football star in Tennessee Williams' *Cat on a Hot Tin Roof*, is in deep trouble. *Cat on a Hot Tin Roof*, first performed in 1955 and arguably Williams' most commercially successful play, represents one day in 1954 in the life of the Pollitts, one of the Mississippi Delta's wealthiest cotton-growing families. As with *A Streetcar Named Desire*, Williams' characters here have become so deeply embedded in American culture (both popular and high) that almost everyone can picture the earthy, swaggering Big Daddy in a crumpled white linen suit or the voluptuous and striking Maggie, dressed in a slip and stalking the bedroom in feline fervor. The viriley beautiful and semi-drunken Brick, his foot in a cast and his morally frozen body sheathed in icy white silk pajamas, also quickly comes to the collective mind. In *Cat on a Hot Tin Roof*, Williams' theater of memory has evolved into a brighter, though still subjectively dense, location. Unlike *Streetcar*, in *Cat on a Hot Tin Roof* the theater of initiation does not have to borrow its masculinity from any other homosocial quarter; the play draws its concepts of masculinity and homosexuality directly from the most homosocial of American institutions, organized sports. As the famous Green Bay Packers' coach Vince Lombardi indicates in the above quotation, from Brian Pronger's *The Arena of Masculinity: Sports, Homosexuality, and the Meaning of Sex*, in the American psyche football isn't just a game, it is the very arena of "supreme confidence" and "super-masculinity."

A critical examination of *Cat on a Hot Tin Roof* presents two crucial problems that must be dealt with at the onset, one textual and the other more subjectively problematic; and both have an important bearing on the theaters of memory and initiation. The play has two very different concluding third acts, and Brick's sexual orientation is purposefully confusing. With his penchant for obfuscation and contradiction, the playwright himself is of little help on either issue. The conventional, standard rationale for the revised third act is found in Williams' "Note of Explanation" inserted between the acts in most published editions of *Cat on a Hot Tin Roof.* Williams maintains that he succumbed to the "creative influence on the play" by its original Broadway director Elia Kazan, who had successfully worked with Williams on both the stage and film productions of *A Streetcar Named Desire.* Apparently, to ensure a more publicly palpable version of *Cat*, Kazan suggested three basic revisions of act three: Big Daddy (who disappears at the end of act two) be reintroduced; Brick should undergo some sort of change, with the emphasis toward positive; and Maggie should become a more sympathetic character.[1] In the revised act three, commonly differentiated as the "Broadway version," Williams makes the suggested changes—and creates a longstanding critical debate that proves more frustrating than enlightening.

In his "Note of Explanation" for the revised third act of *Cat,* Williams writes that Kazan felt the need to change the character of Brick because, "of the virtual vivisection that he undergoes in his interview with his father in act two" (124). Ironically, Kazan appears to have had no compunction to request this same "virtual vivisection" on Williams' original script. However, Marian Price explains that for all the critical consternation caused by Kazan's suggested revisions, Williams himself is more to be held responsible. What began as mere artistic opinion and advice from Kazan prompted Williams to believe that the original version of the play would not become a commercial success, something Williams strongly desired as a public affirmation of his work. Elia Kazan stated several times that when he realized Williams' reluctance to make the changes he simply told the playwright to "leave it as it is." Price argues that her reading of the play "supports the idea that Williams actively embraced the suggested revisions, made them his own, and confidently awaited the play's triumph."[2] She goes on to posit Williams' personal guilt over artistic compromise and homosexuality as the motivating factors ofhis misplaced blame of Elia Kazan.[3]

To complicate matters further, there are actually *four* extant published versions of act three of *Cat on a Hot Tin Roof*.[4] For a 1974 Broadway revival of the play, Williams again rewrote the polymorphous third act, keeping the original intact and only allowing Big Daddy to appear and tell an off color joke. By the time the revival had made it to the stage, Williams had produced an "acting-version" that returned to the old Broadway third act, minus Big Daddy's joke.[5] Given that the primary dramatic action of all of the various versions of act three is the comic bickering over an inheritance, Roger Boxill points out rather facilely, but perhaps trenchantly, that "no version of Act III quite works, because the final act is an afterthought."[6] Aside from the poststructuralist concept of meaning never being firmly fixed, the reader/viewer expects the traditional text itself to remain fixed; these types of textual cruxes always present the daunting (and often prosaic) necessity of a compare-and-contrast critical approach. However, while most modern critics tend to get mired down studying the differences in the original and Broadway versions of act three, none have noticed a more informative approach to the problem. Williams' third act revisions for the 1974 Broadway revival of *Cat* hold the answer, particularly in light of the ways that masculinity inform the play. The only fundamental revision Williams makes to the 1974 script is the insertion and excision of Big Daddy's joke.[7] Given the fact that Williams was more than well aware of the critical controversy caused by *Cat's* unstable third act, it seems incredibly telling that when given the chance to correct the constantly perplexing problem he is more concerned with a dirty joke than Brick's sudden and unexplained change or Maggie's added sympathy. Most critical studies of the play either ignore or dismiss Big Daddy's joke as superfluous to act three. Ruby Cohn, who deems Big Daddy a "colorful character," believes that "his elephantine joke diffuses the dramatic drive."[8] In *A Streetcar Named Desire* the dirty joke actually *infuses* the dramatic drive, bringing into play sexuality, the homosocial, and masculinity—three of the primary dynamics that Williams attempts to bring together in act three of *Cat on a Hot Tin Roof.*

If Blanche DuBois is clearly the protagonist in *A Streetcar Named Desire*, then which character fills that role in *Cat on a Hot Tin Roof*? The play's title obviously indicates Maggie, but the title alone proves deceptive. According to David Savran:

> Among the *dramatis personae*, at least three—Maggie, Brick, and Big Daddy—bear the intense desire and undergo the kind of transformations usually associated with protagonists. To grant a privilege to any one character's point of view is to misread the designs of interdependence and complicity that Williams so painstakingly constructs as a solitary enterprise.[9]

Maggie's tenacity, Brick's ambiguous sexual orientation, and Big Daddy's impending death all represent the complex "interplay of live human beings in the thundercloud of a common crisis," as Williams states in his stage directions for *Cat* (85). There is no question of Maggie's tenacity, a cat just trying to stay on a hot tin roof. Big Daddy is surely dying of bowel cancer. But just how ambiguous is Brick's sexual orientation?

Williams approaches the topic of homosexuality very differently in *Cat* than he does in *Streetcar*. As Mark Royden Winchell points out, "Williams's treatment of homosexuality in *Cat on a Hot Tin Roof* represents an advance over the clichés of *A Streetcar Named Desire*."[10] Gone is the sensitive and nervous young poet Allan and his worldly older friend, replaced by the macho football player buddies Brick and Skipper. These two represent early prototypes of male characters that Williams will continue to incorporate into his dramatic canon. According to Robert Emmet Jones:

> Although many of the playwright's male characters are sterotypes of contemporary ideas of masculinity—athletes, truck drivers, manual workers, studs, sailors, hustlers—they remain passive sexual objects, and other aspects of their personalities

> are rarely explored. . . . And they are types fantasized about by homosexuals. . . . Williams expresses the homoerotic longing that these men might harbor homosexual or bisexual tendencies themselves.[11]

Fortunately, Brick Pollitt, though he does "remain a passive sexual object," is one of the few early Tennessee Williams homoerotic characters whose personality is explored. Unfortunately, for all of the furtiveness and secrecy concerning Brick's true sexual nature, that exploration proves difficult and complicated. However, it is this very concept of secrecy, the choice *not* to know, that leads to a better understanding of homosexuality in *Cat on a Hot Tin Roof.*

Writing in 2002, and from a distinctly twentieth-century perspective on the subject of homosexuality, Harold Bloom believes that without the energy supplied by Maggie and Big Daddy's characters Brick would, "freeze the audience, particularly now, when homosexuality is no longer an issue for an audience not dominated by Fundamentalists, Reagan Republicans, and assorted other mossbacks."[12] Historically contextualizing popular critical commentary, contemporaneous with *Cat's* 1955 Broadway debut, sheds a very different light on homosexuality, masculinity, and the homosocial, and how Williams' combined theaters of memory and initiation both followed and helped define the cultural norms of the era.

In his book *Cultural Politics—Queer Reading* (1994), Alan Sinfield demonstrates how the concept of secrecy, so prevalent in all spheres of 1950s American culture, permeated by fears of post–World War II communism—battered by McCarthyism, influenced the critical reception of *Cat on a Hot Tin Roof.* Sinfield refers to *Cat* as a "scandalous success," but he also points out that popular drama critics of the day had the responsibility of "the nervous restoration of the secrecy that Williams had violated." Sinfield notes that

> This was happening when Brooks Atkinson reviewed the initial (1955) production without mentioning Brick's relationship with Skipper. Walter Kerr, in the *New York Herald Tribune*, acknowledged "the implications" of "an unnatural relationship" but

> complained that *Cat* exhibits "a tantalizing reluctance" to "blurt out its promised secret." In fact, the play is plain enough; Kerr needs there to be a secret.[13]

For Tennessee Williams, and the viewing public, Brick's homosexuality must remain clouded in secrecy, but it must still be expressed. The theater of memory helps the playwright achieve this goal by constant, yet veiled, allusions to homosexuality by all of the major players in *Cat*. The theater of initiation, powered by its need for continuous reiteration, serves to redouble this concept of talking about homosexuality while *not* talking about homosexuality. Both theaters enable Williams to maintain the open secret.

In twenty-first-century hindsight, it becomes clear to most viewer/readers, especially gay ones, that Brick and Skipper are both, without doubt, homosexuals. In his now famous and often quoted section of stage directions from act two of *Cat on a Hot Tin Roof*, Williams shares the core of his dramatic theory with the reader. In this theory he states that "some mystery should be left in the revelation of character in a play, just as a great deal of mystery is always left in the revelation of character in life, even in one's character to himself" (85). The sole, real mystery in the play is Brick's sexual orientation; this mystery, however, is necessary to maintain the open secret status of homosexuality. Alan Sinfield convincingly argues how and why this concept of the open secret exists:

> It helps to constitute the public/private boundary—the binary that seems to demarcate our subjectivities from a public realm, while actually producing those subjectivities—and thus facilitates the policing of the boundary. The secret keeps a topic like homosexuality in the private sphere, but under surveillance, allowing it to hover on the edge of public visibility. If it gets fully into the open, it attains public recognition; yet it must not disappear altogether, for then it would be beyond control and would no longer effect a general surveillance of aberrant desire.[14]

David Savran espouses a similar theory of gay subjectivity and what he refers to as the "guilty secret" of homosexuality, but Savran's theoretical approach to the subject also incorporates the past, represented in Williams' drama by the persistent theater of memory:

> Even more important, this practice acts both to ratify and subvert a psychoanalytical model of personality, for in the same gesture that directs the spectator's hermeneutical gaze toward the withheld secret, it seems to deny the primacy and intelligibility of that traumatic memory, both emphasizing and calling into question the determination of the present by a moment in the past.[15]

As John M. Clum notes about *Cat,* "the tenderness Williams sees as the clear side of his vision here exists only in a stage direction: the cloudiness of homosexuality remains an object of terror, not of the act, but of public exposure."[16] These theories of gay subjectivity represent a direct connection to Tennessee Williams' primary homosexually themed plays, all of which are almost slavishly devoted to memory—the past; and that past is constantly reinforced by the repetition of depictions of masculine, gay initiations.

Even before the dramatic action of *Cat* begins, Williams begins constructing the theater of memory. The only set for *Cat* consists of a large and roomy bedsitting room in the Pollitt plantation house. In the stagecraft "Notes for the Designer" introduction, Williams writes:

> It hasn't changed much since it was occupied by the original owners of the place, Jack Straw and Peter Ochello, a pair of old bachelors who shared the room all their lives together. In other words, the room must evoke some ghosts; it is gently and poetically haunted by a relationship that must have involved a tenderness which was uncommon. (xiii)

We later learn that Straw and Ochello, an apparently unabashedly gay couple, bequeathed the plantation to Big Daddy, whom they took in as a young man and made overseer. As in *Streetcar*, all during the course of the play the reader/viewer will be made aware of a gay past, men in a bedroom. Williams specifically points out that the bedroom must "evoke" the past, and just as the homosexual characters in *Cat* transcend the stereotypical ones of *Streetcar*, the gay "ghosts" have evolved also. Unlike the memories of Allan, which torment Blanche DuBois, Williams goes to great lengths to suggest that the ghosts of Straw and Ochello inhabit a bedroom that is "gently and poetically haunted."

Later in the play, during Brick and Big Daddy's pivotal confrontation, Brick, in a telling assault, will attempt to destroy the memory theater that "must have involved a tenderness which was uncommon."

These gay "ghosts," these gentle specters of homosexuality, Straw and Ochello, serve multiple purposes in *Cat*. The entire dramatic action of the play is trapped within the matrix of their relationship. Williams constructs a kind of narrowing cultural spiral around Straw and Ochello: from breaking with the societal norms of the mid-twentieth century South, to owning the plantation, to sharing the bedroom, and finally to the bed itself. In act one, during a discussion about why Maggie and Brick have remained childless, Big Mamma points at the bed and tells Maggie, "—When a marriage goes on the rocks, the rocks are *there*, right *there*!" (37). The bed comes to represent a successful union, the type of union none of the heterosexual (or ostensibly heterosexual) couples in the play can achieve, and it certainly symbolizes Brick's unfulfilled homosexuality. Judith J. Thompson believes that when the original act three of the play is considered, "the fully realized homosexual relationship exemplified by Straw and Ochello represents the only alternative in the play to either loveless heterosexual couplings or tragically suppressed homosexual longings."[17] David Savran reads Big Daddy as a "carrier of homosexuality," and asserts that "not only has Big Daddy inherited the plantation from Straw and Ochello, but he has also inadvertently passed along at least a glimmer of homosexual desire to his younger son, Brick...."[18] For Roger Boxill, Brick's "glimmer of homosexual desire" becomes unequivocal, when he states, about Straw and Ochello, "it is in their very bedroom, moreover, in a setting described as evocative of their benign ghosts, that the present heir, himself a homosexual, is closeted."[19] For a play that the playwright himself and a plethora of critics have adamantly argued is *not* about homosexuality, there certainly seems to be a lot of "homosexuality" going on—even from page one. For all of the above noted purposes that the Straw and Ochello characters serve in *Cat*, they also function complexly to alter and enhance the way that Williams incorporates the theaters of memory and initiation into the play.

In both *The Glass Menagerie* and *A Streetcar Named Desire*, Williams constructs the theater of memory as a dim stage, not well lighted. He describes the primary set of *The Glass Menagerie* by writing in the stage directions that "the scene is memory and is therefore nonrealistic.... The interior is therefore rather dim and poetic."[20] Thus, the bedsitting room set for *Cat* is also described by the playwright as "poetically haunted," and Williams further suggests this hazy quality by noting that the set designer should consider "a reproduction of a faded photograph of the verandah of Robert Louis Stevenson's home on that Samoan Island where he spent his last years" (xiii). However, Williams also points out that this dimness only represents the background of the play's dramatic action, acts as a sort of atmospheric buffer, when he writes, "for the set is the background for a play that deals with human extremities of emotion, and it needs that softness behind it" (xiii). Indeed, because the foreground of the play is pulled into sharp and bright modernity by "a monumental monstrosity of our times, a *huge* console combination of radio-phonograph (Hi-Fi with three speakers) TV set *and* liquor cabinet,... this monument, is a very shrine to virtually all the comforts and illusions behind which we hide from such things as the characters in the play are faced with...." (xiii–xiv). Williams does not allow the characters in *Cat* to hide or get lost in the dimness of the background; rather it exists to absorb some of the impact from the well-lighted and modern foreground, where the dramatic action is played out. "That softness behind it," the set, is represented by the ghosts of Straw and Ochello, so that the theater of memory can perhaps take up and contain the stark, vivid, and oftentimes brutal theaters of memory and initiation invoked by Brick, Maggie, and Big Daddy—*"that cloudy, flickering, evanescent—fiercely charged!—interplay of live human brings in the thundercloud of a common crisis* (85)*."*

Early in act one of *Cat,* Williams introduces the structure of the foregrounded memory and initiation theaters, the trope of boyhood and games which will be extended throughout the play. In the initial stage directions that describe Brick, Williams makes the point that "he is still slim and firm as a boy" (17). Maggie then immediately refers to him as, "boy of mine!' (17). To extend the concept of boyhood and games further and also to suggest a sexual ambiguity (another dynamic embedded into the play), Williams writes of Maggie "her voice has range and music; sometimes it drops low as a boy's and you have the sudden image of her playing boys' games as a child" (18). Williams weaves actual games into the fabric of the play, games such as football, archery, and croquet, to reflect the more psychically sophisticated games the characters play with sexual orientation and power.[21] Alice Griffin, fully accepting Tennessee Williams' necessary prevarication, his collusion in maintaining the "open secret," writes that "in an interview with *Theatre Arts* magazine Williams said that Brick was not a homosexual, that his self-disgust was the result of living so long with lies." After Williams himself, and apparently Griffin also (writing in 1995!), absolve Brick of his imagined sexual transgression, then we are able to see the "true" crux of Cat:

> It is now possible to view Brick's character in the context of the play as a whole and to see that the question of homosexuality is not the issue. The symbolism of games and game playing, of winning and losing, provides a clue to Brick's disillusionment with the world.[22]

Griffin fails to understand her own clue properly and fully when she argues that Brick's athleticism *only* represents his concept of life, how easily winning can suddenly turn to losing. The game itself then becomes more important than the goal. Brick's goal is twofold and contradictory, to be accepted by his father back into the heteronormative masculine sphere and to reconfigure and reclaim Skipper's memory— how to become/remain a masculine, heterosexual man and still be in love with the memory of his dead friend. No wonder he is so conflicted and emotionally frozen throughout the play; he seems to be playing a losing game.

The study of masculinity has long recognized the influences that organized sports has on the psycho-sexual development of boys. Michael Messner explains:

> For the boy who seeks and fears attachment with others, the rule-bound structure of organized sports can promise to be a safe place in which to seek nonintimate attachment with others within a context that maintains clear boundaries, distance, and separation.[23]

Brick's theaters of memory and initiation have dramatically transformed from that "safe place" into a location where the old rules are tenuous at best, and the structure has collapsed. His attachment to Skipper, despite all of his objections, was intimate. The boundaries were blurred, and the distance was closed. To reachieve proper separation and return to the rules of the game, Brick and Skipper both choose a Draconian route, death: Brick's emotional—Skipper's corporeal.

The memory theater reconstruction of Skipper begins early in act one. While Maggie is railing at Brick about his drinking, she suddenly asks him, "were you thinking of Skipper?"(25). When he evades the question, Maggie tells him:

> Laws of silence don't work.... When something is festering in your memory or your imagination, laws of silence don't work, it's just like shutting a door and locking it on a house on fire in hope of forgetting that the house is burning. But not facing a fire doesn't put it out. Silence about a thing just magnifies it. It grows and festers in silence, becomes malignant.... (25)

Interestingly, Maggie's analogy perfectly expresses how Alan Sinfield's concept of the "open secret" helps society monitor and control homosexuality. If silence about a "thing" just magnifies it, then it also becomes easier to delineate, identify, and contain. This speech also, of course, draws parallels between Brick's predicament and Big Daddy's terminal cancer, and their mutual failure to communicate. In his book, *The Inward Gaze: Masculinity and Subjectivity in Modern Culture*, Peter Middleton relates an anecdote about watching a group of young boys play a game. He perceives two different themes at work:

> One is the way the fantasy of manhood seems to be created out of a bricolage of fragments from the masculine public world, and the other is the difficulties that males, especially males of different ages, have articulating their relations with one another.[24]

Both of these themes are examined by Williams in *Cat.* The component fragments of bricolage, used in an effort to define masculinity, are identified and assembled (for very varying purposes) by Maggie, Brick, and Big Daddy. Most of act two of *Cat* represents a detailed study of a father and son, two men at odds with one another and desperately trying to communicate. The interplay between the foregrounded theaters of memory and initiation, with the contented gay presence of Straw and Ochello hovering in the background as a buffer, enables the characters to explore the "open secret" of homosexuality in the only location it could be explored at the time—at the edges. However, a playwright of Tennessee Williams' talent has the ability to make those edges crackle.

Maggie is the first character in *Cat* to reconstruct Skipper through the theater of memory. The relationship Maggie remembers between Brick and Skipper is described in classical terms of beauty and nobility, yet at the core of her argument, Maggie proves to be disingenuous at least and purely functional at best. At the end of act one Maggie, in an attempt to help Brick overcome his emotional torpor, recalls to Brick his and Skipper's friendship as:

> one of those beautiful, ideal things they tell about in the Greek legends, it couldn't be anything else, you being you, and that's what made it so sad, that's what made it so awful, because it was love that never could be carried through to anything satisfying or even talked about plainly. Brick, I tell you, you got to believe me, Brick I *do* understand all about it. I—I think it was—*noble*! (43–44)

Critics tend to make much ado over this speech, especially considering Williams' penchant for rather frank and obvious symbolism and classical allusions. Earlier in act one, when one of Brick's brother Gooper's many children, one of the "no-neck monsters," enters the bedroom wielding a bow and arrow, Maggie explains that it is her Diana Trophy, a reminder of her archery prowess while a student at Ole Miss (28).[25] Thus, the most obvious critical conclusion to draw (and the one that most critics maintain) is demonstrated by Winchell when he states that "one of the ironies of Williams's play is that its two most overtly heterosexual characters—Maggie and Big Daddy—are also the most tolerant of the latent erotic ties between Brick and

Skipper." Winchell goes on to argue that Maggie's language in describing Brick and Skipper's friendship "elevates it to a platonic status."[26] However, a more important irony can be discerned from Maggie's heterosexual tolerance of latent homoeroticism in her husband, one that passes the platonic for the practical.

The densely complicated structure of the end of act one of *Cat* bears a close reading, because it is within this structure that Williams illustrates how deftly he can shift between and combine the theaters of memory and initiation. And it is in this important scene that the playwright also *frees* Maggie from her often conjectured role of classical goddess-cum-suffering saint. By the end of act one, Maggie is no longer some symbolic representation, some avatar of female acceptance and understanding—she is simply (and complexly) a human woman.

Immediately after Maggie tells Brick that she considers his and Skipper's attachment "noble," she quickly adds, "my only point, the only point that I'm making, is life has got to be allowed to continue, even after the *dream* of life is—all—over. . . ." (44). She stresses that this is her *only* point, and she also repeats an important line from *A Streetcar Named Desire.* When Eunice tells Stella that she must forget Blanche's "story" of Stanley's rape, Eunice says, "don't ever believe it. Life has got to go on. No matter what happens, you've got to keep on going" (133). In the context of *Streetcar*, Alvin B. Kernan calls this "the only truth' that Williams will maintain, you've got to keep on going.'"[27] It may well also represent the only "truth" that Maggie will maintain. "What is the victory of a cat on a hot tin roof?" she asks herself more than Brick, "I wish I knew. . . . Just staying on it, I guess, as long as she can. . . ." (25). In *Cat*, Maggie has a plan, one that represents her neither as a mercenary nor a gold-digging bitch—she wants to survive. This notion of survival informs both Maggie's memory theater construction of Skipper and her perceived understanding and acceptance of Brick's latent homosexuality.

Shortly before her speech about Brick and Skipper and their "noble" relationship, Maggie tells Brick something about his brother Gooper and Gooper's wife Mae, information Maggie thinks that Brick does not realize:

> Mae an' Gooper are plannin' to freeze us out of Big Daddy's estate because you drink and I'm childless. But we can defeat that plan. We're *going* to defeat that plan! *Brick, y'know, I've been so God damn disgustingly poor all my life!*—That's the *truth*, Brick! (41)

She then continues to describe her early life as a traditional Southern "poor relation," replete with family alcoholism, poverty, and lost social position. To save her marriage to Brick, and their inheritance from Big Daddy, Maggie must take the initiative, which includes helping Brick overcome his drinking and her having a baby. For Maggie, the most obvious source of Brick's drinking problem and loss of libido is his guilty memory of Skipper. Defeating Gooper and Mae's disinheritance plan would hardly profit from exacerbating Brick's guilt over Skipper's death. Realizing that she cannot make Skipper's memory vanish, Maggie chooses to valorize it in the only way possible at the time, by linking it to the classical Greek model of male friendship.

In *Cat*, Williams employs the only two models of homosexuality available for public consumption in the 1950s, the classical, ephebophilic, and platonic ideal of Greek friendship and the homophobic, post-psychoanalytic effeminate identity. When Maggie realizes that it is necessary to confront Brick's homoerotic feeling toward Skipper, she must choose between the two, her only options. Later, in his confrontation with Big Daddy, Brick must also choose between the representations, and he opts for the homophobic. Maggie's selection of the classical Greek model, however, allows her to both ameliorate the situation and reiterate a salient point: Skipper is dead. After Maggie tells of Skipper's downward spiral into depression, alcoholism, and drug dependency, it seems as if his laurels had already begun to wither quite dramatically. And Maggie, with her Diana like archer's prowess, aims right for the heart of the matter.

Williams intersperses Maggie's act one memory theater reconstruction of Skipper with images of the theater of initiation, and those images are repeated and reinforced throughout the dramatic action of the play. Immediately after the speech about the nobility of their friendship, she tells Brick:

> Why I remember when we double-dated at college, Gladys Fitzgerald and I and you and Skipper, it was more like a date between you and Skipper. Gladys and I were just sort of tagging along as if we were necessary to chaperone you!—to make a good public impression—. (44)

This scene calls to mind the traditional concept of the gay "beard," when gay men bring a woman along on a social occasion to give the public impression of heterosexuality. However, this double date also fits into the parameters of Luce Irigaray's argument of women being relegated to a commodity by the homosocial interaction of men. Maggie realizes her position in this initiatory dynamic, but she also continues to exploit the homoerotic underpinnings to Brick and Skipper's friendship. When Brick accuses Maggie of naming his feelings toward Skipper "dirty," she says, "I'm not naming it dirty! I'm naming it clean!" (44). Once again, she emphasizes the point that Brick and Skipper's relationship can be safely addressed from the retrospective position of Skipper's death:

> Then you haven't been listenin', not understood what I'm sayin! I'm naming it so damn clean that it killed poor Skipper!—You two had something that had to be kept on ice, yes, incorruptible, yes!—and death was the only icebox where you could keep it.... (44)

For all of the understanding that this speech demonstrates to most critics of the play, it also illustrates the practicality of Maggie's plan. Brick and Skipper's relationship remains "noble" because it is "incorruptible," and it is no longer a threat to Maggie because Skipper is dead.

Maggie next describes in detail the circumstances that lead to Skipper's death. After a football game, one that Brick missed because of an injury, Maggie suddenly told Skipper, "SKIPPER STOP LOVIN' MY HUSBAND OR TELL HIM HE'S GOT TO LET YOU ADMIT IT TO HIM!" (45). This prompted Skipper to make a failed attempt at seducing Maggie, one in which she describes his impotence as, "that pitiful, ineffectual little attempt to prove what I had said wasn't true...." (45). It is this encounter that started Skipper's downward drug and alcohol spiral toward death. David Savarn points out Maggie's role by stating:

> When she attempts to force her way into the relationship (that decisively unsettles the distinction between homosocial and homosexual desire), making love to Skipper, it is because "it made both of us feel a little bit closer to [Brick]," the common object of desire …Since her liaison with Skipper, Brick's repudiation of him, and Skipper's quasi-suicide, Maggie has become the inheritor, the mediator in a now-immobilized erotic triangle between the living and the dead, the woman who desires to be a partner in an impossible and belated erotic fascination, the woman who, in coveting Brick's aloofness, desires his very refusal to desire her.[28]

Savran's remarks, rather unwittingly, constantly return to how death has rendered the entire situation moot—"now-immobilized erotic triangle," and "an impossible and belated erotic fascination." Maggie, while not the simplistic cause of Skipper's death, realizes that it is both the motivating factor for Brick's emotional nihilism, and also represents a way to possibly rectify the damage, by acknowledging the erotic attachment, naming it "clean," and reclaiming Brick's love. She desires much more than his refusal to desire her.

Most critics argue for the fundamental sincerity of Maggie's understanding toward Brick's homoerotic attraction to Skipper, while ignoring some of the direct clues that her understanding is made possible by Skipper's absence. Mark Royden Winchell maintains:

> Had Williams not found Maggie steadily more charming, he could easily have made her into a female Stanley Kowalski. Brick's assumption that she has driven Skipper to his death (much as Stanley helped drive Blanche insane) seems implausible only because Williams convinces us of Maggie's basic sincerity and decency.[29]

And while Maggie is basically sincere and decent, she is not above bending the truth to suit her own needs. This is evidenced by an important incongruity in her memory theater reconstruction of Skipper. Maggie tells Brick that she and Skipper attempted to make love, "because it made both of us feel a little bit closer to you… And so we made love to each other to dream it was you, both of us!" (43). But the play makes it clear that Brick's alienation of affection in his marriage does not begin until after Skipper's death. In act two, Big Daddy bluntly tells Brick, "you started drinkin' when your friend Skipper died" (84). In her concluding act-one speech, Maggie clearly reminds Brick how happy their marriage was before Skipper's death when she says to him, "and we were happy, weren't we, we were blissful, yes, hit heaven together ev'ry time that we loved!" (45). Maggie's sexual encounter with Skipper may have been altruistic on her part, a way to help him feel closer to Brick, but apparently she needed no such liaison to make her feel closer to her own husband.

At the end of her act-one speech, Maggie reiterates both her motives and her position to Brick:

> I'm honest! Give me credit for just that, will you *please*?—Born poor, raised poor, expect to die poor unless I manage to get us something out of what Big Daddy leaves when he dies of cancer! But Brick?!—*Skipper is dead! I'm alive!* Maggie the cat is...*alive! I am alive, alive! I am ...—alive!* (45–46)

Maggie leaves no doubt about her desires, the love of her husband and the money she believes is rightfully theirs. Her "noble" and classically qualified acceptance of Brick and Skipper's homoerotic friendship seems more expedient than open-minded. She harbors no animosity toward Skipper, especially since he is dead. And her memory theater reconstruction of Skipper represents a way to reconcile with Brick, to acknowledge and accept. However, Maggie's theater-of-initiation images of Brick and Skipper clearly illustrate the homosocial ramifications of their relationship, the dense and complex blend of latent homosexuality and masculinity. Interestingly, at the very end of act one of *Cat*, Williams prepares the reader/viewer for the next bombardment of highly charged exchanges, the fierce interplay of the theaters of memory and initiation, when Brick and Big Daddy confront one another over mendacity, drinking, women, sports, and homosexuality. The final image of act one, after the verbal fireworks between Maggie and Brick have concluded, is noted by Williams in the stage directions: *"Brick has replaced his spilt drink and sits, faraway, on the great four-poster bed"* (47). Faraway indeed, he is absorbed back into the gentle buffer of memory, the symbolic bed, created by the ever present ghosts of Jack Straw and Peter Ochello.

In act two of *Cat on a Hot Tin Roof* Tennessee Williams continues the psychic theater construction, but here the theater of initiation into masculinity supercedes the theater of memory. The scene is still Maggie and Brick's bedsitting room, dominated by the large bed, but the room also becomes the site of Big Daddy's sixty-fifth birthday celebration. Brick's physical immobility, a broken leg caused by the previous night's drunken, failed attempt at jumping hurdles at his old high school track, necessitates that the party be brought to him. And just as he does at the start of act one, Williams has one of the characters quickly describe Brick as a boy. Brick's mother, Big Mama, says to him, "oh you bad boy, you, you're my bad little boy. Give Big Mama a kiss, you bad boy you!" (50). With Brick's "boyishness" firmly established, the party soon turns into a fiasco of bickering over Big Daddy's affections (and money) by most of the characters except Brick. These same characters— Gooper, Mae, Maggie, Reverend Tooker, Dr. Baugh—are all complicit in hiding Big Daddy's terminal cancer diagnosis from him. After Big Daddy clears the room, the stage is soon set for his and Brick's act-long confrontation over the exact nature of Brick's problem—what is gnawing at Brick's emotional core. But Brick has the advantage, and the answers, because he possesses more information, and he knows exactly what is gnawing at Big Daddy's core.

The act two scenes which lead to Brick's memory theater reconstruction of Skipper and his vivid, telling theater-of-initiation images are constantly interrupted and intruded upon to demonstrate how difficult it is for the two men, father and son, to communicate, difficult but not impossible. Some of the impediments to communication are represented by the meddling of other characters. When Big Daddy catches Mae eavesdropping on his and Brick's conversation, he tells her, "you was just nothing but *spyin'* an' you *know* it! (62). At the beginning of the confrontation, in a spoken aside, Big Daddy bluntly asks: "*Why is it so damn hard for people to talk?*" (64). It is so damn hard for these people to talk for myriad complex reasons. It is in the stage directions of act two when Williams tells us that *"some mystery should be left in the revelation of character in a play, just as a great deal of mystery is always left in the revelation of characters in life, even in one's own character to himself"* (85). Brick must also maintain the "open secret" of his and Skipper's homoerotic/homosexual relationship. To complicate act two further and problematize communication, we have Brick's famous contention that "mendacity is a system that we live in" (94). When Big Daddy points out that he and Brick have never lied to one another, Brick quickly adds, "but we've never *talked* to each other"(83). However, between the lying and the secrets, the evasions and the furtive suggestions, Brick and Big Daddy do *talk*, and they both manage to shed light on homosexuality, the homosocial, and masculinity—what it means to be gay, be closeted, be straight, be young, be old, be dying, all in the Delta heat of that bedsitting room.

To introduce and diffuse the subject of homosexuality in act two, Williams uses the broadly drawn and comically greedy characters of Gooper and Mae as a catalyst. When Big Daddy brings up Skipper's death, he tells Brick, "I'm suggesting nothing… But Gooper and Mae suggested that there was something not right exactly in your—… Not, well, exactly *normal* in your friendship with—" (84). According to Mark Royden Winchell:

> It would be inexact, however, to characterize Mae and Gooper as homophobic. They undoubtedly support the official taboos against homosexuality, but there is no evidence that they are viscerally offended by the thought that Brick is a "pervert." The only emotions that seem to move them are avarice and envy.[30]

When Maggie broaches the subject of Brick and Skipper's homoerotic relationship, it is in an attempt to ameliorate the past and heal the future; when Mae and Gooper do it, they are exploiting and exacerbating the past for petty greed. They all have personal ulterior motives for recalling and reconstructing Brick's sexual history. Big Daddy then becomes the only character in *Cat* who addresses Brick's homoerotic feelings as a way of helping, a way of understanding Brick's blank emotional state. The irony in this situation, of course, exists in the fact that Big Daddy is portrayed as the ultimate symbol of patriarchal heterosexuality and masculinity. As playwright Arthur Miller believes, Big Daddy represents "the every image of power, of materiality, of authority."[31] A man who has a "lech" for Maggie (19), asks Brick how she is in bed (91). A man who desires a young mistress so he can, "strip her naked and choke her with diamonds and smother her with minks and hump her from hell to breakfast" (72). A man who says about his wife, "but that old woman she never got enough of it—and I was good in bed..." (72). However, it is the "secret" in Big Daddy's hypermasculine heterosexual past that enables him to relate to Brick, and that secret abides in the buffering background memory theater created by the ghosts of Straw and Ochello.

When Brick is aghast at the very idea that people might have thought that he and Skipper were homosexuals, Big Daddy tries to explain and reason with him:

> BIG DADDY [*gently*]: Now, hold on, a minute, son.—I knocked around in my time.
> BRICK: What's that got to do with—
> BIG DADDY: I said "Hold on!"—I bummed, I bummed this country till I was—
> BRICK: Whose suggestion, who else's suggestion is it?
> BIG DADDY: Slept in hobo jungles and railroad Y's and flophouses in all cities before—. (85–86)

More sophisticated members of a 1955 audience probably understood the implications and import of Big Daddy's "bumming" and "knocking" around; most gay men undoubtedly did.[32] With Big Daddy's first remark to Brick, Williams indicates in the stage directions that he speaks *gently*, a word and mood much more befitting the background memory theater of Straw and Ochello than Brick's turbulent foreground memory-theater construction. And as opposed to hearing understanding in his father's implied homosexual past history, Brick simply hears "queer" and begins his long homophobic tirade:

> Oh, *you* think so, too, you call me your son and a queer. Oh! Maybe that's why you put Maggie and me in this room that was Jack Straw's and Peter Ochello's, in which that pair of old sisters slept in a double bed where both of em died. (86)

Williams then assigns Big Daddy the difficult task of becoming the mediator between the gentle background memory theater and the homophobic foreground memory theater. Straw and Ochello's happy, indulged gay past grates against Brick and Skipper's sad, denied gay past. At Brick's denunciation of Straw and Ochello, Big Daddy emphatically says to him: *"Now just don't go throwing rocks at—"* (86). Further to illustrate just how difficult it is for Big Daddy to defend and support an accepted and happy gay history, Williams has him instantly interrupted by the intrusion of Reverend Tooker, looking for the bathroom. As John M. Clum points out:

> Big Daddy will not allow attacks on Straw and Ochello, but his defense is interrupted by Reverend Tooker, "*the living embodiment of the pious, conventional lie*," an interruption that suggests that it is the pious conventional lie that forbids defense of Straw and Ochello. The interruption is Williams's choice: it allows Brick's homophobic discourse to dominate the scene.[33]

Throughout the remainder of act two, Big Daddy futilely attempts to calm Brick's violent outburst. In the stage directions, Williams tells us that "*Brick is transformed, as if a quiet mountain blew suddenly up in volcanic flame*" (87). Big Daddy tries to allay Brick's homophobic rant numerous times, with lines such as, "I'm just saying I understand such—"(87). However, Brick's sublimated homophobia over his homosexual attraction to Skipper has, like the quiet mountain, reached a critical mass, and no understanding or empathy can stop its eruption. When Big Daddy evokes the gentle, understanding memory theater represented by the ghosts of Straw and Ochello, the background buffer, Brick quite literally shouts him down, "YOU THINK SO, TOO?"(87). Until the end of the act, Williams shows the power of the wildly homophobic driven by the unfettered masculine dynamics of the homosocial. Brick's dark, introspective theater of memory (where, just perhaps, he loved Skipper) is eclipsed by his bright and vivid theater of initiation, homosocial and brutal (where, just perhaps, he loved Skipper).

The beginning of Brick's homophobic outburst in act two is fueled by such words as "queer"(86) and *"sodomy!"*(87), but it is his description of Straw and

Ochello's relationship that shatters the buffering background: "Straw? Ochello? A couple of…ducking sissies? Queers? Is that what you—" (88). Williams represents the elderly and ill Big Daddy as too exhausted, physically and emotionally, to defend the positive gay history of the bedroom further, when he says to Brick, "Jesus! Whew…. Grab my hand!" (88). And Brick's refusal, "naw, I don't want your hand…." (88), implies his victory over any memory construction of homosexuality not poisoned by homophobia and the homosocial.

If Maggie's combined theaters of memory and initiation are meant to heal, then Brick's are meant to damage his frozen subjective state further and extend his emotional stasis. To reiterate images of homosexual initiation, Brick, like Maggie, reconstructs his and Skipper's college experiences. However, Maggie's story of the double date, when it seemed more as if Brick and Skipper were a couple, is almost innocent when compared to Brick's college memory and his story of initiation—a vicious fraternity fag bashing. Brick tells Big Daddy:

> Why, at Ole Miss, when it was discovered a pledge to our fraternity, Skipper's and mine, did a, *attempted* to do a, unnatural thing with—We not only dropped him like a hot rock!—We told him to git off campus, and he did, he got!—All the way to…North Africa, last I heard! (88–89)[34]

Acts such as this, in part created by the severe homophobic climate of the 1950s, were not only forgiven in young men, they were usually actively encouraged by the prevailing societal norms. After he relates this story, Brick asks Big Daddy, and also those same prevailing societal norms, "why can't exceptional friendship, *real, real, deep, deep friendship!* between two men be respected as something clean and decent without being thought of as—… *Fairies….*"(89). It is no wonder that Brick's memory-theater reconstruction of Skipper is so toxic and that his initiation-theater reconstructions are so cruel. In Williams' stage directions, immediately following Brick's pained and dramatic declaration of the word *Fairies*, he states that "[*In his utterance of this word, we gauge the wide and profound reach of the conventional mores he got from the world that crowned him with early laurel*]" (89). Those "conventional mores," particularly during the period when Williams was writing *Cat on a Hot Tin Roof* and it was a hit on the Broadway stage, help explain not simply 1950s homophobia but also its lasting negative impact on constructions of American masculinity. According to Michelangelo Signorile:

> The fear that swept gay men at the height of the McCarthy Era cannot be underestimated. It exploited a prevailing fear in American culture at large of effeminate men and instilled it further, even among gay men. Not only would men, gay and straight, not want to appear effeminate lest someone think they were homosexual, but the profusely masculine pose that straight men adopted in the 1950s had a profound effect on gay men that lasted for generations.[35]

Brick's homophobic discourse finally reaches a tenuous dénouement when he tries to explain to Big Daddy his and Skipper's relationship in terms of boyhood and sports, as if homoerotic attraction was simply an adolescent indiscretion expressed and sublimated on the football field—the very arena of the homosocial.

Brick's memory-theater construction of Skipper begins with an implied caveat to excuse their behavior and relationship, and in an attempt to make his explanation more feasible, he ascribes it to Maggie: "Maggie declares that Skipper and I went into pro-football after we left Ole Miss' because we were scared to grow up…" (90). In his detailed study of masculinity, homosexuality, and American organized sports, Brian Pronger illustrates the roots of Brick's homophobia in the context of professional football:

> By making it known that one is gay, one is making it clear that one thinks there is a different legitimate interpretation of the fundamental myths of our culture. This constitutes a basic rejection of conservatism, of the status quo. Hiding homosexuality, on the other hand, *even if it is known that one is hiding*, indicates that one either agrees with the status quo or at least defers to it.[36]

Brick not only seems to agree with the status quo but has deferred to it to such an extent that he has become blank, unable to feel anything except the brief extremes of rage and hate. To defer to the status quo further, Brick's memory-theater reconstruction of his and Skipper's relationship represents a highly edited and watered-down version of events. Brick's story of Skipper's downfall and death is so sanitized that Big Daddy correctly refers to it as "that half-ass story!" (91). And Brick must confess that the story is truly "half-ass" when he admits to leaving out a drunken telephone call from Skipper in which he told Brick that he loved him. Brick's theater of memory is polluted by this initiatory homosexual declaration of love.

Brick and Big Daddy's confrontation ends act two of *Cat*, and Williams has probed homosexuality as best a 1950s American playwright could at the time. Brick's vehement homophobia represents a way for the play to examine a taboo topic and not obviously approve of it. Most gay men viewing a production of *Cat* in 1955, whether they agreed or not, probably well understood Brick's position, his argument. Big Daddy must force Brick to face the truth about him and Skipper, when he says to Brick, "*You!*—dug the grave of your friend and kicked him in it!—before you'd face the truth with him!" (92). And at the end of act two, when in retaliation Brick tells Big Daddy the secret everyone has hidden from him, his imminent death from cancer, the irony of Brick's comment to him is not wasted on a gay audience: "—And being friends is telling each other the truth. . . ." (94).

The multiform concluding third act of *Cat* presents a reader or critic with several problems. In the original version, before Williams made Kazan's suggested changes, one extra memory-theater reconstruction of Skipper exists. This one belongs to Big Mama when she describes the details of Skipper's drug and alcohol induced death (101). This short passage, in which Skipper is represented as basically pathetic, seems primarily expository (and unnecessarily redundant) at best, simply gratuitous at worst; it also appears unchanged in the Broadway version. Big Mama's story is the final mention of Skipper. In both third acts, Straw and Ochello are conspicuously missing by name, and only symbolically appear at the very end, when Maggie attempts to lure Brick into their bed. Even in that manifestation, the Straw and Ochello ghosts have lost their role and power as generators of the buffering background theater of memory. Maggie usurps the homosexual power of their bed, claims it for heterosexuality and her desired impregnation. At the very end of the Broadway version of act three, Williams ironically represents the bed as a sexual shrine of reproduction, an altar, by having Maggie supplicate herself at it: "*then she kneels quickly beside Brick at foot of bed*" (158). Effectively, both theaters of memory and initiation, the homosocial dynamic, and questions of masculinity, all motivating factors for the dramatic action of the first two acts of the play, vanish in the original and Broadway third acts. And they vanish to the detriment of the play, prompting many critics, such as the above mentioned Roger Boxill, to argue that "no version of Act III quite works, because the final act is an afterthought."[37] Williams, who in all probability realized that the problems with act three stemmed from the absence of the dramatic force of the examination of homosexuality and masculinity, attempts to reinsert that dramatic force by reintroducing Big Daddy—creating even more problems and critical conjecture.

Big Daddy's sudden and unexplained reappearance in the Broadway version of act three does appear to be "tacked" on. Thomas F. Van Lann points out, "Kazan wanted Big Daddy brought back in act three because he is such a vibrant and impressive character. But Big Daddy does not belong in act three, for he has nothing more to contribute."[38] But in all of his third-act incarnations, Big Daddy does have something to contribute, the only thing he contributes, a dirty joke. This bawdy story holds some major importance for Williams, as evidenced by the fact that when given the opportunity to rewrite the vexing act three for a 1974 Broadway revival of *Cat* completely, he does nothing more than insert the joke into the original act three, and then remove it again. The subject of Big Daddy's dirty joke demonstrates Williams' attempt to reinfuse act three with the complex mélange of homosexuality, homoeroticism, homosociality, and masculinity which drives the dramatic action of the earlier two acts of the play.

Just as he does in *A Streetcar Named Desire*, Williams has a male character relate a traditional dirty joke to sexualize the situation. And the theme, the hypersexuality of a male animal (a rooster in *Streetcar*), is repeated in *Cat*. On the surface, Big Daddy's joke is rather sophomoric and trite; it involves a father, mother, and young son visiting a zoo. When the son sees that a bull elephant is sexually aroused by a nearby female elephant in heat, he asks his mother about the conspicuous change in the elephant's profile. His mother replies, "oh, that's nothing'!" to which his father adds, "she's spoiled!" (152). Throughout his telling of the joke, Big Daddy continuously asks Brick if his language is too vulgar:

> BIG DADDY:... Ain't that a nice way to put it, Brick?
> BRICK: Yes sir, nothin' wrong with it.
> *And*
> BIG DADDY: ... Ain't I telling this story in decent language, Brick?
> BRICK: Yes, sir, too ruttin' decent! (151–152)

It is evident that the story is meant for Brick's elucidation alone. And while the dirty joke's topic is nominally reproduction, Williams has already displayed his, and Big Daddy's, disgust with heterosexual overfecundity in all of the references to Gooper and Mae's animal-like brood of children. In act two, Big Daddy tells Brick:

> But Gooper's wife's a good breeder, you got to admit she's fertile. Hell, at supper tonight she had them all at the table and they had to put a couple of extra leafs in the table to make room for them, she's got five head of them, now, and another one's comin'. ... (61)

Big Daddy's joke cannot relate to Maggie's sham pregnancy; he tells it before her announcement. So why, exactly, does he tell a story whose punch line is exaggeratedly phallic and for Brick's sole benefit?

If one returns to Peter Lyman's previously noted Freudian support of dirty jokes as an intricate factor of male group bonding, then Big Daddy's story becomes a homerotically charged cautionary tale for his son:

> As Freud observed, the jokes that individual men direct toward women are generally erotic, tend to clever forms (like the double entendre), and have a seductive purpose. The jokes that men tell about women in the presence of other men are sexual and

> aggressive rather than erotic and use hostile rather than clever verbal forms; and... have the creation of male group bonding as their purpose.[39]

Though all of the major characters are present when Big Daddy tells the joke, it seems clear that he is telling it to Brick alone. And Big Daddy is so careful to make his language appropriate, "clever forms (like the double entendre)," that he even seeks Brick's approval. Brick implores him to make the story more explicit, and thus make it a heterosexual male bonding device, when he says of the usage, "yes, sir, too ruttin' decent!"(152). The joke, as basic as it is, is more clever and playful than aggressive and hostile, so its purpose, according to Freud, is seductive and erotic. However, Big Daddy's purpose is a seduction of Brick's subjective sexuality. The punch line of the joke can only be read in one way, that women do not fully understand or appreciate male sexuality, represented by the elephantine phallus. The dirty story serves an identical purpose if the symbolic phallus is replaced with a biological penis. Evolutionary biologist Jared Diamond, in a very nonsymbolic or representational study of gender responses to penis size, indicates that many women find that "the sight of a penis is, if anything, unattractive. The ones really fascinated by the penis and its dimensions are men. In the showers in men's locker rooms, men routinely size up each other's endowment."[40] Interestingly, Brick's homoerotic friendship with Skipper is based in the sphere of sports, where the locker room represents a homosocial location for men to display their bodies—in the absence of women. So Big Daddy's joke, while on the surface patently heterosexual, in the highly structured telling becomes both homosocial and homoerotic.

The bawdy story allows Williams to subvert traditional male bonding in an attempt to return act three of *Cat* to the subject of homosexuality and masculinity, but the playwright fails. Act three, all of the various act threes, fall rather flat, burdened by superfluous comic repartee and a dearth of substance. Big Daddy's inserted appearance and joke, though a highly complicated construction, is just that, inserted to the point of being clumsily intrusive. The primary reason that act three of *Cat on a Hot Tin Roof* is never "fixed" is because it can't be.

As a study of masculinity and homosexuality, *Cat on a Hot Tin Roof* represents a flawed but, nevertheless, compelling work of drama. Tennessee Williams skillfully probes several gay issues in the play, issues that necessitate his somewhat oblique approach. The play's major importance in Williams' canon is how well it illustrates the playwright's ability to create, construct, and reconstruct characters through the complex theater of memory, and then sexualize those characters by recalled and repeated initiatory scenes. The textual problems with the play are a symptom more than a cause in and of themselves. The true difficulty with *Cat on a Hot Tin Roof* stems from Williams' inability to balance the various memory theaters. When female characters alone are given the duty to recreate missing gay characters in Williams' plays, there exists a kind of dramatic equilibrium, as in *A Streetcar Named Desire*. However, in Cat the male characters, Brick and Big Daddy, their masculine subjectivities clashing at every word, throw the dramatic balance off to the point of distraction. Interestingly, in all of Williams' major plays written prior to his publicly coming out in 1970, *Cat on a Hot Tin Roof* is the only one in which two male characters discuss the issue of homosexuality. As if to magnify this point, *Cat* is also the only play of Williams that critics, both popular and academic, insist is *not* about homosexuality. When female characters recreate the missing gay men, they seem to be mitigated of their sexual transgressions. It is only when Brick and Big Daddy, the football player and the man's man, masculine avatars, recreate homosexuality that critics get concerned and worried. As if to acknowledge and indicate this perceived problem, in his next play with a missing gay character, Tennessee Williams returns to reconstruction by women alone—and the theaters of memory and initiation reach an art form.

❋ CHAPTER 3

Suddenly Last Summer

"You think I've got the time to count
your crimes, you pup?
Your guilt consists in this: I want to eat
you up!"
— Ivan Krylov "Wolf and Lamb"

Unlike *A Streetcar Named Desire* and *Cat on a Hot Tin Roof*, Tennessee Williams' *Suddenly Last Summer* (1958) holds no real, firm place in the American collective consciousness of popular culture.[1] More psychologically complex than *Streetcar* and more fully realized than *Cat*, *Suddenly Last Summer*, for its supposed subject matter, tends to generate more controversy than real criticism. *Suddenly Last Summer*, with a compressed four scene structure, is shorter than most of Williams' plays, so he paired it with an older play entitled *Something Unspoken* and gave them the collective title *Garden District*. The paired plays opened on Broadway in 1958. *Suddenly*, set in the elegant Garden District of New Orleans (as opposed to the lower class Elysian Fields setting of *Streetcar*), tells the story of a wealthy widow, Violet Venable, who entices a young psychiatrist, Dr. Cukrowicz, to perform an experimental lobotomy on her niece, Catharine Holly, in an attempt to eradicate Catharine's memory, or fantasy, that she witnessed Violet's son, her cousin Sebastian, eaten alive by starving street urchins in the mysteriously vague Spanish-named country of Cabeza de Lobo. The institutionalized Catharine's mother and brother also figure in the play as poor relations who stand to be included in Sebastian's estate if Catharine will recant, or forget, her gruesome story. *Suddenly* has traditionally been interpreted by academic critics as a modern morality tale, one that examines an inescapable, cruel, and naturalistic world, explored and exploited by the effete dilettante Sebastian, a gay man who cavalierly uses the people around him—family, friends, and strangers. Many early critics were unable to move beyond the linked taboos of homosexuality and cannibalism, even if both were considered from a figurative standpoint. According to S. Alan Chesler, Signi Falk, writing in 1961, argued that *Suddenly* was basically, "another private and very sick view of the world.... Williams has carried his private symbolism to incredible extremes when he would make a decadent artist and aging homosexual, a sybarite who never took a stand for right or wrong...a symbol to represent all men of our time." But as Chesler points out, Falk's literary indignation is woefully miscalculated, because in no part of the play does Williams even imply that Sebastian represents "all men of our time."[2] This type of early critical overreaction to Williams' gay-themed plays is common, as are erroneous readings. Paul J. Hurley, writing about *Suddenly Last Summer* in 1966, from a somewhat more mature and sophisticated critical viewpoint, maintains:

> In that play Williams dealt with homosexuality and cannibalism—disturbing subjects, no doubt—but they do more than shock; they act as metaphors....The point I am suggesting is an important one, and the failure to recognize it has led to considerable misunderstanding of Williams' themes and his methods as an artist. Concentrating on the literal events of the plays, critics have ignored the symbolic function of those events. They have committed the fundamental error of confusing dramatic methods and have treated as realistic theater plays which should be seen as poetic and symbolic.

Hurley is correct in his assessment that many critics before him had made "fundamental errors" in regard to Williams' works, errors precipitated mainly by a social discomfort with expressions of sexuality. Hurley, writing in 1966, demonstrates, "a fairly Victorian vigilance has prevented us from recognizing sexual corruption as an acceptable equivalent for moral degeneracy. For most of us, let's admit it, sex is shock, not symbol."[3] This is particularly true in the case of *Suddenly Last Summer.* In S. Alan Chesler's 1977 bibliographic essay, "Tennessee Williams: Reassessment and Assessment," he astutely notes, "now that the shock value of the play has diminished with the passing of time, other scholars may restudy the work and objectively reassess this neglected masterpiece."[4] And they have—to an extent. *Suddenly Last Summer* differs from *Streetcar* and *Cat* in more than just its absence from popular culture—even today it is still oddly under criticized.

Though still rather scant, more recent critical response to *Suddenly* recognizes that the play's true substance is less about cannibalism and more about memory and ritual initiation. Thomas F. Van Laan believes that "*Suddenly Last Summer* is gaining increasing recognition as one of Williams' best plays because we are finally discovering how it is shaped and what it is about." With its private and contained battle royal between Violet and Catharine as to who will claim and own the only memory reconstruction of the dead poet Sebastian, the play represents Williams' most indulgent exercise in the theater of memory. *Suddenly Last Summer* is, quite literally, a play about memory, so literal that Violet demands to have the biological center of memory excised from Catharine's brain. As Van Laan observes:

> Contrary to much that has been written, it is not a study of Sebastian Venable, sensationalistic or otherwise; rather, it dramatizes a conflict between opposing versions (or visions) of Sebastian, and especially a conflict for supremacy between the two who hold them.[5]

In *Suddenly Last Summer*, this conflict crystallizes the concept of memory reconstruction that informs both *Streetcar* and *Cat.* Sebastian's life, and how he lived it, becomes critically less important than how and who recreates it by recall; thus cannibalism seems less a fitting punishment for his moral transgressions and more an ultimate taboo, amplified by homosexuality. When Tennessee Williams decided to write a play entirely about memory, he wisely decided to make the stakes bizarrely high—a loving, artistic son or a cold, predatory pedophile ironically eaten by his prey. *Streetcar's* dim, fragile theater of memory and *Cat's* bright, complex one both give way in *Suddenly Last Summer* to a fully realized study of how and why characters actively compete to reconstruct the absent. And while the theater of initiation, and masculinity, can be more easily delineated in the two earlier plays, it still exists in *Suddenly*, but on a much more problematic and theoretically dense plane— one steeped in ritual and sexual taboos.

In *Streetcar* and *Cat*, Williams uses the distinctly American masculine activities of poker and football to create the theaters of initiation. Sebastian Venable, with all of his affectations and pretensions, represents a character who would never be involved in such mundane masculine pursuits. Like Blanche DuBois's dead husband, Allan, Sebastian is a poet, a socialite artist who seeks his inspiration and sex globally. His urbanity informs his homosexuality, a type of old-world drawing room queerness. In both visual-image descriptions of the dead Sebastian in the play, we can only picture him in an exquisite, stark white suit or dressed as a Renaissance pageboy at a costume ball in Cannes. His mother tells Doctor Cukrowicz that Sebastian had "An attitude toward life that's hardly been known in the world since the great Renaissance princes were crowded out of their palaces and gardens by successful shopkeepers!"[6] Williams goes to great lengths to de-Americanize the play. First, he sets *Suddenly* in the most exotic and European of American cities, New Orleans. Second, Violet describes her and Sebastian's jet-set lifestyle by mentioning several world capitols and continents as the settings for their exploits—Europe, Asia, South America. Finally, Sebastian meets his fate in the mysteriously named Cabeza de Lobo (*Head of the Wolf*), a country never geographically pinpointed by Williams; however, one can assume from its description that it represents some Third World location. Although, at first, Cabeza de Lobo appears to be located in either Central or South America, it must be somewhere in Europe or at least on the Mediterranean. Sebastian and Catharine travel there from Paris, without a lengthy trip mentioned, and Violet tells the doctor: "They couldn't shut her up in Cabeza de Lobo or at the clinic in Paris" (27). Once again, *Suddenly* differs dramatically from *Streetcar* and *Cat* in that Sebastian is not an American type, a native masculine construction, like the swaggering and overtly sexual Stanley or the all American boy Brick. The archaic Sebastian's theater of initiation must be archaic as well, so it becomes a sexual ritual of symbolic consumption. In the two earlier plays, Williams created ways in which the gay viewer/reader could find pleasure in the theaters of initiation, created by the masculine American homosocial dynamic, even experience pleasure beyond such barriers as suicide and death. In *Suddenly Last Summer*, there is no pleasure, no imagining beyond the theater of memory to a place where two gay men—Allan and his friend, Jack Straw and Peter Ochello, even Brick and Skipper—take pleasure in one another's bodies. In *Suddenly*, there is only a kind of primal terror brought about by a dangerous sexuality, one that consumes and is consumed in turn. Poker and football give way to the ancient Greek frenzy rituals of *sparagmos* and *omophagia*, the wild tearing and eating of raw human flesh. With the theater of initiation rendered horrible beyond pleasure, then the theater of memory becomes the true crux of *Suddenly Last Summer*.

Interestingly, after *Cat on a Hot Tin Roof's* frustrating clash of male subjectivities, represented by the second act confrontation between Brick and Big Daddy, Tennessee Williams returns to female memory reconstruction alone in *Suddenly*. As he did in *Streetcar*, Williams does not allow male characters to participate in and compete for the memory reconstruction of an absent character; only Violet and Catharine vie for that position. As Susan Koprince notes: "confronted with these radically different memories—these multiple voices—the audience must decide which image of an unseen character is ultimately more credible." However, Koprince, like many other critics of the play, wrongly contends that "so dominant is his presence that Sebastian Venable, a figure who never appears in person in *Suddenly Last Summer*, actually succeeds in taking over the drama—emerging, one could argue, as its true major character."[7] Nominally, just as *Cat* has multiple protagonists, *Suddenly Last Summer* has two, Violet and Catharine. Relating directly to

Thomas F. Van Laan's earlier stated belief, about the play, that, "we are finally discovering how it is shaped and what it is about," Judith J. Thompson points out, "even as Mrs. Venable and Catharine narrate their antithetical memory stories of Sebastian's life and death, they act as the major antagonists in his story's reenactment." If Violet and Catharine are considered antagonists, then Thompson's contention agrees with Koprince's, that Sebastian is the play's main character. Thompson does, however, clearly illustrate *Suddenly's* complicated dramatic structure, often ignored at the expense of the sensationalism of cannibalism:

> As dramatically realized, then, the play is structured not in the sequential pattern of a story told, then reenacted, but by the *simultaneous* revelations of the fate of Sebastian and the fate of Catharine—thereby heightening the suspense of each revelation and creating emotional tension by withholding the full understanding of their analogical significance until the play's very end.[8]

Thompson shows how Williams, by the play's structure, has used another method to reinforce memory, a method that has moved beyond simple repetition and one that actually informs meaning in *Suddenly's* complex narrative form. But, figuratively, the *true* major character of the play is neither the women nor the dead Sebastian—it is the theater of memory.

As he does in *Streetcar* and *Cat*, Williams begins *Suddenly Last Summer* with a detailed stage direction in which he describes his concept for the play's set, and this set contains as much information about the play as its structure does. He writes:

> *The set may be as unrealistic as the décor of a dramatic ballet. It represents part of a mansion of Victorian Gothic style in the Garden District of New Orleans on a late afternoon, between late summer and early fall. The interior is blended with a fantastic garden which is more like a tropical jungle, or forest, in the prehistoric age of giant fern-forests when living creatures had flippers turning to limbs and scales to skin.* (9)

The set is often interpreted by early critics as a background for the play's literal and figurative study of evolution and naturalism, represented by Violet's story of the trip she and Sebastian took to the Encantadas, the Enchanted Isles, better known as the Galapagos Islands. On this trip, one of Sebastian's numerous searches for a proof of God, they witness thousands of sea turtle eggs hatch on a beach, and then the natural selective slaughter as the hatchlings try to make their way to the sea, the majority only to be viciously eaten by sea birds before they reach their destination. However, later critics such as Leonard Quirino take note of Williams' set directions and maintains that "Williams suggests that the mode of the play is to be abstract and ceremonial rather than naturalistic and the action that will unfold abstractly expressionistic rather than merely literal." Quirino believes that Williams' primary abstraction, represented by the blended Victorian mansion and junglelike garden, "fuses the human and the vegetable realms as part of one cosmically destructive scheme."[9] But there also exists another way in which to view the set, one that helps to create and define the theater of memory.

From a Freudian standpoint, the set of *Suddenly* is structured to reflect the human unconscious, the foundation of memory, the part of Catharine's brain and psyche that Violet wants the doctor to cut out and destroy. Williams is specific when he writes that the interior of the Gothic Victorian mansion is *blended* with the junglelike garden, replete with the appropriate sounds: "*there are harsh cries and sibilant hissings and thrashing sounds in the garden, as if it were inhabited by beasts, serpents, and birds, all of savage nature....* (9). No domestic interior could represent the strict order of the consciousness as well as an American Gothic Victorian sitting room, just as no setting could represent the wild and dark, chaotic and terrible depths of the human unconscious as well as a prehistoric jungle—and they are blended. In a classically psychoanalytic study of Nathaniel Hawthorne's short story, "Young Goodman Brown," Wilfred L. Guerin draws an identical analogy:

> On one level, then, the village may be equated with consciousness, the forest with the dark recesses of the unconscious. But, more accurately, the village, as a place of social and moral order (and inhibition) is analogous to Freud's superego, conscience, the morally inhibiting agent of the psyche; the forest, as a place of wild, untamed passions and terrors, has the attributes of the Freudian id.

With this idea in mind, Violet and Catharine's battle for the memory reconstruction of Sebastian becomes both ironic and tragic. Regardless of which one triumphs, she ultimately will lose, just as Brick Pollit is playing a metaphoric game that he cannot win. The winner will be in the same position as Young Goodman Brown, and Guerin reminds us, "as mediator between these opposing forces, Brown himself resembles the poor ego, which tries to effect a healthy balance and is shattered because it is unable to do so."[10] In response to Paul J. Hurley's "*Suddenly Last Summer* as Morality Play,'" the only other critical source on the play that even mentions Hawthorne, Judith J. Thompson notes, "not Hawthorne, but his contemporary and admirer Melville is explicitly invoked by the play's literary allusions."[11] While this is true, Hurley simply utilizes a comparison between Tennessee Williams and Hawthorne to define, equate, and perhaps essentialize Sebastian's homosexuality with evil:

> To look about oneself for manifestations of sinfulness and to become so overwhelmed by the viciousness of humanity that one begins to see cruelty and vulgarity as the only truths about human nature is, for Williams, as it was for Hawthorne, a fearful sin.[12]

In *Suddenly*, Williams has moved beyond a staid nineteenth-century notion of sin and how we must pay for it, to a modern realm where sexuality is a basic component of identity and subjectivity, and a complex marker for masculinity. To emphasize this point further, he extends the Freudian setting conflict, the anxiety created by the tension between consciousness and unconsciousness, *out* from the Gothic Victorian mansion—to the city and the world.

The city of New Orleans also becomes a site for memory reconstruction when Williams represents it in terms of consciousness and unconsciousness. Thomas J. Richardson believes that Williams was "influenced significantly by the exotic unreality of New Orleans, so much, in fact, that the city became an informing image for his art." Richardson's argument for New Orleans' role in Williams' plays is temporal, dividing it into a city of night and a city of day. Richardson demonstrates that Williams wrote about:

> a city defined as undercurrent of sin, release, depravity, particularly violence and sex.

> …The city of night and release was a place where one could attempt escape from restrictions, inhibitions, the burdens of responsibility and time, and live only for the fulfillment of the moment. However, the city of night is always followed by the city of day, and the world of history and time can never be escaped.[13]

This concept, that New Orleans as a city of night represents a type of unconscious sphere and physical embodiment of the Freudian id, is evident in *Suddenly Last Summer.* The act that originally prompts Catharine's neurosis and causes Sebastian to ask her to accompany him on his summer tour is her rape, late at night in the French Quarter. Catharine leaves a Mardi Gras Ball at a downtown New Orleans hotel after her date passes out from drinking; she is offered a ride home by a young married man who first drives her to the fringes of the French Quarter and rapes her. Williams emphasizes the darkness of the scene, both figurative and literal, when Catharine says:

> We stopped near the Duelling [sic] Oaks at the end of Esplanade Street. …Stopped!—I said, "What for?"—He didn't answer, just struck a match in the car to light a cigarette in the car and I looked at him in the car and I knew "what for"!—(65).

Only the dim illumination of the burning match gives Catharine a hint at the reality of the dark situation, enveloped in physical darkness. When she tells the story, in the stability of daylight, Violet has already dismissed its validity by telling everyone present, "she'd lost her head over a young married man, made a scandalous scene at a Mardi Gras ball, in the middle of the ballroom" (57). Later, when Catharine relates the tale of Sebastian's cannibalistic death, Williams has her describe the scene in an almost preternatural bright white light cast by a glaring noon day sun, as if to imply that the theater of memory is a place defined by extremes—pitch black or blazing white—the outer boundaries of the order of consciousness. As Richardson says about Tennessee Williams himself, he "turned in his art to the exotic unreality of the city of night, the fringe of his consciousness, and made it his reality."[14] However, Williams also turned to the very geography of New Orleans for a similar purpose.

In scene four of *Suddenly,* Dr. Cukrowicz questions Catharine under the influence of a truth serum drug he has administered. When she tells the doctor that she realized that Sebastian wanted her as a traveling companion so she could procure young men for him, to demonstrate her worldliness Catharine tells the doctor: "I knew what I was doing. I came out in the French Quarter years before I came out in the Garden District…." (81). Richardson points out that

> The time-honored dividing line between the French Quarter and the American commercial and residential sectors, including the famous Garden district, is Canal Street…. Traditionally, Canal Street defines the contrasts of the American-French city which include past vs. present, Protestant vs. Catholic, age vs. youth, wealth vs. poverty, inhibitions vs. a joie de vivre, and a clearly bilingual society.[15]

In regard to *Suddenly*, one could easily add to these pairings consciousness vs. unconsciousness and superego vs. id. The married man drives Catharine from the order of the Roosevelt Hotel ballroom, on Canal Street, to the dark and libidinal French Quarter, the Duelling Oaks at the end of Esplanade Street, the street which marks the eastern boundary of the Quarter. On the other side of Esplanade Street are the Elysian Fields, the setting for *A Streetcar Named Desire*.[16]

The dilettante poet Sebastian is also a habitué of the French Quarter. His mother tells the doctor how Sebastian only wrote one poem a year, "which he printed himself on an eighteenth-century hand-press at his—atelier in the—French-Quarter—so no one but he could see it…." (14). Violet's hesitations, indicated by Williams' use of dashes, indicates that she is couching her terms too carefully. The reader can easily assume that other activities, "so no one else but he could see it," were going on at Sebastian's French Quarter "atelier"—perhaps some of that "joie de vivre" Richardson noted, common in the Quarter and in opposition to the inhibitions of the Garden District. Steven Bruhm interprets these geographical elements and boundaries as helping to define Sebastian's homosexuality when he states, "the topography here is interesting …it separates the workings of the libidinal economy from the political economy." Bruhm then makes an argument that relates directly to the concept of homosexuality as an "open secret," the dynamic so well illustrated in *Cat on a Hot Tin Roof.* However, Bruhm uses an economic and spatial model in his study of *Suddenly*:

> But while the French Quarter may well represent sexual freedom, that freedom is... shadowed by the adjacent city of puritan ethics and economic commercialism. The libidinal economy is constantly being surveyed by the political economy, so that the two worlds are not divided as much as they are defined by each other, by the overwhelming sense of *difference* that each represents to the other.[17]

Topography informs and helps to create sexual meaning in *Suddenly*, just as Alan Sinfield demonstrates with his "open secret" theory of public and private boundaries: "it helps to constitute the public/private boundary—the binary that seems to demarcate our subjectivities from a public realm, while actually producing those subjectivities—and thus facilitates the policing of the boundary."[18] Thus Bruhm correctly contends that "Williams is exploring how, in the field of homosexual desire, the commercial sensibility of the American city surrounds the erotic topography of Sebastian Venable's sexual behaviour, and becomes complicit in what it seeks to condemn."[19] New Orleans, with its many dual natures, represents the very foundation of the human psyche, the conscious and the unconscious, the realm of the theater of memory. In *Suddenly Last Summer*, as if to emphasize the point, Williams expands this concept—he makes it global.

Violet and Sebastian Venable are, in the 1950s vernacular, jet-setters, wealthy people with enough time and money to travel to any world location—a symptom of the ennui of the rich. Most of their destinations represent traditional haunts of the jet set. In scene one, Violet tells the doctor that Sebastian:

> had a perfect little court of young and beautiful people around him always, wherever he was, here in New Orleans, or New York or on the Riviera or in Paris and Venice, he always had a little entourage of the beautiful and the talented and the young! (22)

It is only when Sebastian feels the need for spiritual fulfillment that they venture out from the clean, well-ordered places, almost penitently, as if enlightenment cannot be found or achieved in the consciousness represented by "civilized" cities. Violet tells the doctor about the first of these spiritual trips, to the Galapagos Islands. She quotes Herman Melville's description of the islands:

> Quote—take five and twenty heaps of cinders dumped here and there in an outside city lot. Imagine some of them magnified into mountains, and the vacant lot, the sea And you'll have a fit idea of the general aspect of the Encantadas, the Enchanted Isles—extinct volcanoes, looking much as the world at large might look— after a last conflagration— end quote. (15)

A far cry from the well structured, planned boulevards of Paris or the canals of Venice, the primal Encantadas represent the ultimate topographical landscape of the human unconscious. And what Violet and Sebastian witness there, the violent slaughter of the sea turtles by the predatory birds, represents the disorder and fury of the id, not a complex, naturalistic manifestation of the godhead or a reflection of Sebastian's "evil" homosexual nature. The traditional critical interpretation of the trip to the Encantadas is best represented by Thomas P. Adler:

> *Suddenly Last Summer* is a modern morality play, revealing not what good is, or what God is, but rather what evil is. And what God is not. Sebastian went looking for a clear image of God in the Encantadas islands and thinks he found the desired image in the birds of prey devouring the newborn turtles.[20]

Apparently, two regular and natural occurrences, a necessary population control feeding and Sebastian's homosexuality, represent evil for Adler, if not for Tennessee Williams. Most critics, wholly disregarding Sebastian and Violet's capricious and dilettante lifestyle, are all too ready to consider Sebastian's search for God as the true location of meaning in *Suddenly Last Summer*. This might well be the case if Williams had not included a second spiritual journey for the Venables, mother and son; and this one, like the problematic third act of *Cat on a Hot Tin Roof*, is patently and dramatically comic.

On the second of these spiritual journeys, Sebastian and Violet travel to the Himalayas so Sebastian can enter a Buddhist monastery. Violet tells the doctor that he "had gone so far as to shave his head and eat just rice out of a wood bowl on a grass mat" (20). When Sebastian decides to renounce all worldly goods and give his fortune to the monks, Violet "saves" him, at the expense of returning to her dying husband in New Orleans. She rescues him from what she calls, "those sly Buddhist monks" (20):

> I got him through that crisis too. In less than a month he got up off the filthy grass mat and threw the rice bowl away—and booked us into Shepheard's Hotel in Cairo and the Ritz in Paris—. And from then on, oh, we—still lived in a—world of light and shadow.... But the shadow was almost as luminous as the light. (21)

They flee the dark unconsciousness, represented by the remote and mystical Himalayas, and return to the bright conscious world of the city. Violet's phrase, "world of light and shadow," reflects the play's use of binaries, conscious and unconscious, civilized and uncivilized, but she also shows that these binaries will not hold when she says, "but the shadow was almost as luminous as the light." The dark experiences of life *should* become as enlightening as the bright ones because the two cannot be separated. Neal B. Houston believes that "mother and son continue to live in their own chiaroscuro world"[21]—giving Sebastian and Violet's life together the depth and complexity of a Renaissance painting, one of a never ending party occasionally interrupted by a quick search for God.

The final geographical and spatial blending of conscious and unconscious sets the stage for both Catharine's theater of memory and Sebastian's death. While in Cabeza de Lobo, they exist in a world that is bifurcated by economics and space. In scene four, while under the influence of a truth serum, Catharine tells the doctor that she and her cousin spent most of their time at "a beach that's named for Sebastian's name saint, it's known as La Playa San Sebastian, and that's where we started spending all afternoon, every day" (78). When Catharine tells the doctor that La Playa San Sebastian was a public beach, Violet immediately contradicts her: "That Sebastian would go every day to some dirty free public beach near a harbor? A man that had to go out a mile in a boat to find water to swim in?" (79). Catharine explains that: "No, it wasn't the free one, the free one was right next to it, there was a fence between the free beach and the one that we went to that charged a small charge of admission" (79). Later we learn that the innocuous sounding fence is actually a barbed wire barricade to keep starving, homeless locals separated from the tourist beach. It is only when these young men breach this barricade of class, of order and disorder, consciousness and unconsciousness, that Sebastian and Catharine enter a nightmare world. When Catharine tells the doctor that people began to follow Sebastian, he asks who and she tells him, "the homeless, hungry young people that had climbed over the fence from the free beach that they lived on" (82). They flee the beach and go to a restaurant, only to find the same ubiquitous fence separating its courtyard from the public beach:

> it was between the city and the sea, and there were naked children along the beach which was fenced off with barbed wire from the restaurant and we had our tables less than a yard from the barbed wire fence that held the beggars at bay ....There were naked children along the beach, a band of frightfully thin and dark naked children that looked like a flock of plucked birds. (83–84)

It is at this point in the play that the reader first connects Cabeza de Lobo and the feeding frenzy that Sebastian witnessed in the Encantadas; the predatory and starving children are described as a flock of hungry birds. However, it is also at this point in Catharine's tale that the beach experience clearly represents a conflict between consciousness and unconsciousness, memory and fantasy, truth and illusion. To illustrate his fear at confronting his own demons, his dark id, Sebastian tells Catharine: "Don't look at those little monsters. Beggars are a social disease in this country. If you look at them, you get sick of the country, it spoils the whole country for you…." (84). Catharine's story, her memory-theater reconstruction of Sebastian and the events that lead up to his death, thus becomes a way of looking at the starving children, making them be seen, giving substance to the things we would rather forget or deny. In scene three, Catharine's brother, George, afraid that her story will preclude him from Sebastian's estate, says to Catharine: "You got to drop it, Sister, you can't tell such a story to civilized people in a civilized up-to-date country!"(47). In *Suddenly*, Tennessee Williams has created two "countries," the land of consciousness and the land of unconsciousness, the id and the ego, the dark and the light, reality and illusion—and all of the characters, like all people, have dual citizenship.

In scene three, immediately after George accuses Catharine of telling an uncivilized story in a civilized place, her mother asks her why she invented such a tale. Catharine tells them: "But, Mother, I DIDN'T invent it. I know it's a hideous story but it's a true story of our time and the world we live in and what did truly happen to Cousin Sebastian in Cabeza de Lobo…." (47). It is this quotation, more than any other section of the play, that caused early critics to read *Suddenly* as a modern morality play. Even for Williams, who by his own admission wrote clumsily at times, the quotation seems rather awkward and contrived, less a plea for belief and more a cautionary tale. Writing in 1958, and from a literal standpoint, Williams probably did not intend to indicate that rich American tourists, regardless of their sexual orientations or moral standings, were at risk of being eaten by starving children in third-world countries. However, on a figurative level, the story becomes more reflective of prevailing social attitudes about homosexuality in the 1950s, an era previously examined by Williams in *Cat on a Hot Tin Roof.* Sebastian's death represents a sacrifice of his personal happiness by and through the free expression of his homosexuality, and his theater of initiation is a traditional ritual of that sacrifice. In scene four, when Catharine tells the doctor that she was trying to save Sebastian, the doctor asks her from what and she replies:

> Catharine: Completing— a sort of!—*image!*— he had of himself as a sort of!—*sacrifice* to a!—*terrible* sort of a—
> DOCTOR: —God?
> Catharine: Yes, a—*cruel* one, Doctor! (64)

If one considers Sebastian's spiritual journeys authentic, a true search for meaning and enlightenment, then the naturalistic "god" he witnesses in the slaughter of the turtles is cruel indeed. Judith J. Thompson believes that

Sebastian is on a "self-consuming quest to sacrifice his own corrupt flesh to the rapacious life force he had envisioned in the Encantadas."[22] And, of course, with the religious subtext of the play, Sebastian's death also represents a corruption of the Christian ritual of the transubstantiation of the Eucharist, emphasized when Catharine tells the doctor that the hungry street urchins begged Sebastian for: "*Pan, pan, pan!* … The word for bread, and they made gobbling noises with their little black mouths" (84). According to Andrew Sofer:

> In Williams' theology, the sacred host consumed by the faithful is, in the last instance, one's own body. Sebastian Venable is sacrificed to the pagan god he reveres: the savage god of the turtles, his own divine image.[23]

However, assuming that Sebastian is sacrificed to "his own divine image" begs a rather tired, old and subtle criticism of his homosexuality, and one often critically applied to Williams' gay male characters—abject narcissism.

In his standard reading of *Suddenly* as a purely modern morality play, Paul J. Hurley posits that Williams uses homosexuality as a metaphor, "not only because it is probably the most common of sexual aberrations but because it also suggests vividly and emphatically the tendency of many men and women to retreat altogether from their society and to surrender all attempts to remain related to their fellow man." Indeed, Hurley's thesis for his famous essay, "*Suddenly Last Summer* as Morality Play,'" states: "Turning in upon oneself and away from the concerns of one's fellow man represents a sort of self-cannibalism; man may be consumed by his own inversion."[24] Thus, Sebastian's homosexuality represents a kind of greedy and selfish self-love, bereft of the social altruism and magnanimity inherent in heterosexuality. Interestingly, and perhaps conveniently, Hurley fails to note that all of the heterosexual characters in *Suddenly*—Violet, Catharine, Dr. Cukrowicz, George, Catharine's mother—appear to suffer from this very same social deficiency. Steven Bruhm comes closer to the truth about homosexuality, masculinity, cannibalism, and sacrifice in the play when he argues from an economic standpoint that:

> This system uses cannibalism as a trope for the social anxiety surrounding homosexuality. It exaggerates the anxiety of one male's relationship with another, of a *mutually consumptive* bond between men, and then turns the trope against itself.[25]

Bruhm's argument leads directly back to *A Streetcar Named Desire* and *Cat on a Hot Tin Roof*, connecting all three plays as separate studies of how homosocial/homosexual interaction depends on the commodification of women, making Violet and Catharine's battle for the memory-theater reconstruction of Sebastian doubly sad and ironic.

Violet attempts to construct a memory of her son that is idealized, almost to the point of being mythologized. In scene one, in a conversation with the Doctor, Violet claims control of Sebastian's memory, a duty she says that he gave to her when he became ill as a young man: "Violet? Mother? You're going to live longer than me, and then, when I'm gone, it will be yours, in your hands, to do whatever you please with!" (13). Violet must explain to the Doctor that Sebastian meant "of course, his future recognition!—That he *did* want, he wanted it after his death, when it couldn't disturb him ..." (13). Her memory reconstruction of Sebastian also involves an effort to make her son effete to the point of being asexual, a preemptive attack on what she knows is Catharine's memory of Sebastian as predatorily sexual. Violet tells the Doctor:

> My son, Sebastian, was chaste. Not c-h-a-s-e-d! Oh, he was chased in that way of spelling it, too, we had to be very fleet-footed I can tell you, with his looks and his charm, to keep ahead of pursuers, every kind of pursuer!—I mean he was c-h-a-s-t-e!—Chaste....(24).

Of course, without his mother by his side in Cabeza de Lobo, Sebastian fails to keep ahead of his pursuers. Williams implies that it is almost as if Violet must now metaphorically outrun Catharine, defeat her for Sebastian's memory, escape from Catharine's identity-consuming story just as Sebastian tried to escape from the hungry boys. Violet tells the Doctor that her claim to Sebastian's memory reconstruction receives its validity from her connection to him in life: "This sounds like vanity, Doctor, but really I was actually the only one in his life that satisfied the demands he made of people" (25). After

Sebastian's death, Violet claims the right to his memory as a poet and artist, and the focus of that memory becomes Sebastian's volume of poetry, more a religious relic than a book. In the stage directions, Williams describes how Violet presents the poetry book to the Doctor for his perusal: "*She lifts a thin gilt-edged volume from the patio as if elevating the Host before the altar. Its gold leaf and lettering catch the afternoon sun. It says* Poem of Summer. *Her face suddenly has a different look, the look of a visionary, an exalted* religieuse" (13). It is with this same religiouslike zeal that Violet attacks Catharine's memory of Sebastian, denying it to the point of having it biologically cut out from even existing as a possibility. However, the Doctor realizes that Catharine's memory construction of her cousin must be carefully examined before it can be surgically removed—like a malignant tumor.

Catharine's memory reconstruction of her cousin, Sebastian, has little to do with either chastity or art. Although brutal, Catharine's Sebastian is also more human and flawed. In scene four, during her interview with the Doctor, Catharine discusses Sebastian's annual artistic output, his "Poem of Summer" for the summer he spent with her. When confronted with Sebastian's empty notebook, the one he usually kept notes in for his annual poem, Catharine admits: "Yes, you see, I failed him! And so, last summer, we went to Cabeza de Lobo, we flew down there from where he gave up writing his poem last summer… ." (77). Catharine understands that Sebastian's poetry, never once read by anyone, was as effete as the poet himself. She also realizes that the poetry was only a manipulative ploy of his mother's. When Violet accuses her of breaking some sort of tacit trust of helping Sebastian to create, Catharine tells her: "Yes! Yes, something had broken, that string of pearls that old mothers hold their sons by like a—sort of a—sort of—*umbilical* cord, *long-after…*" (77). For Catharine, Sebastian's vocation as a poet simply represents another means by which Violet controlled him; whereas, Violet sees his poetry as a clear indication of Sebastian's identity. Ironically, after her rape and subsequent disillusionment, Catharine's definition of love perfectly describes Violet and Sebastian's relationship. Catharine tells the Doctor: "Yes, we all use each other and that's what we think of as love, and not being able to use each other is what's—*hate....*" (63). Ultimately, Catharine realizes that her only connection to Sebastian must be in the form of a substitute mother figure. When the Doctor asks Catharine in what way she loved Sebastian, she replies: "The only way he'd accept:—a sort of motherly way. I tried to save him, Doctor" (63). So, unlike Violet, Sebastian's true mother, the surrogate mother, Catharine, realizes and recognizes his weaknesses and his humanity, his homosexuality and his libertine tastes. When these two polar identities of Sebastian collide, the chaste aesthetic vs. the decadent homosexual bon vivant, Williams sets the stage for a battle that neither side can win. The true Sebastian becomes lost in the fray, the casualty of a memory war.

Like Hawthorne's Young Goodman Brown, whoever wins control of the memory of Sebastian, Catharine or Violet, will be left with too many conflicts to create a healthy and complete memory-theater reconstruction ever. To complicate the matter further, Violet and Catharine's competition truly is a type of inversion, such as the one Hurley argues for in regard to homosexuality. They are futilely attempting to co-opt and use his memory much in the same way he used them. As Steven Bruhm points out:

> women are the material in a hierarchical system of exchange that allows an interdependent relationship between men, so that, in essence, Sebastian's homosexual liaisons operated on a principle of commercialism in which one object was exchanged for another of equal value. In this case, Violet and Catharine were exchanged momentarily for Sebastian only because that kind of exchange would facilitate homosexual liaisons in a hegemonically heterosexual world.[26]

Both Violet and Catharine want to use Sebastian's memory as a kind of commodity: Violet to preserve the status of a loving son and poet and Catharine to save herself from being lobotomized. The irony (and perhaps proof) exists in the fact that the homosocial exchange system worked, to a point, for Sebastian, but fails for the women characters. As Andrew Stofer notes: "In Violet's memory theater, only the mother could satisfy her son's appetites, and she is willing to destroy her niece to keep her central exhibit intact."[27]

Suddenly ends with a cryptic line from the cool, logical Dr. Cukrowicz: "I think we ought at least to consider the possibility that the girl's story could be true. …" (93). Over and above the fact that he qualifies his assertion twice, most critics point out his use of the word "girl" to identify Catharine. According to Stofer, "his use of Violet's dehumanizing phrase the girl' does not bode well for Catharine, who has struggled so hard for recognition as a subject in her own right."[28] Throughout the entire play, the doctor has referred to her as "Miss Catharine." The other telling fact of his use of "the girl" in reference to Catharine is found in scene one, when the doctor tells Violet about his first "successful" lobotomy, and he only refers to the patient as "the girl." It seems as if Violet Venable, the mother, will ultimately win possession of her son Sebastian's memory-theater reconstruction, and that Catharine's memory will be excised, physically and psychically, from her brain and mind—but mother's victory will only be a Pyrrhic one.

Suddenly Last Summer remains as Tennessee Williams' most realized dramatic examination of the theater of memory, a literary device which interested him from his very first play. As a study of masculinity, *Suddenly* presents certain difficulties; chief among these is the fact that Williams almost actively precludes the audience/reader from participating in any kind of pleasure from Sebastian's homosexuality. Allan, Blanche's gay husband from *Streetcar*, commits suicide and, in essence, also sacrifices himself because of his homosexuality. In *Cat*, Skipper has already killed himself because of his sexual desire for Brick, and the sexually conflicted Brick is slowly sacrificing himself up on the pyre of alcoholism. However, in both earlier plays, by craft and manipulation of the theaters of memory and initiation, Williams leaves room for a certain kind of pleasure in the homosexual male pairings, a pleasure derived from gay male masculinity. *Suddenly Last Summer* is quite different. To call Sebastian Venable an unsympathetic character seems superfluous. Perhaps the reason that Williams appears to indulge the theater of memory in *Suddenly*, at the expense of the theater of male initiation, can be found in the play's very structure, the dual levels of consciousness and unconsciousness, the superego and the id. Those naked, starving children on the bright beach of Cabeza de Lobo, the ugly, hungry beggars whom Sebastian cannot face, are symbolic of what inhabits our unconscious, all of the innocent people or things that we think, rightly or wrongly, we have treated badly. In the end, the true ritual of initiation is how we reconcile our guilt and our pleasure, our pain and our happiness. If we allow our memories to grow teeth, they will ultimately consume us.

As early as 1947, Tennessee Williams was one of the few American writers, of any genre or popularity, who was willing to explore the topic of homosexuality in his work; his subtlety and complexity at doing so are astounding. He possessed all of the traditional attributes that identify an American Southern artist, the two most important of these being the absolute need, almost desire, to tell stories and knowledge that the best stories always come from the same place—the family. His plays represent a kind of confession, not so much to guilt, but to experience. That literary confession extends to a sharing and the ritual involved in becoming part of something, an initiation. An examination of the theater of memory is not a new approach to Williams' plays, but when that theater also provides a method for the playwright to infuse his writing with complex concepts of masculinity and homosexuality, new critical locations appear. Michael Moon's theory, that repetition of ritual sexual encounters helps gay men form an identity and subjectivity denied them by the heterosexual world, informs Tennessee Williams' gay-themed plays in the various theaters of initiation. Susan Koprince believes "Despite the diversity of his dramas, Tennessee Williams essentially tells the same story over and over again. He records the yearnings of the loveless, the cries of the desperately lonely."[29] Not only does he tell the same story over and over again, he also tells it in the same way, yet each play stands as an individual achievement, a tribute to the playwright's immense talent. Williams resurrects dead characters and makes them the focus of a story. He tells sexual secrets, the kind that all human beings have, in the bright light of day, in a dingy apartment, on a vast plantation, in an elegant mansion. And he tells them over and over again, as if to reinforce both their existence and importance. Women are his narrators of choice; men seem to muddle the duty with their homosocial bravado. As a person, Thomas Lanier Williams was a gay man. As the early playwright, Tennessee Williams, he was too popular, too successful, to be that gay man, at least in his plays. And Thomas Lanier Williams knew what it was like to seek out stories, representation of any kind, that painted a picture of homosexuality and masculinity, a knowledge that he could not completely deny to Tennessee Williams. There, in the privacy of a room or the darkness of a theater, if the readers or viewers are willing, they can see beyond the suicide, the alcoholism, the denial, even the destructive self-consumption, and take some pleasure in the picture—two gay men.

❋ CHAPTER 4

In Love with Masculinity: Sex, War, and the Southern "Boy" in the Novels of Charles Nelson

"A book about being young, male, American, and in love with masculinity..."
—Mark Simpson on *The Masculine Marine*

Southern writer Charles Nelson has only two novels to his credit: *The Boy Who Picked the Bullets Up* (1981) and *Panthers in the Skins of Men* (1989); both titles are lines from Rimbaud poems.[1] The books, the latter a sequel, concern the adventures of Kurt Strom, called "Doc" by his friends, a closeted gay navy medic and ex-professional baseball player who volunteers for military duty during the Vietnam War. The first novel is set primarily in Vietnam from 1966 to 1967, and the second is set in the United States in 1968, after Kurt returns stateside and remains on active duty. *The Boy Who Picked the Bullets Up*, something of an underground gay classic novel, often appears dichotomously on bibliographies of the best gay fiction and best Vietnam War fiction.[2]

Nelson, reclusive to the point of being problematic for bibliographical purposes, did grant a rare interview to gay journalist Rich Grzesiak in 1989, shortly after the publication of *Panthers in the Skins of Men*. In the interview, Grzesiak refers to Nelson as "a conservative Southerner," and Nelson himself states that he "live[s] in a small Southern town."[3] Over and above Nelson's Southern background, the novels have a distinctly Southern flavor to them. Kurt Strom grows up in Louisiana, and several of his friends and acquaintances in Vietnam are also Southerners. Though the first novel is set primarily in southeast Asia and the second in the American northeast, they are both informed completely by Kurt's acute Southern disposition and sensibilities. Also, *Boy* is written in epistolary form, all narrative letters written by Kurt to friends and family back in the States. Though not necessarily distinct to Southern writing, letters almost always seem to play an important or pivotal role in the narrative structure of Southern fiction, reflecting the inbred Southern penchant for letter writing. In her work, *Epistolary Responses: The Letter in 20th Century American Fiction and Criticism,* Anne Bower notes that when Southern writer Lee Smith's epistolary novel *Fair and Tender Ladies* (1988) was first published it received a review in the *Times Literary Supplement* calling it both "credible" and "sonorous." Bower believes that the novel's "sonority derives from individualized orthography, syntax, and vocabulary. ..."[4] *Boy* obtains this same sense of credibility and sonority for similar reasons; Kurt's letters all have the ring of a colorful Southern tale, very colorfully told.

Nelson's protagonist, Kurt Strom, is obsessed with two things, sexual conquests and masculinity. And his sexual conquests are always straight-identified men. Nelson views the books as "picaresque erotic tale[s]."[5] The novels are both patently written in the picaresque tradition, with a ribald main character and episodic adventures; however, they can also be read as a psychologically and equally complex modern version of Choderlos de Laclos's eighteenth-century epistolary French classic, *Les Liaisons Dangereuses.* As with de Laclos's courtiers, Nelson's characters are playing very sophisticated erotic games here, and most of them are predicated on the pursuit of some avatar of traditional masculinity. In *Panthers*, Kurt tells one of his gay friends: "I desire the archetype: the soldier, the sailor, the policeman, the fireman...."[6] De Laclos's French aristocrats use their sexual games and dalliances to further their intrigues and politics, exploiting both social class and positions of power. Kurt and his friends do the same, enmeshed in the Byzantine rules and rank of the United States military. When Kurt questions Montchanin, a heterosexual man that he and his buddy Nick seduced, he asks him:

> "What did you think when you stood naked?"
> "My skin tingled. Whatever went down seemed out of my control."
> "You liked being passive?"
> "Liked it? No. I just waited. I had no expectations."
> "What did you think when Nick went down on you?"
> "An officer is sucking my prick. Hot damn!"
> "Psychological pleasure?"
> "I hardly felt it, I had such a sense of power." (*Panthers* 154)

Nelson even has one of the characters point out the similarities and differences between their modern sexual games and those written about by Choderlos de Laclos in his eighteenth-century work. Diana, a bisexual actress who helps Kurt seduce straight men through elaborate schemes, says of their adventures:

> We enjoy these games because they challenge our intellects, prove the force of our personalities and the power of our beauty, and are fun. We're modern bourgeois descendants of the characters in *Les Liaisons Dangereuses*; Heaven forbid that we become as vicious and competitive as they. (*Panthers* 206)

Both Nelson novels address homosexuality (and heterosexuality) blatantly; they are raw and graphic in their representations of gay sex—one of the primary dynamics that seems always to blur that imaginary line between pornography and erotica. Though just as sexually provocative for its time period, *Les Liaisons Dangereuses* is now considered a literary masterpiece for its depiction of eighteenth-century French social structure. Albeit Kurt Strom and his decadent friends are not aristocrats, their sexual adventures reflect this same concept of social structure, with the sphere being the United States military of the 1960s and the sexuality being between and among men. As Maurice Charney argues in his foundational book, *Sexual Fiction* (1981):

> One person's curiosa are another's dirty books, and, as Ned Polsky points out in his important essay, "On the sociology of pornography," "pornography" has meaning only in relation to the criteria of social class. There is no intrinsic reason why the courts privilege middle-class pornography by such code phrases as "redeeming social value" and "community standards" while attacking the more raucous and cruder pornography of the non-cultivated classes.

Of course, raucous and crude, as evidenced by Chaucer's *The Canterbury Tales*, need not preclude literary merit, style, wit, social commentary, and importance. Charles Nelson's well-written novels encompass all of these elements. Charney uses the term "sexual fiction" to characterize and identify the genre. According to him, "in sexual fiction the interest in sexuality is continuous throughout the book and not just confined to certain episodes."[7] As artist and cultural critic Juan Davila states: "Once it is transferred to culture, pornography loses its genital voice and one can begin to penetrate the different ideologies at play."[8] Nelson's novels set a plethora of those different ideologies into play.

The Boy Who Picked the Bullets Up and *Panthers in the Skins of Men* function to redefine many beliefs about masculinity, homosexuality, and the military, both cultural and literary. "Of all the sites where masculinities are constructed, reproduced, and deployed," David H. J. Morgan argues, "those associated with war and the military are some of the most direct."[9] This military/homoeroticism dynamic has a rich and varied past in history as well as literature. Micha Ramakers points out that

> It is possible…to trace a long tradition of coupling homoerotic desires to warriorship/military life in literature, such as the legends of the mythical heroes Achilles and Patroclus, Gilgamesh and Enkidu, or David and Jonathan. …Such tales obviously appealed to the imagination of a twentieth-century minority that saw its masculinity denied and its desires and relationships outlawed.

However, Ramakers also theorizes that these representations only exist in the abstract, a gay fantasy of the military: "These examples…are more about fantasies of warriorship and the erotically charged brotherhood that accompanies it, than about contemporary soldiers and their uniforms."[10] Nelson's works do appeal to the coupled gay fantasies of masculinity and the military, but they are also about real contemporary soldiers, perhaps the reason that both novels are often cited as excellent and accurate fictional accounts of an American soldier's life in Vietnam during the war. Nelson, himself a

Vietnam War veteran, admits that both books are highly autobiographical, including the homosexual adventures. In the Grzesiak interview, the author refers to the books as "memoirs."[11] Nelson's writing also inverts, and perhaps subverts, Michael Moon's theory of redundant gay initiation, predicated on the concept that gay men have to witness repeated sexual acts performed by strangers because they lack a fundamental sense of heterosexual initiation, what he refers to as "common rites of passage," usually experienced in such masculine spheres as sports and the military.[12] Kurt Strom, Nelson's protagonist, professional baseball player and soldier, represents both spheres of traditional masculine culture, and he introduces heterosexual and straight-identified men into repeated acts of homosexual initiation. Kurt believes that heterosexual men lack a gay "common rite of passage," one that he feels is his duty to help them experience, and the novels' episodic structures create an overwhelming sense of repetition. Kurt explains to a friend his purpose for repeated and impersonal homosexual liaisons: "I attain satisfaction by teaching attractive straights the felicity of the very same man-to-man sex that they ridicule queers for enjoying. I gain revenge upon unattractive heterosexuals by denying them such refreshment" (*Panthers* 238). In essence, Kurt Strom is attempting to personally deconstruct the social sexual order, and in this process he helps to redefine homosexual masculinity by actively forcing gay sexual situations on any man he finds attractive and then forcing those same men to face and consider what they have done. His Southern charm is one of many tools, or perhaps weapons, in an entire panoply.

The Boy Who Picked the Bullets Up

"The problem with straight men is that they're repressed. The problem with gay men is that they're not."

—Mark Simpson, in *Military Trade*

For an epistolary novel, *The Boy Who Picked the Bullets Up* has a rather cautionary and inauspicious beginning. Kurt Strom's very first letter, sent from the Chelsea Naval Hospital in Boston on 2 August 1966, begins:

> *My dear Paul,*
> The Post Office returned my last letter after a note had been added: WRONG PAUL CARROLL. "Had there ever been a right Paul Carroll?" I wondered.[13]

Traditionally, letters only have meaning if they are actually read by the person for whom they are intended, completing a dialog. All of the letters in *Boy* are written by Kurt to friends and family; there are no replies. This creates, essentially, a limited first-person narrative structure. The reader must assume that the dialog has been completed. Kurt, a twenty-four-year-old gay man from Louisiana, has two years of college, two years of playing minor league baseball, and a rather impressive sexual history under his belt. From his first letter, the reader learns that he has recently volunteered for military duty, in the Navy, during the height of the Vietnam War, and he is currently stationed at a navy hospital in Boston, awaiting his orders for Vietnam. The epistolary structure of the novel is both meaningful and complicated. The letters span a time period from August 1966 until July 1967, and Kurt writes letters to four different people: his grandmother, whom he refers to as "Mom," back in his hometown of Bonifay; his cousin, Chloe; a former baseball teammate, Arch; and finally his gay confidante, Paul. Some letters are one paragraph while others are pages long, and with a postmodern playfulness, some of the letters are long poems, self-contained short stories (replete with dialog and traditional structure), lists, and even sports rosters. The letters are in no particular sequence, except chronological, but there is parity of numbers. Kurt writes each recipient approximately fifty letters, excluding two letters that he writes to his sister Karen after their mother dies. In total, the novel consists of two hundred and four letters. As one would suspect, the letters are all appropriate to the recipients, not just in terms of their sexual content, but also in terms of their descriptions of the horrors of the war. Kurt also concludes all of his correspondences with either an aphorism, a line from a song, a witticism, etc. all emblematic, oftentimes ironically so, of the theme of the letter.

The letters Kurt writes to his grandmother and female cousin, Chloe, represent the most likely of wartime missives back home to the family; most of these concern family matters, local gossip, and details of his quotidian activities in the military. The letters that he writes to his baseball buddy, Arch, contain the most harrowing and horrible of the war stories, with only vague references to sexual escapades, and even those are slyly couched as heterosexual. Finally, the letters that he writes to his gay friend, Paul, an art professor, contain detailed information about Kurt's homosexual conquests. Kurt relates several of the same stories to each recipient, which creates an interesting literary dynamic. The reader possesses four versions of the same incident, each specific to the individual letter recipient's position as either female or male, friend or family, and aware or unaware of Kurt's homosexuality. Thus, it is in the letters to Paul and Arch that Kurt's most obvious commentaries on masculinity occur; and those are always set on two of the most important social playing fields of masculinity—the battlefield and the bedroom. For Kurt Strom, both of these are primary locations of engagement.

From Kurt's very first letter to Paul, the reader learns that the protagonist is, at twenty-four, worldly, urbane, and well traveled; he is not a fresh-faced country boy right off the farm. Kurt writes about Boston: "a cultural bonanza of museums, theaters, and libraries; and a profusion of students, sailors, and Irish-American laborers contributed to a rich, full life in Boston" (11). Kurt soon leaves Boston after he is assigned to the Marine Corps (in fact, a part of the Navy) as a medic, and the remainder of military experiences in the novel are directly connected to the marines. In an effort to explain the Marine Corps to his buddy, Arch, Kurt writes that "only one creed inspires a marine: *A hard cock has no conscience*, unless one hails from the Deepest South where cock means pussy, but I think that's just a matter of semantics and not of religion, as Marinedom is" (40). The statement raises several pertinent points in regard to sexuality, masculinity, Southernism, and the military. Throughout the novel,

Kurt exploits this philosophy, depending on the sexual frustration of young men, all but sequestered from women, for his homosexual conquests. It is also interesting to note his qualification of the semantic difference between the use of "cock" and "pussy" in the deep South, which is, as a matter of fact, true. The statement implies Kurt's belief in a type of inherent and discursive bisexuality, one where, according to circumstances, the line separating heterosexuality and homosexuality becomes effectively blurred, allowing him to cross it easily with minimal social repercussions. Finally, his assertion that the Marine Corps represents a kind of religion to its members underscores the almost devotional reverence paid to the institutional masculinity of the military, especially in the Marine Corps.

In the same letter, Kurt writes about the marine appellation "grunt," and says "marines march past continuously, always in groups, and each marine is in step with the rest of the group; as they march, they grunt" (40). Its need for strict conformity thus noted, the Marine Corps, as one of the ultimate groups of symbolic, institutionalized masculinity in our culture, practically defines the term "cult masculinity." According to celebrated gay psychotherapist Dr. Charles Silverstein: "In its most extreme form I call it *cult masculinity*, in which symbols of masculinity exert more influence over behavior than the need for love. Cult masculinity is excitement seeking carried to its most extreme form."[14] In *Boy*, Nelson combines war and homosexuality, both obsessed with cult masculinity and its symbols, and creates the character of Kurt Strom, the *ne plus ultra* representation of excitement seeking carried to its most extreme form. In his critical study, *Military Trade* (1999), of both civilian and military gay men who are fixated with servicemen as sexual objects, Steven Zeeland argues:

> No theory of sexuality can adequately account for personal quirks. But most military chasers can be said to have in common a passion for an organic, embodied, archetypal, "authentic" masculinity; for immersion in *numbers* of servicemen; and for a "pure" homosocial; camaraderie or "buddy love"—but one that allows for sex between men.[15]

Zeeland's argument, based on both cultural theory and years of actual interviews and research into the subject, yields an interesting point in the reiteration of the need constantly to qualify masculinity with words such as *organic*, *embodied*, *archetypal*, and "*authentic*." From Zeeland's research, and Kurt's fictional experiences, the military's structure and codified definition of what it means to be masculine provide the quintessential environment to immerse oneself in the pursuit of masculinity, the " pure' homosocial camaraderie or buddy love'—but one that allows for sex between men." Kurt writes in a letter to Paul, "and I am surrounded by six hundred ruthless and horny youths. All in all, it's not half bad" (124).

The first explicit example of the military's obsession with masculinity is contained in one of Kurt's first letters from Vietnam that he writes to Paul. It details a mandatory group lecture on masturbation that he participated in at Camp LeJeune, before he was deployed to Vietnam. The lecture, conducted by a drunken admiral, borders on both the comic and the bizarre, but it also reinforces the military concept of a patently phallocentric definition of masculinity. Kurt writes:

> The admiral staggered to the podium dragging a three-foot-long plastic penis behind him. He held it up for display; then he commenced his lecture. "This is something we've all got. You sure better not be in the Navy if you don't. Not this man's Navy." (71)

The warning is both figurative and literal, in all male military terms: Only a real man has a penis. The lecture, on genital hygiene and the perils of masturbation, is accompanied by the admiral's constant, absent minded stroking of the grossly exaggerated penile simulacrum. Kurt says, "the admiral fondled the penis and continued" (71). The lecture eventually reaches the unavoidable pun on penis size, masculinity, and control of the homosocial order in an all male environment, when the admiral says:

> "Mighty important little organ. Or mighty important big organ, as the case may be." He winked lewdly and stroked the gargantuan pecker he cradled in his arms. I steeled

> myself and looked around to see 499 men staring at the stage, contemplating the admiral and his plastic penis.
>
> "You have to keep it clean," he was saying. "Wash it every day, but don't rub too hard. You wouldn't want *that* to happen, not with other real men in the showers. This is for the women of America." I decided I liked neither the man nor his message. (72)

The admiral links masculinity and American military manhood directly to the phallus, with phrases such as "this man's Navy" and "not with other real men in the showers." Ironically and homosocially, he makes all of these masculine abjurations while lovingly, and perhaps unconsciously, masturbating the huge penis. His warning of a supposedly unwanted or accidental erection in the group showers, what he demurely refers to as *that*, as if the mention of the word alone can compromise the homosocial order, runs counteractive to Kurt's homoerotic philosophy of the military, why he decides he neither likes the man nor the message. Peter Lehman, in his book, *Running Scared: Masculinity and the Representation of the Male Body*, explains why the admiral's exhibit penis is grotesquely huge and why "accidental" erections should be avoided or at least concealed from other men: "Our culture has so much invested in the construction of sexual difference around the sight of the penis that the penis must be hidden or dramatically exaggerated." Lehman also demonstrates how recent critical theory has reread Freudian psychoanalytic separation of the phallus and the penis and how representations of both influence concepts of masculinity. According to Lehman, "the phallus dominates, restricts, prohibits, and controls the representation of the male body, particularly its sexual representation.... although the penis and phallus may be theoretically separable, they are linked in actuality, and linked in a way that has specific consequences for both the theoretical concept of the symbolic phallus and the literal male body and the penis."[16] In *Boy*, Nelson realizes this concept by representing the penis as both the phallic symbol of power and a sexual representation of the male body; it becomes the locus of masculinity. Throughout the novel, Kurt uses the concept of the "accidental" erection to both identify and seduce his fellow soldiers, whose penises are not "for the women of America" alone. In Charles J. Levy's essay, "ARVN as Faggots: Inverted Warfare in Vietnam," he examines how homosexuality and its threat to masculinity was an important factor in the training of Vietnam era marines. Levy points out:

> Homosexuality appeared in two contradictory themes of basic training. On the one hand, homosexuals were the enemy....On the other hand, marine recruits were called "faggots" by their drill instructors during boot camp. By compelling these men to accept such labels, the drill instructors achieved on a psychological level the same control that they had on a physical level....[17]

Kurt writes a letter to Paul, dated 12 January 1967, that details the military's use of homophobia in its training of Vietnam era soldiers. After Kurt arrives for duty in the jungle, during what he terms "Paranoia Week," he describes a "seminar in Homosexuality to celebrate Paranoia Week," conducted by one Lieutenant Sanford. Kurt explains in the letter:

> Marines are trained to hate queers. Marines take great offense when they are called queers. Should a recruit be unable to hack basic training, he is known as a queer. Whenever a marine fucks up, he is assumed queer. It's rock bottom to these guys. The pits. A queer has no reason to live, so he's best done away with. Kill a queer for Uncle Sam. (188)

At the conclusion of his seminar on the threat of homosexuality to the Marine Corps, Lieutenant Sanford says: "I believe the government should stand all faggots before a firing squad. If I ever thought that one of my men was a faggot, I'd shoot him in the back and call it self-defense"(188). Homosexuality, apparently constantly lurking in the midst, is constructed as a threat to masculinity and American culture as menacing as any enemy, including the North Vietnamese.

Kurt utilizes a form of this same psychological process, the military's constant obsession with the power of homosexuality, already instilled in the marines, to seduce them, once again inverting and undermining the homosocial order of the military and providing straight-identified soldiers with a homosexual initiation. While in training at Camp LeJeune, Kurt visits his family back in Louisiana. He successfully seduces a soldier on the bus ride back to the base. While changing buses in Atlanta, Kurt sees the soldier and walks up to speak with him. Kurt writes in this letter, "he hissed, Stay away from me, faggot "(33). In the light of the bus station, Kurt has become the enemy again, the "faggot." He writes of this remark, "I could only assume that he hoped to wound me" (33). In this statement, *wound* takes on both an emotional and martial meaning. In the darkness of the bus, just as the drill instructors call recruits "faggots" to gain a psychological and physical advantage over them, Kurt performs the same kind of interpellation, transformed into the physical act of sex. In *Sexual Fiction*, Maurice Charney argues:

> The most striking feature of sexual fiction is its thorough sexualizing of reality. All perception is eroticized and the world becomes, as in Leo Bersani's formulation in *A Future for Astyanax*, a theater for the enactment of our desires, "constantly open to—always ready to be penetrated by—our desires."[18]

Writing about homoerotica, sociologist Tim Edwards argues that most of the homosexual scenes of the genre are predicated on the notion of "contextual transgression." What appears as a normal situation, such as riding a bus, suddenly becomes sexual. Edwards maintains:

> The intensity of the sexual action is immediately connected to this transgression....such transgression is an essential ingredient of all gay sexuality, in view of the general social presupposition of heterosexual normality, which is so strong that any gay scene inevitably is also transgressive at a social level.[19]

The homosexual scenes in *Boy* thus become socially transgressive, disrupting the accepted social order by representing both gay and public sex. In a study of gay men and public sex, Laud Humphreys explains why this type of homosexual behavior actively resists social sexual norms when he explains that for Western people:

> sex is invested with personal meanings: interpersonal relationship, romantic love, and an endless catalog of sentiments. Sex without "love" meets with such general condemnation that the essential ritual of courtship is almost obscured in rococo accretions that assure those involved that a respectable level of romantic intent has been reached.

> Both the appeal and the danger of ephemeral sex are increased because the partners are usually strangers to one another. The propositioning of strangers for either heterosexual or homosexual acts is dangerous and exciting—....[20]

It is also incredibly socially transgressive; so Kurt Strom not only causes havoc with military concepts of homosexuality and masculinity, he also constantly disrupts the existing social order with his recreational pursuit of public gay sex. Kurt deconstructs, and reconstructs to his own advantage, the very basis of military organization. According to military sociologist Bob Connell: "It is the *relationship* between forms of masculinity—physically violent but subordinate to orders on the one hand, dominating and organisationally competent on the other—that is the basis of military organisation."[21] Kurt, an enlisted man, assumes the power usually only relegated to officers in the military, but as opposed to using it for discipline and strict obedience, he is using it for sexual control and domination. The very foundation of his sexual games is domination and organization; he *always* elaborates a plan for his homosexual conquests. Kurt transforms the traditional *relationship* between forms of military masculinity into a single dynamic, effectively breaking down the existing binary relationship between officer and soldier. He achieves this by playing games. As Mark Simpson points out in his study of masculinity and war movies, "war films may be texts of masculinity, but the biggest lesson they have to teach is that being a man is a game, albeit a deadly one."[22]

The earliest indication of Kurt's homosexual exploits as a high-stakes game with serious consequences comes in a letter to his friend Paul, written shortly after he arrives in Vietnam. Kurt is offered duty in a military mental ward, a duty he declines but not before visiting the ward and observing the patients. Symbolically, most of the soldiers are playing games, primarily cards. However, three of the soldiers play a common board game with the indicative name *Sorry*. Two of the *Sorry* players are "a pair of tubby, middle aged marine gunny sergeants." Kurt learns that the two sergeants had recently been discovered in their hut engaged in "*soixante-neuf*." He writes to Paul:

> It sounds comical, but after twenty years or so in the Crotch (the Marine Corps), they will spend several months in the brig at half-pay for the crime of sodomy, be issued an undesirable discharge, lose their pensions, and learn that their families have been notified of their prodivities. I wonder whom they so offended. (92–93)

After noting several other homosexual patient/prisoners in the mental ward, many of these attractive younger men, Kurt writes to Paul that he declined the duty for fear of too much temptation with men who had already made their sexual interests known: "It was tempting, but I'm afraid I couldn't have resisted touching the untouchables." Kurt's single-sentence concluding paragraph to this letter indicates both his recognition of risk and his eagerness to play: "Still, without danger the game grows cold" (93).

Long before and long after the Vietnam War era, United States military proscriptions against homosexuality in the ranks have been severe and fervently pursued. The military is an organization that constantly polices the homosexual while tacitly embracing the homosocial. Homosociality lends itself to the construction of masculinity in the military and to a reciprocal construction. According to Michael S. Kimmel, "masculinity is a *homosocial* enactment. We test ourselves, perform heroic feats, take enormous risks, all because we want other men to grant us our manhood."[23] All of Kimmel's "qualifications" of manhood are inherent in military duty, particularly during wartime; however, the military must appear to actively avoid actual homosexuality. Morgan, recognizing the complexity of the military, explains, "if in the armed services one finds an ideological emphasis on homosociability and heterosexuality, it is, as is so often the case in a complex society, a complex ideological unity compounded of several, sometimes contradictory, strands."[24] Allan Berube quotes a 1982 (fifteen years after Kurt's fictional year in Vietnam) Pentagon directive on homosexuality, calling it the military s "strongest antigay policy to date":

> "Homosexualityis incompatible with military service," the directive explained, because it undermines military discipline, creates security risks, and gives the military a bad reputation. Even a member of the armed forces who "has stated that he or she is a

> homosexual" or "desires" to "engage in homosexual conduct" is considered a threat to the military under these rules.[25]

In 1993 President Bill Clinton's controversial and self-explanatory gays-in-the-military "Don't Ask - Don't Tell" policy was codified from executive order into law, a law that still maintains in 2006. Regardless of the law's intent, gay men and women are unceremoniously drummed out of the United States military, with dishonorable discharges, everyday—simply for being gay. Interestingly, the "Don't Ask - Don't Tell" law perfectly proves Alan Sinfield's theory of the "open secret," (discussed here, in detail, in chapter three), used to create and police the boundaries of homosexuality. With all of the traditionally strict and firmly entrenched prohibitions against homosexuality in the military in mind, Kurt well realizes what the consequences of his "games" might be, but he plays them anyway. For him, these games do not necessarily "undermine military discipline." Rather they shift it to his sexual favor. It all depends on how you play the game.

In Kurt's letter, dated 16 November, to his gay confidant, Paul, he bemoans the fact that he cannot find suitable sexual conquest candidates in his company. He writes to Paul: "A vow of celibacy should be easily honored here.... My ability to fantasize will be challenged by my surroundings" (134). Kurt then supplies Paul with a list that delineates his criteria for sexual attraction. This list informs the entire structure of the novel, and it also offers a study of how Kurt relates to men as sexual beings through elements such as attractiveness, race, and masculinity. He writes to Paul: "Three corpsmen share my tent and company duties and are, in order of their undesirability: (1) fat, (2) black, and (3) near-sighted" (134). "Fats," an ostensibly heterosexual man, falls short of Kurt's strict, and traditional, standards of male attractiveness. He tells Paul that "Fats is a bulbous-nosed, bad-tempered blond, lacking eyebrows, eyelashes, and probably pubic hair. I doubt that he's changed his underclothes since coming into his full growth which, like his stench, is considerable" (134). Apart from his appalling lack of personal hygiene, "Fats" represents the physically unattractive heterosexual male in Kurt's erotic lexicon. Michelangelo Signorile identifies a cultural dynamic, prevalent in the gay world, that also tends to "spill over" when gay men sexually objectify straight men, as Kurt does.

Signorile argues that "it is not difficult to see that many if not most of us become both the rigidly objectified as well as the rigid objectifier, holding ourselves and *each other* to rigid standards of physical beauty. These standards become a significant, if not the most important, characteristic in choosing a mate or sexual partner."[26] As a closeted gay man, Kurt is proud of two facts: that he can pass as straight, and that he is physically attractive, and he is disdainful of heterosexual men who fail to meet the standards he holds for himself. His theory can best be summed up as: If a gay man can look this butch, this macho, this masculine, this handsome, then why can't you, with your vaunted heterosexuality? In a previous letter to Paul, concerning the first jungle patrol, Kurt writes that when a Sergeant Pinkerton forced him to strip so the sergeant could apply insect repellant to him, "regardless, I was determined above all to be brave and butch, so I merely asked, in my roughest and deepest voice, Okay, Sarge, tell me what to do'" (129). With his masculinity established, Kurt also assumes that the straight-identified sergeant and marines objectified his body when they "gathered to watch the action" and the Sarge told him, "You're in pretty good shape, ain't you, Doc?" He feels no compunction about turning this objectification around and aiming it squarely at heterosexual men in the process of reviewing their likelihood as sexual partners.

The second of Kurt's "undesirables" on his list is identified as "black." He writes to Paul that "Soul Brother goes by Splib, a nomenclature that I'm told those of the persuasion find inoffensive...Splib speaks only to his Brothers" (134). In part, it is the African American soldier's self-isolation that bothers Kurt: "He has stacked boxes around his cot, behind which he disappears for days on end. I resent the crowding the boxes cause, and I find his isolation impenetrable" (134). Unlike Kurt, the closeted gay man, the African American soldier is also marginalized, but easily identifiable. Because he cannot, or will not, "pass" he has constructed a real, physical closet in which to remain, only relating to his "Brothers." Interestingly, Kurt actively avoids the company of his homosexual "brothers," fearing he will be "outed" by association, making his mental closet as impenetrable as Splib's stacked boxes. In an earlier letter to Paul, dated 12 October, Kurt writes about the circumstances surrounding his discovery of other gay soldiers in his company in Vietnam. After furtively planning an assignation in the dark with an unknown marine, when they meet the next night Kurt realizes that the man is "my hoochmate the lab technician, a prematurely aged nervous nelly. Hardly my type" (95). Kurt uses the pejorative term "nelly," common among homosexual men to identify an effeminate gay man. He then informs Paul: "Anyway, he filled me in about Who's Who, in which I am probably now listed. Sadly, my sisters rank among the homeliest of the battalion personnel; I cannot imagine being tempted again" (95). The term "sisters," as Kurt rather derisively uses it, is common among gay men in reference to their gay friends and acquaintances. In their examination of gay men and homophobia Driggs and Finn note: "such epithets sometimes express familiarity or affection, but more often they show an underlying disdain for gay identity."[27] Used in Kurt's context, "sister" becomes an ironic term of gay brotherhood, just as he refers to Splib and his African American friends as "Brothers." Splib, however, seeks out the company of his brothers, while Kurt finds his "sisters" lacking in the requisite masculinity and physical attractiveness he requires for his sexual conquests.

Kurt makes no attempt to penetrate the African American soldier's cardboard citadel. He writes in the letter, "besides, have you ever tried to get directions from a nigger?" (134). Though no formal or academic critical work exists on Charles Nelson's fiction, the few popular forms, such as book reviews and interviews, that address the two novels often cite Kurt's seemingly racist attitude toward African Americans. Rich Grzesiak, a long-time popular gay journalist and literary critic, who has always had a close relationship with both the gay publishing and gay readership communities, writes in his interview with Charles Nelson, "blacks found Kurt Strom a racist." When Grzesiak asks

Nelson's reaction to the charge of racism in his books, Nelson at first historically contextualizes his work:

> I don't feel I have to defend myself. Some of my critics are stupid—they're saying it's all right for Kurt to think this way in 1968, but Mr. Nelson, this is 198_, and you should know better. That's ridiculous, because I'm narrating these books in Kurt's words.[28]

Though simplistic, Nelson's theory has a basis in valid cultural criticism. In her essay, "African American Lesbian and Gay History: An Exploration" (1998), eminent critic Barbara Smith examines the interaction between white gay men and African American men, both gay and straight, in the 1950s and 1960s. Smith first contests Tracy Morgan's argument that white gay men of this period found racism, " useful,' in terms of the wages of whiteness' thesis in assisting white gay people to attain greater social and cultural privilege as, at least, not black' outcasts in American culture...." Smith demonstrates that any perceived notion of gay racism was, in fact, more historically and culturally motivated. According to Smith:

> Although excluding Black men might have had the result of minimally enhancing white gay men's social position, their original motivation for such exclusion was no doubt based upon unquestioning conformity to the racial status quo. Morgan does not take into account that racism, white supremacy, and segregation were universally institutionalized, accepted, and practiced by whites of all classes, genders, sexual orientations, and geographic regions.[29]

As Nelson himself points out, he is narrating the voice of a character firmly entrenched in 1960s social values, and a character who is also rather blunt in his opinions and ideas. As Smith so astutely notes about this historical period: "The average white person did not have to decide to exclude Black people from every aspect of their social, economic, and personal lives. U.S. society was organized to ensure that this would always be the case." Thus, Kurt's attitude toward the African American soldiers that he serves with in Vietnam reflects the broader societal attitude of the time; however, Nelson's further comments on racism, in the interview, extend beyond this historical contextualization of racism in his work. These ideas have much more to do with building a closet—either of cardboard or subjectivity.

In the interview with Grzesiak, Charles Nelson tells him the reason he thinks his writing might be considered racist:

> I was a sissy when I was growing up, and got picked on a lot. As I grew up, I became very sensitive to angry people, so all my life I've avoided them, even in the service—and that's not easy there. An awful lot of blacks are angry, so I just stay away from them. I don't want to be around this anger.[30]

So, Kurt Strom is not the traditional Southern melodrama racist, but a character whose creator recognizes and acknowledges the anger inherent in marginalization, why both Kurt and Splib choose to build walls around themselves. Kurt does make several African American men, in both novels, the subjects of his homosexual conquests, but he also holds these men to the same strict standards of masculinity and physical attractiveness as the white men.

The final man on Kurt's list of sexual "undesirables," number three, is referred to as "nearsighted," an interesting designation for the homosexual member of the trio of failed sexual objects, one that perhaps relates to Nelson's own early traumas as a "sissy," picked on by other adolescents—the predictable "queer" with glasses. His description of the third corpsman is informative:

> The bespectacled one never goes on patrol....Queenie passes her days tastefully decorating her corner of the tent with silk scarves from Bangkok. Despite her friendliness, Queenie can give me little counsel, and her back issues of *Contemporary Living* are uninformative. (134)

Kurt's description of his tent mate indicates his strongly internalized homophobia which informs both novels. Once again, he uses gay forms and terms in an ironic and derogatory context, the term "Queenie" for an effeminate gay man and the feminine personal pronoun "her." However, unlike Kurt's subjective isolation and Splib's physical isolation in the tent, "Queenie" appears to be, in part, celebrating his identity, festooning the muddy hooch with silk scarves, being friendly as opposed to reserved and isolated. With his sarcastic comments about the decorating magazine, Kurt displays his contempt for a gay man's attempt at establishing both identity and a little domesticity in the face of the abject horrors of jungle war. With these same comments, Kurt's sexual behavior, his need to seek out and seduce only straight-identified men, raises serious questions about why and how homophobia has become so embedded in the psyches of many modern gay men.

The social engine that drives masculinity, homosexuality, and internalized gay homophobia is both simple and complex. According to Driggs and Finn, "it may seem self-evident, but it's easily overlooked; gay men are brought up in the context of all of society's rules and expectations for males." They rather facilely warn gay men "you probably have been influenced by society's standards of masculinity."[31] Indeed. In Gregory K. Lehne's influential essay, "Homophobia Among Men: Supporting and Defining the Male Role" (1980), he argues primarily that homophobia in Western cultures is a tool used to control and monitor traditional male sex roles. Lehne posits that "the male role is predominantly maintained by men themselves. Men devalue homosexuality, then use this norm of homophobia to control other men in their male roles." One of the major cruxes of Lehne's theory is "homophobia is only incidentally directed against actual homosexuals—its more common use is against the heterosexual male." And while this assertion may well contain some truth, Lehne all but ignores gay homophobia as well as actual homophobia directed toward gay men, as if it has little or no part in this masculine social process. He does, however, point out, and then quickly abandon, the fact that "effeminacy itself is highly stigmatized in the homosexual subculture." This statement begs the obvious question, why? Why is Kurt Strom so obsessed with seducing heterosexual men into an initiatory rite of male sex, while actively and often harshly condemning other gay men, those more easily identifiable by traditional concepts of homosexual effeminacy that Kurt holds in high contempt? The first part of the answer has much to do with *Boy's* setting, the military during war time. With highly visible, strictly codified, and stringently enforced rules and regulations concerning homosexuality, the military defines Lehne's basic tenet:

"When homosexuality is stigmatized, homophobia exists as a device of social control, directed specifically against men to maintain male behavior appropriate to the social situation."[32] Kurt, the closeted gay athlete and soldier, "buys in" to this theory, which further problemitizes the answer. Who had decided, for Kurt, just what was "male behavior appropriate to the social situation" in the wartime jungles of Vietnam in 1966? And more importantly, how does a man having sex with ostensibly heterosexual men maintain this appropriate behavior?

In Michelangelo Signorile's book, *Life Outside,* he details how gay men have been influenced by what he terms "crises of masculinity," historical points that changed how masculinity has been defined and enforced. These points also represent "the historical moments when anxiety about masculinity peaked, which resulted in shifts in how men who had sex with men perceived one another." Kurt's wartime experiences, in the Vietnam of 1966, fall directly in the aftermath of what Signorile considers one of the seminal "crises of masculinity" in the twentieth century, the McCarthy Era of the 1950s, (discussed here, in detail, in chapter three, in regard to Tennessee Williams' play, *Cat on a Hot Tin Roof).* Signorile points out that the McCarthy era, with its gay witch hunts which equated homosexuality with insidious Communism, had a tremendous and lasting impact on how American men, gay and straight, reacted to effeminacy:

> It exploited a prevailing fear in American culture at large of effeminate men and instilled it further, even among gay men. Not only would men, gay and straight, not want to appear effeminate lest someone think they were homosexual, but the profusely masculine pose that straight men adopted in the 1950s had a profound effect on gay men that lasted for generations.

In a large part, this "effect" manifested itself in internalized gay homophobia, and Kurt Strom is the homosexual product of the generation at the height of this period. When Kurt expresses his distaste for homosexual men, he is, like his perceived racism, simply reflecting the prevailing, almost oppressive, social norms of the time. Unable to deny his physical and sexual attraction to other men, he basically ignores traditional identities of *gay* and *straight* and essentializes all males into sexually attractive or unattractive. This concept has the complexity of being both revolutionary and conservative at the same time. Kurt breaks down an old, established sexual binary, but for the most conventional of reasons, to conform. And as Signorile points out, society had done much of the work for Kurt; it had essentially defined whom he finds sexually attractive:

> The sexual object-choice that gay men found themselves increasingly attracted to may have been dictated by the larger heterosexual male population and what it defined as "manly" at a time when both gay and straight men alike were experiencing acute anxiety surrounding their masculinity. The effeminate homosexual continued to become at best someone to avoid, even among a great many gay men themselves.[33]

Thus, Kurt exists in a world of military homophobia, created to maintain appropriate masculine behavior, and a world of masculinity that not only disapproves of effeminate homosexual men; it also fears them. Kurt ends one of his letters with an old Southern aphorism: "There's them that kiss ass and there's them that beat ass and there's them that merely shake it from side to side"(158). Kurt, in all meanings of the axiom, does all three, but the way he "shakes it from side to side," both his ass and the social structure, should not be diminished by such a simple adverb as "merely."

To illustrate his internalized homophobia further, Kurt's next letter to Paul also involves a story about an effeminate gay man. Kurt's appellation for this man, a fellow navy corpsman and acquaintance from training back in Boston, is another pejorative term for a homosexual man, supposedly indicative of his effeminate behavior; Kurt simply calls him "Miss Priss." Kurt learns that Miss Priss is assigned to a neighboring company in the jungle, and he receives an invitation to tea. After some gossip, Kurt tries to ascertain the sexual proclivities of the more attractive members of Miss Priss's company: "I learned nothing about a couple of beauties I casually pointed out; Miss Priss is somewhat insipid, with only good to say about people. I could see what was good about the men I pointed out; I wanted to know a little of the bad" (142).

Like Kurt's gay tent mate, "nearsighted," who had embellished his tent space with silk scarves and decorating magazines, creating a domestic space, Miss Priss brews mint tea and serves it in delicate china teacups along with some fruitcake from, as Kurt explains, "Mumsie." However, unlike his description of "nearsighted's" gay domestic haven, the very avatars of heterosexual masculine sexuality, the "hard," handsome Sergeant Pinkerton who had earlier slathered Kurt with insect repellant and the quintessential hardcore marine, Corporal McGrath, invade Miss Priss's gay domestic space, looking for Kurt who is due for a patrol. McGrath, a taciturn fellow Southerner, represents the embodiment of Kurt's fantasy marine: butch, tough, and straight. In a later letter to Paul, one that consists entirely of a long, narrative poem about the soldiers that he serves with, Kurt writes a paean about Corporal McGrath's military skills and sexual power; these two elements combine to describe McGrath as a "stealthy panther," a beast hardly appropriate company for the fussy Miss Priss (320).

Much to Kurt's chagrin, Miss Priss offers the sergeant and McGrath fruitcake and tea in the "tiny china cups." On the way back to their company, McGrath asks Kurt: "Is that old sissy a buddy of yours?" (142). Miss Priss, apparently easily identifiable as gay because of his tea cups and manners, suddenly becomes a liability to Kurt's closeted identity, and he quickly defends himself by answering: " Merely a friend of a friend.' I replied courageously" (142). Kurt's attitude toward Corporal McGrath also represents the complexity of his sexual identity, gender, and masculinity. After he denies his connection to the gay-identified Miss Priss to McGrath, Kurt adds: "McGrath cast me a suspicious glance. Yesterday I caught him staring at me several times. I felt just like a tall dyke in drag" (142). The "boy" realizes and acknowledges his own performativity of gender, but like every other theoretical social system of behavior, he has subverted this one also. Even if Kurt's "drag" comment was made derisively, it is nonetheless telling.

"Just like a tall dyke in drag." Kurt means, of course, that McGrath's gaze, which he perceives as sexual in nature, reconfigures him as female, but not just any female identity. Kurt must become a lesbian impersonating a man, a "dyke in drag." Kurt's obsession with masculinity disallows him to effeminize himself in any way, but made the object of desire by McGrath's heterosexual gaze, Kurt must at least alter his sexual identity, tweak it in some way.

Kurt's next letter to Paul, dated 22 December, once again concerns the hypermasculine marine, McGrath. In describing his attraction to McGrath, Kurt points out that, like himself, McGrath was a high school athlete, a "twelve-letter" man. Kurt writes about him, "I find any physical contact desirable" (167). By planning and subterfuge, Kurt manages to get his next ambush duty with McGrath. While preparing for the night, Kurt splashes on Aqua Velva After Shave, which he reminds Paul is the aftershave "for the Man's Man," denoting both heterosexual masculinity and homoeroticism (168). After they settle in for ambush duty, the scene turns sexual, when McGrath begins masturbating to pass the time. Their casual and folksy exchange, while highly homoerotic, is also indicative of the rather blasé attitude about situational homosexuality between southern raised males: Kurt, the Louisiana boy, and McGrath from Mississippi, the "golden beast of the Delta":

> "McGrath, are you poundin' your pud again?"
> "Sorry, Doc, I'll stop."
> "No! Go right ahead. I've halfa mind to join you." Silence. "McGrath, I believe I will join you."
> "Go to it, Doc."
> Despite the companionable feeling, I wasn't satisfied. "Would you like me to give you a few whacks, buddy?"
> "I'd take to it kindly, Doc," he replied.
> My hand replaced his hand upon his sex. "Would you mind giving me a little help?" I asked.
> McGrath obliged with easy grace. "Sure, Doc." (168)

The encounter leads to a heated homosexual experience in which "we stripped and each of us placed his sex in whatever orifices would accommodate." Kurt writes to Paul that after they finished the encounter, he attempted to kiss McGrath: "But when I tried to give him a little smooch, McGrath pushed me away" (168). McGrath's reply to the proffered kiss represents the complex code of masculinity and homosexuality inherent in the military, so much so that it sounds axiomatic: "You can fuck a marine," he snarled. "But you can't fuck with a marine" (168).

Kurt appears to believe that because he has submitted to homosexual sex, McGrath can accept a fluidity of his sexuality based on a type of masculine confidence. As Zeeland notes:

> But Marines are not ordinary men. …having survived the hell ofboot camp, Marines are fitted with an armor or supermasculinity that may allow them to play with the man-woman binarism secure in the belief that, whatever they do, they will always land back on top. Sometimes they may even come to see through the binarism.[34]

McGrath's Marine Corps "supermasculinity" allows for acceptance of the physical act of sex between two men; from Kurt's letter description of the encounter, McGrath allows himself to be anally penetrated by Kurt. However, Kurt's offer of a post-coital kiss ironically represents a gender boundary which McGrath is not willing to cross. In an interview with a man obsessed with homosexual encounters with straight-identified marines, Zeeland quotes him as saying: "You tell them to do something sexually, and they basically do it. They'll do anything but kiss, because that's queer. They're the epitome of male masculinity."[35] With his tautological emphasis of "male masculinity," the interviewee once again expresses the irony that marines will have homosexual sex with another man, keeping their "male masculinity" intact, as long as there is no emotional expression represented by a kiss. McGrath's response to the kiss, "you can fuck a marine…. but you can't fuck with a marine," embodies a plethora of sophisticated culture dynamics which drive both heterosexual and homosexual concepts of masculinity. According to Brian Pronger, "that the expression getting fucked' has a nonsexual, profane use is significant." This significance is found in the construction of the traditional man/woman binary, the same binary that Kurt hopes McGrath has deconstructed by dint of his "supermasculinity." Pronger argues that when the word *fuck* is used as profanity, in all of its many guises:

> Such uses of the word, although not intended to convey erotic meaning, originate in a perspicacious understanding of its culturally created erotic meaning, which is that being fucked is a denigration. That sense of denigration comes from heterosexual discourse where the person that gets fucked is a woman, a man's mythic inferior.

McGrath's casual acceptance of getting "fucked" exists because he so adamantly refuses to being "fucked with," actively resisting the inferior female position, as dictated by societal norms. He and Kurt can both safely remain the Aqua Velva "Man's Man," in all meanings of the term—men nobody can "fuck with." As Pronger points out: "Fucking is that act in which the power relations between men and women are embodied. The profane, and nonsexual, use of getting fucked' reveals the true meaning of the sexual act of getting fucked in our culture."[36]

Though he does not get a kiss from McGrath, Kurt remains relentless in his pursuit. He writes to Paul that after McGrath tells him that "you can't fuck with a marine," he becomes all the more sexually attractive: "I was dismayed for a moment, but oily persuasion repaired the rupture and white heat again warmed the jungle" (168–169). Kurt's use of the word "rupture" indicates his knowledge that he has split a binary, and because you can "fuck a marine" but cannot "fuck with a marine," they do just that to repair the break. Brian Pronger addresses this notion, that "real men" are not the subject of receptive anal sex, the one major taboo that violates accepted, traditional social tenets of masculinity: "Men who are receptive are worse than failures, they have betrayed their dominant position and made themselves like women.'" Pronger also shows that male violation of the anal sex taboo represents a type of ritual, one that celebrates a transcendent experience: "Getting fucked, therefore, is the deepest violation of masculinity in our culture. Enjoying being fucked is the acceptance of that violation, it is the ecstatic sexual experience in which the violation of masculinity becomes incarnate."[37] Kurt has managed to place himself in an ideal environment, the military (particularly the Marine Corps), in which to play his games of homosexual initiation through subversion of masculine norms. The Marine Corps, with its rigid code of masculine behavior, actually enables, in part, its members to reconfigure the "passive" and "active" roles in homosexual practices. Zeeland notes that "some Marines I have known claim that Marines view being penetrated not at all as female, but as a *manly* test of endurance that, successfully withstood, leaves the bottom with *more* power." He quotes a Marine Corps officer, "Captain Eric," as stating that "it takes a lot more masculinity to be a bottom than to be a top." To support his remark, "Captain Eric" adds a "favorite DI [Marine Corps Drill Instructor] aphorism: "Pain is weakness leaving the body."[38] Interestingly, these men have equated passive anal penetration with performance and function, and as opposed to pleasure, sex becomes an act to be endured and withstood, connected to pain and weakness. They have, in effect, masculinized receptive anal sex, equating it to a feat of accomplishment, one that gives them more *power*. Ironically, the straight-identified marines in Nelson's novel serve to legitimize homosexuality by their furtive homosexual actions. As Pronger states: "The legitimacy of homosexuality lies not in its loyalty to orthodox masculinity, but in its violation."[39] Homosexuality becomes a way for them to wrest more *power* from the masculine social structure of the military. To illustrate this point, Kurt ends the letter about his sexual encounter with McGrath with one of his epigrammatic quotations: "And a man's a man for a' that." (169). From Robert Burns' "A Man's a Man," a poem listing the acts and attitudes which make a man a man, this line indicates that Kurt and McGrath both understand that part of their masculinity is defined, and perhaps even amplified, by the violation of its strictures and restraints.

In his letter dated 19 January 1967, Kurt tells Paul about his first experience with being "caught" in the game by his superior officer, Sergeant Pinkerton. Pinkerton takes Kurt aside and says to him: "McGrath tells me you and him got it on" (196). Kurt never discovers whether McGrath told the sergeant to assuage guilt over the homosexual encounter or as simple boasting. He even surmises that McGrath might have been using the homosexual encounter to get discharged from the Marine Corps and sent back home: "People have shot off their toes to get out of Nam; McGrath's is a better method and just as effective.

Well, at least I wasn't pregnant" (196). Regardless of McGrath s motivation for confessing, once the homosexual game is made an issue, the sergeant must deal with it. How sergeant Pinkerton deals with the homosexual encounter between two of his men represents not only a military approach to the subject, but also a common one. Kurt, in an effort to diffuse the situation and find out if the sergeant is using the accusation as a subtle come-on, immediately goes on the defensive. In response to the sergeant's statement, he says: "We sure did, Sarge. I'm here to take care of y'all, am I not? You think you might like to try it? I'd be more than happy to oblige" (197). After Sergeant Pinkerton good naturedly turns down Kurt's offer, he chastises Kurt with a traditional avuncular warning about "boys will be boys" situational and facultative homosexuality:

> I know it's tough out here, Doc, and a guy who looks like you is probably used to a lot of pussy. We'd all like some pussy, and what you and McGrath done is just what we used to do back home when we was kids and didn't have no pussy. The Marine Corps, though, don't like it. They want you to be a man, and a man don't do kid stuff. That's what it is, Doc. It's kid stuff. You and McGrath should know better than that. I don't care that you done it. It's just that the Crotch don't like it. If they found out, they'd boot your ass to the brig. They'd think you was queer. I know you're not queer, and I know you're a good doc. I'd hate to lose you because of something dumb. (197)

After his strict warning, the sergeant musses Kurt's hair, as if he were a boy, and Kurt is twenty-four years old. David H. J. Morgan points out that, traditionally, "the less official accounts of military life suggest the operation of a double standard, the toleration of homosexual relationships so long as they did not threaten the wider patterns of good order and discipline."[40] By telling, admitting, or confessing to Sergeant Pinkerton, their immediate superior officer, McGrath problemitizes his and Kurt's homosexual encounter. Over and above their transgression of military code, the sergeant sincerely seems to be more concerned with losing a good medic, Kurt, and his best marksman, McGrath, so their homosexuality becomes boyish and "dumb." Pinkerton is certain that the two soldiers cannot be "queers;" they are far too masculine for that. They are simply immature and naive. This approach to homosexuality in the military, particularly during wartime, is apparently common.

Gay journalist Randy Shilts' 1994 comprehensive examination of gays in the United States military, *Conduct Unbecoming: Gays and Lesbians in the U.S. Military*, records an anecdotal situation from the Vietnam War which directly reflects Kurt and McGrath's admitted homosexual encounter. Interestingly, this story involves a navy medic attached to the Marine Corps, Kurt's duty in *Boy*, and occurs during the same year as Kurt's fictional letter, 1967. Shilts' description of navy medic Jess Jessop could easily be used to describe Kurt Strom: "As the medic for his Marine squad, Jessop also bore the veneration that Marines heap upon their Navy Doc.' Jessop was his men's physician, their nurse, their counselor and father confessor." Unlike Kurt, Jessop was formally charged with homosexuality, which he denied, telling the Office of Naval Intelligence: "No, I'm not a fucking queer." However, Jessop's defense of his heteronormalcy was identical to Sergeant Pinkerton's contention about Kurt, that he was too good a soldier, too masculine to be queer. The inquest found that Jessop "could not be a faggot because he was a good sailor."[41] As in Nelson's novel, as long as a soldier maintains certain culturally accepted "norms" of masculinity and adequately performs his duties, his occasional homosexual transgressions can be relegated to either fabrication or immature behavior. Jessop, just like Kurt, fully realized that he was gay. He had also learned how to play the game.

One of the next letters Kurt writes to Paul, dated 8 March 1967, is apparently in reply to an admonishment. He tells Paul: "I'm certain you mean well with your warning. And I appreciate it. But you're being hypocritical when you accuse me of ... living for sex to the detriment of better things'" (239). Ever the opportunist, Kurt reminds Paul that the very military environment of wartime invites sex as a means of dealing with the tension: "I'm surrounded by steel-eyed, swashbuckling, ruthless, sexy, and stupid men. I shall bait my hooks well: These fish will bite" (239). Once again, Kurt constructs the marines as mythic symbols of rugged masculinity, romantic and dashing—yet gullible to his southern charm. For all the soldiers' ruthlessness, Kurt's own mythic sexuality and powers of seduction reduce them to mere fish, easily hooked and reeled in. This letter also details the exploits of other gay marines whom Kurt feels do not measure up to his same level of sexual proficiency, maintaining his mania for comparing himself to other less successful homosexual conquerors, *lesser* gay soldiers. The first is an unnamed corpsman, a sort of failed version of Kurt who does not even earn an identity in his letter, who plies marines with alcohol and pornography only to undermine his seductions with what Kurt calls a "shattering climax: I'm sorry, but I love you'" (239). Love, anathema to Kurt's sexual philosophy, is replaced with power and idealistic notions about masculinity as a challenge and a game, something to be tested and absorbed, not denigrated by an abstract concept such as romantic love. In Nelson's sequel, *Panthers in the Skins of Men*, Kurt and Paul discuss love, face to face. During their dialog, Kurt says:

> Romantic love is a panacea for loneliness nurtured by advertisers, film-makers, and inferior novelists to sell their products. It's an antidote for adventure, a catering for an effeminate need for security. Romance fulfills a woman's needs for pornography. (200)

Over and above his contention that romantic love is a created "product," used to placate the lonely consumer, Kurt considers it an "antidote for adventure," an obstacle in the attainment of conquests and masculinity. Romantic love simply caters to "an effeminate need for security," with "effeminate" denoting the weak male, the *un-masculine* man, hetero-or homosexual, who needs security more than daring exploits. To damn romantic love completely, Kurt relegates it to pornography for women. Love then becomes a marker for the surrender of true masculinity, a concept that, in Kurt's world, is predicated upon constant sexual victory.

The next two examples, in this letter, of *lesser* gay men in Kurt's company represent two separate spheres of power, spiritual and physical. One is a priest, the other a doctor, and the story Kurt relates to Paul reflects how all three men provide different types of succor to the injured marines in their collective care.

Kurt views both men as congenial sexual competition. The company's Catholic chaplain, Father Kerry, "sits next to the beds of the more attractive patients and murmurs soothingly, wiping their brows with his right hand as he rubs their lower abdomens with his left" (239). This is, of course, Kurt's sexual technique, minus the homily. In the previous letter to his cousin, Chloe, Kurt said of Father Kerry, "he's always consoling the maimed and the dying, whatever their faith. I like him, although I'm of no faith myself" (238). On the contrary, Kurt's faith is purely humanistic and centered in his ego. He jokingly writes to Paul that Father Kerry's "perversity dismays me; we share the same taste, and as he cruises the ward during the day, he can usually get to my favorites before I can" (240). Kurt makes no distinction between the priest's pastoral duties and his sexual predilections, fusing the two into a type of complete care of both body and soul. Father Kerry's daily rounds become "cruising," and trump Kurt's chances to *console* the injured soldiers. His admiration for the gay priest also stems from his dislike of the company's Protestant chaplain, who never visits the hospital tent, and who Kurt believes has no true interests in the enlisted men: "...his consolation is directed toward predestined officers" (238). Officers are only to be dominated, not courted or coddled. Only enlisted men, whose power is represented solely by their masculinity and sexuality, interest Kurt Strom.

Kurt's encounter with Dr. Schiller is spurred by guilt over the death of a young marine, a wounded man with a fatal and unstoppable embolism headed toward his heart. To help alleviate a high temperature, Kurt tears off the marine's clothes:

> In his delirium, the boy alternated between an impassioned acceptance as he caressed me and a sudden clarity, when he would hiss, "I'll get you for this, faggot." Like his consciousness, his erection ebbed and flowed. Father Kerry had been perfoming ablutions when I arrived on the ward and had apparently relieved the boy's less critical congestion. (241)

Though in different surroundings and circumstances, this sexual encounter is strikingly similar to Kurt's earlier seduction of the soldier on the bus. Even the ambivalent responses and Kurt's descriptive verb match, almost verbatim. Kurt writes in that early letter to Paul: "he hissed, Stay away from me, faggot'"(33). Both reactions employ the word "hiss," which implies an impassioned and even violent reaction undermined by both soldiers' acceptance of Kurt's proffered sex. The use of the pejorative term "faggot" by both men in reference to Kurt seems to be an attempt to define his identity as separate from theirs, though both men are sexually compliant. Both men also issue a warning to Kurt, a type of perfunctory refusal that, like the use of "faggot," serves to protect their own sense of masculinity and heterosexuality.

In his next series of letters, Kurt explains that his company has been moved from their previous Chu Lai location to the much larger city of Da Nang, a city that also has a much higher population of American military personnel. Kurt, assigned to a bustling Marine Corps medical unit, finds Da Nang to be a thriving location for furtive homosexual encounters among the soldiers, indicating that situational homosexuality is somewhat proportional to numbers. In a letter to Paul, dated 17 March 67, Kurt begins: "I have good news and I have bad news" (258). The difference between the two will become important by the end of the letter. The "good news" is that when he first arrived in Da Nang, Kurt immediately went looking for "signs" of homosexual activity around the base, and found them in the most traditional, predictable, and common place, the Marine Corps PX bathroom. He writes to Paul: "Still, I take a certain perverse enjoyment in using the facilities. And I could hardly help noticing a huge glory hole between the two stalls" (258). The glory hole, a small hole (or in this case a large one) surreptitiously cut in the wall between two public bathroom stalls and used for anonymous oral sex, becomes a sign for Kurt that homosexual activity is prevalent at the Da Nang base. Other gay "signs" include the graffiti written boldly on the bathroom walls, snippets of homosexual doggerel that Nelson reproduces in the text, with a postmodern playfulness, in all bold capital letters, indicating its prominence as a sign to which both gay and straight marines have access:

YOUNG AND CLEAN
STRONG AND LEAN
6' 1" OF RUGGED MARINE
HAIR OF YELLOW
EYES OF GREEN
HERE AT 1500 EVERY TUESDAY TO FUCK ASS

THE HORNIEST MOTHER FUCKER IN NAM
DROPS BY EVERY WEDNESDAY MORNING
TO CHECK OUT WHAT SOME OTHER
HORNY MOTHER FUCKER
MIGHT HAVE IN MIND (259)

This type of public toilet signaling by gay men, the glory hole and the graffiti, demonstrates the ubiquity and transgressive nature of public, casual sex for many homosexuals. For Kurt, the signs are exciting and comforting; he writes to Paul: "It was all very friendly and familiar, even in Arcady" (259). His use of the literary term, "Arcady," is ironic, considering that the term denotes a place of pastoral innocence, hardly the description of a public men's room in a military PX; however, because Arcady can also be used to symbolize a kind of promise land of plenty, the bathroom is the homosexual liaison point for numerous young and attractive soldiers, a true gay Arcady. To prove the point, in his next letter Kurt writes: "Paul, that place is a gold mine. You'd hardly believe the legions of studs who wander into the bathroom for reasons that would shock the Pentagon" (261). With only its purely functional use as a location of biological evacuation and hygiene considered, the toilet seems non-erotic, almost anti-erotic. But Ramakers points out the importance of bathrooms and bathroom sex in the social interactions of gay men:

> Gender-segregated and with the inherent sexual connotations of urination and defecation, they [public bathrooms] are an ideal site for homosexual contact. Public toilets are therefore indeed "oases of eroticism." They also provide(d) much needed, but scarce, opportunities for gay men to create social as well as sexual networks. Research carried out both in Britain and in the United States suggests that for many

> decades public toilets played a particularly important role for (especially but not only) working-class gay men.[42]

Kurt relies on the predictability of these social and sexual networks for his homosexual conquests. Being a closeted gay man, he also well understands how they work. When Ramakers states that public bathrooms appeal to mainly working-class gay men, he assumes the probability of their being closeted. Nelson can easily transfer this same probability of class and homosexual behavior to the marines in Vietnam, especially the enlisted men who are almost all working-class—Kurt's primary sexual target.

Kurt shows no fear of being caught cruising the PX bathroom; this is the "good news." After spending an unsuccessful Friday morning in the toilet, looking for sex, he writes comically, and militarily, to Paul of his persistence: "Like MacArthur, however, I shall return" (259). Like most gay men, he ignores the "heterosexual anxiety" of the bathroom, considering it more opportunity than danger. Lee Edelman, in his essay, "Tearooms and Sympathy, or, The Epistemology of the Water Closet," argues:

> that the men's room, whose very signifier...enshrines the phallus as the token not only of difference, but of difference as determinate, difference as knowable, is the site of a particular heterosexual anxiety about the inscriptions of homosexual desire and about the possibility of knowing or recognizing whatever would constitute the "homosexual difference."[43]

Edelman's essay concerns the anxiety caused in 1964 by the arrests of several Washington D. C. government employees caught having homosexual sex in public restrooms. His thesis implies that the high level of tension caused by the incidents stemmed directly from the public's collective fear that homosexuals were becoming "unidentifiable," masquerading as masculine men, stable family men, government men. The bathroom becomes a site for knowledge, a location where difference is recognizable, blurred, and feared, where a heterosexual man might actually distinguish a homosexual man and accidentally give him an identity. It is a dangerous liminal space that must be *policed.* The U.S. military recognizes the social dangers, the threat to heterosexual masculinity, posed by the "cruisy" men's room. As recently as 1989, Randy Shilts reports of a sting operation carried out by the Naval Investigative Service in Okinawa, Japan, "where the NIS secretly installed videocameras in a public restroom at a picnic ground at Camp Lester.... Their cameras documented an impressive amount of sexual activity among at least forty servicemen or civilian military employees." The military displays the need to watch the boundaries secretly and punish the *crime*, what they term "sexual impurity" and "indecent acts."[44] Bathroom sex among men, if nothing else, assails the heterosexual masculine fortress of pure and decent sex, strictly defined by military code and, one assumes, practiced by all servicemen. Kurt *watches* the bathroom also. His approach to the bathroom utilizes only the "recognizable" factor of this social equation, the "inscriptions of homosexual desire," which allow him opportunity for homosexual conquests with the straight-identified marines. Like most gay men, Kurt's finds pleasure in the bathroom and its sexual environment; his anxiety is generated from far different quarters—the "bad news."

The "bad news" Kurt reports to Paul illustrates where and how Kurt fears reprisals for his homosexual activity. While back in the United States for his mother's funeral, on a return flight stopover in San Franscisco, Kurt met, "a pair of dreary things who could talk only of drapes and soufflés" (259). As a favor to the effeminate gay couple, he accepts an address of a friend of theirs, a soldier currently serving in Vietnam, and a promise to write the man a letter. When Kurt does write to the soldier, in what he calls a "moment of weakness," he is horrified to receive a reply from an army hospital where the man is being imprisoned and treated for homosexuality. Though the letter is sad and rather pathetic, "Why didn't you write sooner...I was so lonely...My sergeant was so desirable," Kurt realizes the danger that it poses to his own personal safety as a closeted gay man: "Jesus Christ! They censor the letters of psychos. The fool! Any minute now, I expect a huge furry paw to clamp down on my shoulder and a gruff voice to growl, Come with me, boy'" (259). Kurt fears the unknown military power, which has the ability (and the right) to reach from nowhere and punish the "boy," assuming a patriarchal role. This is the same power that populated the mental hospital, written about in the earlier letter, with men who had transgressed heterosexuality and posed a threat to military masculinity. In that letter (92–93), Kurt asked the question that resonates as the subtext of his fears expressed by the letter he received from the gay prisoner: "I wonder whom they so offended?" (93). The "cruisy" bathroom at the PX, replete with all of its gay signs and markers, while maybe not safe, still represents the knowable. As Kurt put it, "it was all very friendly and familiar." The fear that somewhere someone *official* would read the letter written to him by the prisoner represents the unknowable. To make matters more complex, the power is also paternal, considering the military's usurpation of the role by way of its inherent *in loco parentis* status. Kurt knows that his sexually explicit letters to Paul are safe. In one of his earlier letters, he wrote to Paul: "Speaking of mail, I've confirmed that the battalion's censors send corpsmen's mail on without reading it. Now I can really dish the dirt" (174). This third-party interruption in the epistolary dialog, the mysterious "censor," presents more of a threat, vague though it is, to Kurt's homosexual pleasure than any real threat of being caught having sex in the PX bathroom. As Michel Foucault astutely notes in *The History of Sexuality, Volume One*, the very ability of power to work "is proportional to its ability to hide its own mechanisms…for its secrecy is not in the nature of an abuse; it is indispensable to its operation."[45] However, while he fears this unknown power, Kurt also finds it exciting and titillating, as evidenced by his earlier homosexual fantasy of humiliating a lieutenant. As he explained the fantasy to Paul, four of the officers that he found sexually attractive stand behind two way mirrors and "they watch us." In the next series of letters to Paul, Kurt becomes acutely aware of how thrilling his sexual games can be when he flaunts his obsession in the face of military power. Just as in his fantasy, officers begin to enter—from behind the mirror of power.

In his next series of homosexual adventures and letters to Paul, Kurt documents his association with two officers, Air Force pilots Steve and Don; with this pair, Kurt also begins to explore how military power and sexual power combine and intertwine. Kurt begins his letter to Paul, dated 22 March 1967 from Da Nang, with a teasing hint: "But I am the only person at Med Battalion who has seen Saigon, and I can't tell a soul" (261). Kurt first meets Steve, "a dashing hard-eyed air jockey wearing a flight suit," while cruising the PX bathroom (261). Though at first Steve shows no sexual interest in Kurt, he does invite him on a cargo flight to Saigon. As Kurt points out, this trip presents a high level of danger for him personally: "I was flirting with a charge of AWOL and several weeks in the brig" (261). After blatantly defying military authority, Kurt deftly manages to get out of duty and sneak away. He and Steve fly to the capitol city of Saigon and check into a hotel, a room Kurt calls "a fitting seraglio" (262). Kurt's encounter with the captain illustrates an intersection and interaction of several of the sexual dynamics that he pursues, such as specularity, scopophilia, masculine drag, and military power. Steve, a married man whose civilian job was as an illustrator for an advertising agency in Los Angeles, wants to *look* at Kurt, to appreciate his masculine beauty from an artist's perception:

> "Hold it right there." he moved to a desk and picked up a sketch pad. "The face grabbed me as soon as I saw it. I had to sketch those bones. But I never expected the body. Holy mackerel! Don't move." Steve walked around me for twenty minutes, flipping pages over as he filled them. I stood stunned. A captain! As I got used to the idea, and as I measured Steve's happy intensity, a carnal reaction set in. (262)

This encounter bears several striking similarities to Kurt's first sexualized experience with an officer, Sergeant Pinkerton, who helped Kurt dress for his first jungle patrol in Vietnam. Both officers, Steve and Pinkerton, are described in terms of hardness, denoting both power and sexuality, Pinkerton as "my lean, hard sergeant" and Steve as "hard-eyed." (129, 261). Both officers make an aesthetic observation of Kurt's body; thus Kurt makes note of their eyes; Pinkerton tells him: "'Strip down,' demanded my lean, hard sergeant.... Strip all the way down,' ordered my bronzed, blue-eyed sergeant" (129). And both make very pointed comments about the masculine beauty and perfection of Kurt's body. After Kurt has stripped naked before him, Pinkerton says, " you're in pretty good shape, ain't you, Doc?'" (129). Steve expresses a similar impression about Kurt's nude form: "The face grabbed me as soon as I saw it. I had to sketch those bones. But I never expected the body. Holy mackerel!" As an officer, an ostensibly straight man, and artist, Steve is not only representative of power and masculinity, he also embodies a discerning perception of beauty, a "hard-eyed" objective appraisal of Kurt. Through what Kurt perceives as a sublimated sexual attraction, Steve, the artist, creates various simulacra, the hurried sketches, of Kurt's nude body. Presumably, Steve's interest in Kurt is purely aesthetic, while Kurt's interest in Steve is sexual, as indicated by the fact that he becomes erect while being drawn. Steve uses his power as an officer to spirit Kurt away to Saigon, and his power as an artist to objectify Kurt's body sexually. He also employs his official status to elevate Kurt's. When Kurt exits the hotel room shower, naked, he observes, "Steve, dressed in a captain's uniform, was leaning over the bed laying out a second uniform." After Steve has sketched Kurt's nude body, he points to the officer's uniform and tells him, "You'd better put that on. It should fit.... We're eating at the officers' club" (262). The officer's uniform represents power, masculinity, and danger to Kurt; impersonating an officer in the military is as egregious an offense as going AWOL. However, because Steve, and his friend Don, are both officers, Kurt must become an officer, in appearance at least, to socialize with them. In his previous homosexual encounters with other marines, all enlisted men, Kurt functions on their rank and social level, but when he interacts directly with officers, he must be elevated to their status, even if he desires to seduce them, to assume some of their masculine and military power sexually. The uniform enables him to accomplish this act.

In Zeeland's *The Masculine Marine*, a Marine Corps captain explains the importance and the allure of the same type of uniform that Kurt dons as *straight drag* :

> *Zeeland:* What does the Marine Corps dress blue uniform symbolize to you?
> *Captain Eric:* It forces you into an erect posture, forces you to hold your head up. You look proud; you look like you've got it all together. It's a very good-looking uniform. And I think that symbolizes this attitude of "I am going to be as precise and perfect and

> excellent as I can be." That's why the standards for these uniforms are very strict. We must have gone through a dozen uniform inspections before we got out of Quantico.[46]

The marine's description of the uniform gives it its own power; the uniform "forces you" to look and act in a certain manner. The uniform, for the officers, is appearance translated into action and attitude. When Kurt dresses in the captain's uniform, he becomes transformed to the point that when he, Steve, and Steve's friend, Don, meet at the Officers' Club, Kurt regales them with fictitious stories of his heterosexual prowess. He also indicates the performative nature of the evening when he writes, as an aside to Paul: "Steve was fascinated by my stories about Paulette Carroll (I hope you don't mind my putting you in drag) and gently inquired whether I preferred older women" (263). The irony is represented by the fact that Kurt, with Captain Steve's assistance, has put himself into drag also. Kurt inhabits the uniform so well, and the masculine power role as officer, that when he is first introduced to Don, the major "expressed amazement at my rapid advancement through the ranks" (263). Major Don, another of Nelson's avatars of heterosexuality and masculinity, described by Kurt as, "a short wiry blond dude on the right side of devastating," serves as a sexual foil to his friend, Steve (263). Steve's homosexual curiosity is tested by Kurt's physical beauty, while Don views Kurt as a sexual equal, a straight stud like himself. In a rather comic turn, they compare erotic stories, both being the sexual hero of their own tale, as to how many and how avidly they have seduced women. Kurt, of course, gender switches his stories, transforming his male sexual conquests into women for the sake of the heterosexual bragging rights narrative competition. After a night of heavy drinking among the three men, Kurt finally seduces Captain Steve, while Don is asleep in the next room; it seems only fitting and predictable that the macho Don walk in on the act.

Nelson introduces the Air Force officers, Steve and Don, to put Kurt on a different sexual playing field than the one he is used to, the enlisted grunts back in the tents of Da Nang, where he can only fantasize about sex with officers. The setting and characters shift from the jungle to the city, from tents and ditches to hotel rooms, from privates to majors and captains, from the more basic soldiers to the educated and more sophisticated officers. The only constant is represented by Kurt's malleability and talent to charm himself out of bad situations. When Don discovers Kurt *in flagrante delicto* with Steve, he storms from the hotel room. Kurt asks Steve how Don will react to what he witnessed, and Steve tells him, "Tell everybody. Write my wife. Ruin my career" (265). However, none of these imagined punishments for heterosexual transgression happen. Instead, Don falls completely into Kurt's hands by sexually testing him, a test where the only passing grade is to be butch enough to have sex with men and still maintain masculinity—Kurt matriculated in this school long ago. Steve and Don make a special flight to Da Nang just for Don to confront Kurt, and over dinner Kurt instinctively knows how to rectify the situation: "Steve seemed nervous and said little. I did my butch act: cars, chicks, raping, maiming, killing… I got no applause" (269). His "butch act" is further augmented by the fact that he has once again dressed in the Air Force captain's uniform. After Don leaves them alone, Kurt and Steve engage in a complex dialog which delineates the boundaries of homosexuality and masculinity for the Air Force officers. Kurt asks Steve:

> "Did I pass the test?"
> Steve laughed. "Yeah."
> "What if I'd flunked?"
> "You didn't."
> "What if?"
> Steve sighed. "Don's got an exaggerated notion of masculinity. He…"
> "He hates queers."
> "Yes, But you're not…" (270)

Don's "exaggerated notion of masculinity" is predicated upon constantly indulged heterosexuality and supported by active homophobia. As Kurt maintains, he "hates queers"; however, that hatred is defined by the stereotypical effeminate homosexuality that Kurt shuns as actively as the heterosexuals. Don witnessed the two men engaged in a full-blown homosexual act; for it not to be *queer* Don must hold up both men to a personal, and societal, standard of masculinity that precludes any queerness. Kurt's "butch act," his sports career, his physical attraction, his charm, his sexual nature, even the officer's uniform, all become tools in resisting Don's concept of "queer." Not difficult, considering it is the same definition of queer that Kurt employs for the internalized homophobia that drives him to seek sexual encounters with only straight-identified men.

In this same letter to Paul, Nelson uses Captain Steve's character, the officer and artist, to explain, in part, Kurt's attractiveness to heterosexual men and the unexplainable and common ambivalence they have toward having sex with him. No other character in the novel, thus far, has mused on why he succumbs to Kurt's sexual allure. About their sexual encounter, Steve tells Kurt, "I had to justify what I was doing....It was too new. I'd never even thought about...I was afraid. I couldn't justify what I felt. I wasn't sure what I felt" (270). As with several of his earlier sexual conquests, Kurt exploits this sexual confusion, generated by his charm, physical appearance, and alacrity. Steve, the artist, seems more impressed with the powerful aesthetic aspect of Kurt's masculine homosexuality:

> "Then I decided that my aesthetic judgment was the key. Don appreciates getting it on with a beautiful woman, but he feels that any woman is better than no woman. I happen to disagree. I refuse to make love to a woman who's ugly or whom I can't respect. I'm an artist... a sold-out artist maybe ...But I can still appreciate beauty. And you are, my friend, except for that scar along your head. Hey! Look at me." He ran his hand through my hair and traced the scar. "It might be too provoking if you were flawless." (271)

Steve running his hand through Kurt's hair draws another sharp parallel between him and the previous officer, Sergeant Pinkerton, whom Kurt found sexually desirable. After his lecture to Kurt on homosexuality in the military, Pinkerton also mussed Kurt's hair indicating his boyish charm and beauty and mitigating the sergeant's attraction to him; however, Steve, because of his artistically acute sense of beauty, indulges himself in the act. Steve's aesthetic rationalization of his homosexual desire toward Kurt implies a Platonic concept of male beauty, appropriate in a novel obsessed with the subject. In a study of male beauty, interestingly entitled "Beauty (re)Discovers the Male Body," Susan Bordo makes the Platonic connection between the male body, sex, and beauty:

> In *Symposium*, he [Plato] describes the beauty of the body as evidence of the presence of the divine on earth, and the original spur of all "higher" human endeavors (as well as earthly, sexual love). We see someone dazzling, and he or she awakens the soul to its natural hunger to be lifted above the mundane, transitory, mortal world.…the beautiful body of another becomes the inspiration for a lifelong search for beauty in all its forms, the creation of beautiful art, beautiful words, beautiful ideals. …

Steve, the "sold-out artist," who has given his talents to commercialism (his stateside job as an illustrator), becomes so enamored of Kurt's physical beauty that he remembers what Platonic aesthetic transcendence can achieve, in this case even a breaking down of heterosexuality. Even his reminder to Kurt that his beauty is flawed by the scar reflects the Platonic. As Bordo points out, "It's our nature to be imperfect, after all, and anyone who tries to overcome that limitation on earth is guilty of hubris—according to the Greeks."[47] Kurt's scar ironically ameliorates his masculine beauty, saves it from being "too provoking." Steve's friend, Don, can forgo beauty for heterosexual desire, indicating that he lets his body think for him as opposed to his mind. For these foil characters, Steve represents the mind and Don represents the body. It is Don, the body, who has the "exaggerated notion of masculinity," one that applies only to sexual orientation, the conquest of women, and the rejection of "queers." Steve, the mind, can appreciate Kurt's beauty and transcend his former notions of masculinity and sexuality. The anxiety created between these two representative characters embodies Kurt's own conflicted nature, his obsession with heterosexual male beauty and his internalized homophobia and disdain for effeminate gay men, the "queers," the failed homosexuals. To illustrate this very point, the same letter includes an anecdote of the sexual success and failure of a masculine gay man and an effeminate gay man.

While in Saigon with the two Air Force officers, Kurt decides to see the city, and while wandering about meets a handsome, friendly army private named Greg. Greg invites him back to his apartment and, like Kurt's sexual *modus operandi*, Greg employs a planned seduction, a sexual game with Kurt as the prize. Kurt, amused at the sexual ruse, asks him bluntly, "Does this work? …The whole set up" (275). Greg, the army version of Kurt, explains the success of his homosexual game/plan for seducing American military men in Saigon: "the boys need a place to hide after dark. They're lonely, Greg explained with a grin, and horny, and afraid of being tossed out on their ass should they not prove amenable. The set-up was hard to resist" (275). The success of Greg's elaborate "set-up" is compared, in stark relief, to the next character who literally suddenly enters the picture:

> Before we could leave for the USO, the door opened and an apparition walked in, a limp-wristed, eye-rolling, queen so nelly they could have heard the swish across the Mekong River. When she saw me, she gave a little scream, lisped "Excuse *me*," and slipped back outside.
>
> I turned to Greg. "What ever was that?"
>
> Greg groaned. "My roommate." (275)

Nelson, as he has done previously in the novel, uses derogatory gay argot to give the reader a vivid impression of the roommate. Steve and Don represent the mind and the body, while Greg and Leigh (note the feminized form of the traditional male name, "Lee") represent the masculine, butch gay man and the effeminate, "queer" gay man. Leigh decides he can play the same sexual seduction game that has worked so well for Greg and Kurt, so he finds a soldier whom Kurt describes as "butch as he could possibly be," and brings him back to the apartment while Kurt and Greg are there. After some comic coaching from Greg and Kurt ("He's drunk a pint of sloe gin. What do I do now?"), Leigh attempts to bed the drunken soldier. Greg and Kurt's dialog exchange about the situation is telling:

> "I can't believe it," said Greg. "Leigh hasn't had sex during the eight months we've been here."

"You're kidding?"

"I thought he was asexual. I can't believe it." (278–279)

Leigh, the obviously feminine homosexual man, has been sexless, so much so that Greg thinks he is "asexual," and has either failed at or refused to play the complicated "butch" gay seduction game he sees played out in front of him constantly. Earlier, Greg told Kurt, "Leigh makes himself scarce. …He'll stay down in the TV room until we've gone to bed" (275). Predictably, Leigh's seduction plan goes terribly wrong; he is too "queer" to make it work. He dramatically runs into the living room from the bedroom, screaming, "Oh, God! Oh, God!… I'm ruined…Ruined" (279). When Greg and Kurt enter the bedroom, they find the drunk soldier naked with his rifle drawn and screaming, "Fucking faggot…Fucking faggot" (279–280). Though more malicious than Kurt's gay epithets used to describe the effeminate Leigh, the angry soldier's remark represents the same homophobic contempt. After Kurt and Greg manage to calm the soldier and get him out of the apartment, they must tend to the hysterical Leigh: "We carried Leigh to his bed, put cold compresses across his forehead, and gave him a sedative. It took several minutes of sobbing and hiccoughs before we could understand what happened" (280). Leigh's overreaction is meant to be comic, but it also illustrates how "queer" gay men can only fail at playing the "butch" game of heterosexual, masculine seduction. Leigh had to ask Greg and Kurt for all of the rules, the instructions that they so readily are able to follow. When they finally do ascertain what happened in the bedroom between Leigh and the drunken soldier, the answer, which abruptly ends the anecdote and is once again meant to be comic, explains why the effeminate gay man has failed so miserably at the game: "Leigh," said Greg sternly, "you're never supposed to kiss them" (280). Leigh, the "failed" gay man, broke the most basic rule of homosexual sex with straight-identified soldiers, the dictum Kurt learned when he seduced Corporal McGrath and offered him a kiss back in the jungle: "You can fuck a marine," he snarled. "But you can't fuck with a marine" (168). The overly emotional Leigh, as evidenced by his hysterical reaction to the incident, seeks a feminine marker of affection from the soldier—a kiss. The masculine Greg's warning to him is paternal, instructive, and strict; he advises Leigh "sternly" on how to become a sexually successful *man*.

Directly after the episode with Leigh and the drunken soldier, Kurt manages to reconcile his mind/body sexual dichotomy represented by the two Air Force officers, Steve and Don. Don, whose exaggerated notion of masculinity involves both the constant sexual conquest of women and exaggerated homophobia, finally succumbs to Kurt's male sexual attraction; however, the incident also represents a highly ritualized and sexualized reenactment of the war raging on around the characters. When Kurt returns to the hotel room he shares with the two officers, Don engages him in a conversation. Kurt notes, "the talk was desultory until Don brought up the topic of homosexuality. He wanted to know about my first time. I felt like a hooker with a john" (280). Because Kurt considers the truth banal, "I embroidered a tale in which Pinkerton held a .45 to my head and forced me to go down on him. …and I liked it'" (280). In this fantasy Pinkerton, Kurt's commanding officer back in the jungle, *forces* Kurt to perform as a homosexual against his will by using military action, a service revolver held against his head. Kurt makes Don think that homosexuality is situational, a side effect of the war, so it does not threaten heterosexual masculinity. When Don considers Kurt's position, as a gay medic among so many young and attractive males, he becomes sexually aroused at the idea and says, "I'm a medic, alone in a room with several young chicks lying naked in their beds" (280). Don then uses the most trite and traditional rationalization for homosexual sex between non-gay-identified men when he says to Kurt, "I've been thinking, you know, head's head, no matter who gives it" (281). His statement clearly indicates that he has attempted to rationalize homosexual sex with Kurt, so much so that he asks Kurt for reinforcement of the idea when he asks, "Kurtie baby, you understand what I'm saying?" Kurt writes to Paul, "I understood. I just mistrusted him" (281). Kurt's inherent mistrust of Don's obvious sexual advance stems from Don's almost vitriolic homophobia, a major defining factor for his own sense of masculinity; Kurt suspects a game at best, a trap at worst. When Don displays his erect penis to Kurt, Kurt responds, "Major, if you only had a gun pointed at my head, you couldn't keep me off it" (281). Because he is truly suspicious of Don's motives, Kurt's statement seems to be an almost unconscious reenactment of his forced fantasy sexual initiation with Sergeant Pinkerton. The next day, while Don is flying Kurt from Saigon back to Da Nang, they reconstruct the forced, martial homosexuality. Kurt writes to Paul, "I was buckled into a little mesh hammock-type seat, my ass an inch off the floor, and my eyes level with Don's crotch. He pulled a water pistol from his pocket and squirted me in the face. He grinned and unzipped his flight suit" (282). This reenactment of Kurt's spurious "first time" homosexual experience serves to reflect the violence of war, people forced at gunpoint to obey, and Don's ritual initiation into the world of gay sex. Don's masculine and official control become the means by which he can have sex with another man, and Kurt has defeated the reluctant heterosexual male body along with the mind by playing an elaborate game. To illustrate the point, in his next letter to Paul, Kurt writes that Don and Steve return to Da Nang to visit him. While Kurt is having sex with the physical Don, the intellectual Steve enters the room. Steve's artistic and intellectual natures come into play when he is portrayed, at first, as a voyeur: "I looked at Steve who was standing in the doorway. He was looking at me. As I set to work on Don, Steve shut the door behind him and moved to the bed to watch" (304). However, the sexual intensity of the scene overcomes Steve's intellectual reticence to compromise his heterosexual masculinity in front of his best friend, his straight buddy. As Steve willingly joins in the sexual scene being enacted before him, Kurt writes to Paul that he made the *coup de grace* of his sexual games with straight identified power figures represented by the two Air Force officers; he penetrates Don while Don is forced to perform oral sex on Steve, and Kurt refers to the act as "returning the favor." His statement does not seem ironic in the context of the scene. Kurt ends this letter with the epigram:

> "Drink now and love, Democrates: for we
> Shall not have wine and boys eternally" (304).

The classical epigram not only recreates the irony of a pastoral homosexual world imbedded in a war-torn jungle Hades, it also portends a radical shift of locale and social structure in the novel.

The final section of *The Boy Who Picked the Bullets Up* becomes a complex mixture of community, masculinity, Southern homosociality, and postcolonialism. Kurt writes to his cousin, Chloe, that the high command in Vietnam has transformed a former civilian project into a strictly military one. The project is called "CAP:" Combined Action Platoon, and its primary stated purpose is to allow American military personnel to aid Vietnamese civilians with medical and social assistance. CAP's secondary, and furtive, purpose is to aid the military in ferreting out Viet Cong communist sympathizers in South Vietnamese villages. When Kurt learns that his commanding officer, Sergeant Pinkerton, will be in charge of a CAP unit, he immediately volunteers; however, he is refused the duty by the Marine Corps medical chief. When Pinkerton pleads with the Chief to allow Kurt to become part of his team, the Chief's reply sets the tone for the remainder of the novel. The Chief half jokingly asks Pinkerton, "What the hell is this? You queer for Strom or something?" (308). The men who become part of the CAP unit, most of them Southern, form the nucleus of a community that is, indeed, *queer*. When a colonel briefs the men on their conduct while serving the Vietnamese village, he lists several *DON'Ts*; refraining from sex with the local women is stressed by being repeated four times. Kurt, of course, considers this forced military abstinence as sexual opportunity. He writes to Paul, "I am to live in a remote encampment with some very horny marines who are specifically ordered to refrain from fucking women. Let's hear it for Colonel So and So" (314).

Kurt introduces his fellow CAP members by writing Paul a long, narrative poem outlining each man's background, from social position to geography, sexual attractiveness to athletic ability, once again reflecting his penchant for listing and ranking, a type of postmodern control of a situation. Most of the soldiers, by Sergeant Pinkerton's design, are Southerners. Pinkerton, himself a Texas "good old boy" type, represents the center of the community. The other members run the gamut, socially and geographically: Corporal McGrath is a Mississippi "red neck;" Herndon is a Virginia "aristocrat," educated at Dartmouth; Tennessee is a traditional farm boy, work horse type; and the sole African American member, Bluege, is a Baton Rouge native (319–324). CAP duty also removes and relieves the men from the direct combat and jungle patrols of Da Nang, creating an environment where the war is always in the background as opposed to the foreground. Like Joseph Conrad's *Heart of Darkness* with its African locations and Marlow's fascination with the unknown, the "blank spaces on the map" that intrigued him, Kurt too realizes the blank and deceptive nature of the jungle. He writes to his grandmother about the little, isolated village of Bou Bou Phu, his CAP duty post, "As usual, I'm uncertain as to where I am. I've seen our location on maps. It appears to be twenty miles inland from Da Nang. But if I learn nothing else from Vietnam, I'll always know that appearances can be deceiving" (326). For Kurt, this assertion is far more than spatial; it applies to the outward appearance of the war and heterosexual masculinity, and his constant uncertainty as to just where he is.

The unusual location of the CAP unit, originally a regulation military camp near the village, plays an important role in the creation of a community in the novel. While reconnoitering in the surrounding jungle, the marines discover a derelict, Western-type paradise isolated and hidden in the mountains. Kurt writes to Paul:

> Atop a nearby butte, we found a deserted villa, made some repairs, and moved into it. Our translator learned that a wealthy French family from Da Nang had abandoned the villa after the debacle at Dien Bien Phu. LaSalle says the older Vietnamese hate the villa; they hint at a curse. I have little desire to know more. (332)

The French colonial villa represents the folly of Western colonization and conquest of Vietnam and a type of futile oasis of Western culture in the tropical jungle. With its grand architecture, terraces, and a huge swimming pool, it stands in stark relief to the wild foliage that hides it. The villa is so overrun by nature that it is covered in creepers and insects; Kurt names it "Cobra's Folly." However, the villa also creates a home for the soldiers, one that is not transient, cold, and military like their usual tent hooches. Kurt writes, "Indented in one wall is a fireplace; Pinkerton has placed snapshots of his wife and his three little boys upon its mantel. My library fills a built in bookcase next to my bed. …I dreamed again the other night I was at Manderley" (322). His reference to the mysterious manor house in Daphne DuMauier's *Rebecca* and the translator's report that the native inhabitants consider the ruined villa to be cursed both give the location an ominous and foreboding sense. Nevertheless, the men use their skills to repair the house and make it a home.

Kurt's first seduction of a straight-identified marine at the villa further illustrates Nelson's portrayal of Kurt's homosexuality as a game and his sexual actions as initiation. Barry, a young radio man whom Kurt describes as "Superman" because of his glasses, becomes the antithesis of the failed gay man from Kurt's first jungle duty assignment, the nearsighted and bespectacled "Queenie." Barry represents another of Kurt's avatars of pure male sexuality; however, Barry, unlike the earlier representations, is neither vaguely dangerous nor a bad boy. He is the embodiment of boyish innocence and naiveté. Kurt writes about Barry:

> Barry wore eye-glasses, which turns me off. On the beach, however, he shucked those glasses and his clothes and displayed one of the most beautiful bodies I've had the pleasure of viewing. Had I not already come to know him as a friendly puppy dog of a kid, I would have been too much in awe of his bronzed good looks, heavily muscled body, and glorious butch walk to speak to him. (346)

Just like Clark Kent, the mild-mannered farm boy who can remove his glasses and transform himself into the mythical icon of masculinity, Superman, Barry achieves the same kind of transformation in Kurt's mind. However, Barry *is* a simple and good-natured farm boy, not a super hero. Kurt decides to seduce him by exploiting his position as medic and warning Barry about the perils of masturbation—unless performed correctly. Kurt turns his demonstration into a game, and as he writes to Paul, "Barry loved it. So did I. We enjoyed it even more the following night" (347). To extend the concept of his seduction as a game further, when Kurt and Barry are interrupted, *in flagrante delicto*, by an intruder in the radio room of the villa, Kurt instructs Barry to play a simple game to throw suspicion while he investigates. Kurt tells Barry, "Say I went to the store and bought an apple and a banana'" (348). Barry fails to understand the alphabetical game, and in an attempt to explain it to him, Kurt sexualizes it. When Kurt quickly, and comically, looks for the intruder as he explains the game, he lists an apple, a banana, a cherry, and for the letter "D" a dildo. Barry asks, "What's a dildo?" (348). Interestingly, the reader also learns that while they were engaged in sex, Barry had removed his glasses: "By this time, Barry had his rifle loaded and locked. I handed him his glasses… (348). To become Kurt's icon of heterosexual male sexual power, Barry must remove the glasses, which make him appear innocent, inept, and perhaps a little too similar to the nearsighted, failed gay men whom Kurt holds in disdain. The alphabet game also becomes a part of their sexual activity, as if what they do is simple child's play, and thus forgivable, as opposed to fully realized sex between two men. Kurt writes to Paul, "And Barry is fascinated by the Apple, Banana, and Cherry' game. We go all the way to Z' every night. He considers the game as foreplay" (348). Kurt's seduction of Barry, his innocence and devotion, represent initiation and game playing, but they also represent how Kurt has the nascent ability to approach true emotional attachment with another man. Barry, with his puppy dog fealty, appeals to the hardened and cynical Kurt, whose main form of emotional involvement with men has, up until this point in the novel, been elided in favor of sex, in return for pure masculinity.

The masculine domesticity of the villa becomes compromised by the introduction of one of the few developed female characters Nelson introduces in the novel. Shelia, a sort of *bon vivant* hippy girl and the sister of Frick, one of the marines at Bou Bou Phu, travels wartime Southeast Asia in search of fun. Kurt laments to Paul that before her arrival all of the men ran around the compound naked, as if the villa were a masculine retreat, a refuge from women; however, "now everyone wears cut-offs. Shelia's presence negates all my good work. It will take weeks after she leaves before things get back to normal" (351). "Normal" for Kurt implies an almost adolescent desire for the absence of women who interfere with the natural camaraderie and sexuality of men. He writes, "Barry and I have had to be circumspect to the point of abstinence." And, as Kurt points out about Barry, Shelia has the power to make the soldiers miss their girlfriends and wives back home, "and he's reminded of his lost lady . . ." (351). To stress Shelia's effect on the soldiers at the villa further, Kurt begins his next letter, to his cousin, Chloe, by stating, "You've wondered several times about the tension among men without women" (352). Interestingly, it is only the young woman whom Kurt corresponds with who is curious to know about how men behave in the absence of women. Apparently, none of his male letter recipients have asked the question, as if men naturally understand (or perhaps tacitly are not overly concerned) how men act without women. Kurt explains Shelia's impact on the soldiers when he writes to Chloe that, on her first day there, Shelia went swimming, wrapped herself in a brief towel, joined the marines, and said, "You guys look as if you haven't seen a girl for months." Kurt's response indicates his homosexual disdain for the young woman's interruption of the homoerotic pastoral nature of the villa: "I don't think I'm going to like her at all" (353). If she reminds the heterosexual marines of their female sexual partners back home, she simply reminds Kurt that there exists a strong and almost insurmountable competition for a gay man intent on seducing straight-identified men.

Not long after Shelia's arrival at the villa, Nelson plunges the characters back into the thick of the war on jungle reconnaissance patrols, similar to the earlier patrols Kurt participated in when he first arrived in Vietnam. These patrols interrupt the calm and camaraderie of the Bou Bou Phu masculine refuge. With all of the marines anxious and tense over the new wave of dangerous duty, Nelson slowly begins to structure the break down of order and masculine control at the remote villa. The first example to illustrate this point represents how Kurt's sexual games and initiations backfire when improperly practiced by one of his sexual acolytes. Sergeant Pinkerton accidentally sees

Kurt and Barry engaged in sex; from Kurt's vantage point he realizes they have been seen, but Barry does not. Pinkerton tells McGrath, Kurt's most constant and macho sexual partner, about the incident, which allows Nelson to set the stage for a debacle, almost a pastiche, of Kurt's sexual initiation game. The earlier example of failure of Kurt's straight-identified sexual seduction by someone else occurred when the "failed" effeminate gay man, Leigh, attempted to seduce the drunken soldier and proved unsuccessful because of his emotional reaction to the purely sexual situation. McGrath fails for just the opposite reason—unemotional cruelty. McGrath confronts Barry and Kurt about their homosexual activity when he says to them, "Barry is it true what sarge tells me? That you're a cocksucker?…The sarge tells me you suck old Doc's peter." He attempts to cajole Barry into performing oral sex for him, and when Barry balks, McGrath says, "Don't I turn you on none? I'll bet old Doc turns you on. He is pretty, ain't he?"(388). McGrath consciously confronts Barry and Kurt with the dynamic of straight-identified male homosexual attraction being based upon physical appearance and masculinity, manliness and sexual prowess. He even tells Barry, "I'll get you hotter'n a firecracker." When Barry refuses his demand, McGrath distorts and corrupts Kurt's sexual game. Apparently neither sophisticated enough for guile and subtlety, like the gay Kurt, nor emotional and effeminate like the gay Leigh, the straight-identified McGrath resorts to simple cruelty. He threatens Barry by telling him, "You want me to write to your daddy and tell him 'bout you and Doc? Git on down there, Barry." His appeal, to the disdain and disapproval of the father, represents a total deconstruction of the game of homosexual initiation. McGrath either knows the rules too well or does not know them at all. Regardless, the reaction is the same. Father figures can be aware of the game. Surrogate fathers can be aware of the game. Fathers other than one's own can be aware of the game. True fathers can never be aware of the game—never. Kurt's reaction to the forced sex scene proves problematic and telling. He writes to Paul, "There appeared to be no resistance. Barry proved a good marine. He did as he was told. I know. I watched" (388). The implication is, of course, that Kurt received sexual pleasure from his voyeuristic position, though Barry is not only his sexual partner but also his good friend. The allure of the homosexual initiation rite, though tainted by McGrath's viciousness, still maintains, still excites, and, thus, must be viewed by the sexually constructed Kurt. After Barry performs oral sex on McGrath and the marine leaves, Barry apologizes, over and over, to Kurt for what happened. Kurt simply tells him, "Don't you pay it no never mind, Barry" (389). However, Kurt knows that the act he witnessed, and what it represents, will become divisive and damaging to all of the relationships at the villa, as if a sexual thread had been pulled. His directly following letter to his cousin, Chloe, plainly states, "my family in Bou Bou Phu splinters into unhappy loners..." (389). "Splinters" implies a shattering as well as simple factioning, a bold break.

A week after the incident with McGrath, before Barry and Kurt can reconcile, they both go on jungle patrol. Barry, as advance point man, trips a wire and explodes a grenade which disembowels him. Kurt gets to him before he dies, and cradles him in his arms. Barry wants to play the "Apple, Banana, Cherry" alphabet game as he dies in Kurt's arms, the game that once represented a kind of innocent foreplay for them. Barry's death marks the beginning of the total end of male domesticity and homoerotic camaraderie at the villa. In his next letter to Paul, dated 5 July 1967 and a week after Barry's death, Kurt writes about the final incident that illustrates the destruction of relationships among the marines and Kurt's forced homoerotic "initiation" at the point of McGrath's rifle. While on patrol with two other marines, McGrath forces Kurt to perform sexually for all of them. McGrath puts Kurt into the same place he forced the innocent Barry into, that of sexual victim; however, the worldly Kurt can hardly be threatened with a letter to a father. McGrath, realizing that Kurt presents a more complex problem than Barry did, resorts to simple violence, wartime tactics. He tells Kurt and the other marines to get undressed, and when Kurt refuses, McGrath say to him, "You too, Doc. I'll shoot your ass, too, you fucking cocksucker..." (398). All of Kurt's fantasies about forced homosexual sex among straight-identified soldiers come true, and transforms into distaste and disgust when he realizes that he is not in control of the situation, that it is real beyond his fantasy construction. In the following letter, when his grandmother writes to Kurt that his little brother, Neil, is planning on joining the military, Kurt responds, "Learning that Neil has enlisted in the Army depresses the bejesus out of me. No one should suggest within my hearing that it will make a man of him" (399). Kurt knows better. The military, with its structure and discipline, no more makes men than it makes peace; it makes soldiers. Men cannot be *made*, not by masculinity, war, office, or responsibility. The only true thing the military can make is war, as Kurt and the other marines at the villa soon find out.

The precursor to total destruction of the Bou Bou Phu villa as a masculine refuge occurs when Kurt and Sergeant Pinkerton go on a jungle patrol alone. Pinkerton, the handsome Texas cowboy and married father, the man who first paternally scolded Kurt for his "boyish" homosexual indiscretions, represents the final and ultimate challenge to Kurt, the most impressive initiation, a symbol of the father that Barry so feared would learn his secret. While waiting in the bush, Pinkerton brings up Kurt's sexuality and the questions it generates:

> "Doc, you ain't queer, are you?"
> "Yeah, I am."
> Pinkerton stiffened; then he relaxed. "No, you ain't. I seen you play ball. You're faster than any of us. And stronger. And smarter. Doc, you ain't queer." (401)

Pinkerton's simplistic belief system precludes the concept that a masculine man, strong, athletic, and smart, could possibly be a homosexual. He only identifies as homosexual men who fit Kurt's parameters of the "failed" gay man, the effeminate and emotional homosexual who seeks more than sex from men. Kurt's physicality alone is enough for Pinkerton to doubt his homosexuality, so much so that he even tries to convince both Kurt and himself of heterosexual masculinity: "Doc, you ain't queer." Kurt then writes, "I took Pinkerton's face between my hands and kissed him. He accepted it. I slid my hand under his belt. He accepted that, too, and more" (401). Ironically, Kurt's seduction of the sergeant begins with a kiss, the marker of affection and emotion; then it proceeds to sex. This seduction represents the culmination of Kurt's Vietnam "duty," a quest to initiate straight identified men into the realm of masculine homosexuality, though in his earlier conquests affection came later. With Pinkerton, the father figure, affection is primary. After they make love, Pinkerton grabs Kurt's face in what Kurt thinks is the prelude to another kiss; however, Pinkerton whispers in his ear, "Doc, something's out there. You wait here. I'll be right back" (401–402). Sergeant Pinkerton never returns from the jungle. Kurt has artfully seduced the father, affectionately and passionately made love to him, perhaps the most successful of his initiations, and the father has disappeared—forever, leaving Kurt abandoned and alone in the wilds of the primordial and dangerous jungle. Freud would be very interested.

The remainder of this letter documents Kurt's journey back to the villa at Bou Bou Phu, where his story of Pinkerton's disappearance is a precursor to the novel's representation of the total break down of order. The South Vietnamese attack the villa, and as Kurt writes to his buddy, Arch, "They've wiped us out. Everybody's dead" (405). The enemy from without takes advantage of the enemy from within, the dissent and tension, the ruptures and factions, caused by the homosexualization of the male relationships at the isolated villa, removed from the "normal" sphere of the surrounding war. Few survive. Interestingly, Shelia, the interloping woman, the symbol of heterosexual normalcy at the all-male villa, takes up a machine gun and a knife and fights her way out, filling a traditionally masculine role that all of the male soldiers fail to achieve, that of war hero. McGrath, Kurt's failed acolyte of homosexual initiation, the marine who cruelly and violently forced the other men to perform oral sex on him, is symbolically wounded in the throat. Kurt writes to Arch that he found McGrath "drowning in his own blood from a wound in his throat" (406). Kurt later learns from a medic that "McGrath will be on a respirator for the rest of his life" (417). And Kurt, archly and symbolically, is wounded in the buttocks, the primary location of male homosexual pleasure. He writes, "I felt a sharp sting in my ass; then a big black mass of pain washed over me" (406). After the medics pick him up and take him to a field hospital, Kurt sees some of his former friends, other medics, tending to his wounds, and he writes to Arch, "It's unmanly to admit, Arch, but that's when I started to cry" (406). Kurt's obsession, even with the destruction of the villa and most of his initiates, remains with masculinity, and he also maintains the basic tenet of that masculinity, heterosexual or homosexual, not shame that he felt "unmanly" but shame that he could admit it. Kurt's lessons in masculinity and manhood, the ones that he taught and learned, become enlightening but draconian. And he has one final lesson to learn about homosexual initiation, masculinity, and games.

Kurt's final letter about his experiences in Vietnam, written to his gay confidant, Paul, has no date, the only letter in the novel without one, as if when the letter was written time had either stopped or been suspended. The letter, a rambling, disjointed, and at times rather incoherent story, begins ominously enough: "Please excuse the printing. Left handed. I'll tell you" (419). Kurt tells Paul of his last military duty, medic on a medical helicopter. His horrific story involves the helicopter striking an aerial mine, exploding, and killing all aboard except Kurt, who is left in the wreckage along with several charred bodies. The narrative thread of the story becomes difficult to follow, because the reader learns that after emergency surgery Kurt became addicted to field-administered morphine. The military transports Kurt to a hospital in Okinawa, Japan, where he is mysteriously smuggled out by a man named Vince. Kurt writes, "Vince said he wrote letters. I never answered. I always answered letters" (419). The novel's epistolary structure has, thus far until the very end, been completely dependent upon Kurt's talent and penchant for writing letters, his need to correspond. The reader immediately recalls the letter Kurt received from the gay "friend of a friend," a man imprisoned in a military stockade for homosexuality, and a letter that identified Kurt as homosexual; it was also the only letter to which Kurt did not respond. The letter prompted Kurt's fear of the unseen and patriarchal military power that could easily punish him for his closeted homosexuality, his breach of accepted masculinity. Vince takes the heavily drugged Kurt to a small house, a domestic setting, and leaves him with Joe, an older man who also represents a punishing patriarchy, though this dynamic is a true pastiche of Kurt's gay initiation rites. Joe beats and abuses Kurt and forces him to play a game, a very structured sexual game:

> Then he made me learn lines from a piece of paper and he slapped me when I couldn't remember them and pushed me against the wall but I finally did. I knocked at the door and he said come in son and I said Dad what does circumcised mean and he showed me and made me blow him. Joe said I favored his son. (419)

Kurt's usually elegant, witty, and well-constructed prose becomes almost childlike. McGrath, Kurt's pupil who failed to play the straight-identified homosexual initiation game properly, was a young man, like Kurt, a son. Joe, the older man, represents the horrors possible when a father is a failure at initiation, when a father misunderstands the rules of the game, when a father even *plays* the game. Sergeant Pinkerton, Kurt's military father figure, succumbed affectionately to Kurt's sexual prowess, then disappeared forever. Joe inverts and corrupts the nature of the initiation, carefully planning the game, even to the point of a script, and he rapes Kurt. This time, the father will *not* disappear, so Kurt must. He escapes from Joe's house, and is spirited away by two compassionate Air Force officers who sneak him aboard a flight headed for the United States.

Kurt's concluding few paragraphs find him in the care of a Green Beret who is driving him cross country from California to the soldier's "old Kentucky home…" (420). He is in the care of a fellow Southerner. Though still addicted to the morphine, Kurt struggles to return to his home, east and to the south, to the only place he can heal, psychically and physically. The letter is written from the Nevada desert where the two men camped: an environment completely, diametrically opposed to the steamy jungles of Vietnam. He writes to Paul that the Green Beret "calls me Spaceman," a name that implies both his drugged condition and also his journey through time, space, and experience. Kurt's last request of Paul brings the narrative to an end and a circular course back to the beginning. He plans on stopping in Colorado to visit Paul and writes, "Have a stiff drink and a warm bed and a cute little snow bunny for the Green Beret and you and me will go downstairs and sit in front of the fire and have another drink and I'll tell you all about it" (420).

Relentlessly,
Kurt

And tell he does.

> "War talk by men who have been in a war is always interesting; whereas moon talk by a poet who has not been in the moon is likely to be dull."
> —Mark Twain, *Life on the Mississippi*

After he realized that he was gay in the late 1960s, celebrated Southern novelist Armistead Maupin made a decision:

> He did not want to spend his life as an outcast. There was, he thought, one solution. Maupin's father had always believed that history provided every generation of southern males with a war in which they could prove their manhood. Maupin would move beyond his guilt and prove he was a man: He would volunteer for Vietnam.[48]

Maupin's southern father's belief, that war could prove or even construct manhood, remains common, especially in the South. During the American Civil War, the U. S. Military Academy at West Point was such a bastion of southern military power and influence that it had to be closed for the duration of the conflict. Charles Nelson's character in *The Boy Who Picked the Bullets Up*, Kurt Strom, like Nelson himself, is the product of this masculine and militaristic tradition. Kurt discusses some of his own father's World War II experiences in the South Pacific in a letter to his grandmother, illustrating the line of duty (*Boy* 143). Kurt's military duty, however, also serves his obsessive pursuit of masculinity, his need to understand it, get it from others, give it to others. His status, as a closeted and straight-identified homosexual man, gives him an objective position from which to view the variform nature of masculinity and how it works or fails to work, but it is his need to initiate other men into his world of masculine homosexuality that gives Nelson's novel its complexities and importance. The book's epistolary structure provides a built-in episodic framework which helps support and define its complicated treatment of Michael Moon's theory of redundant gay initiation. Though we live in a culture in which frank fictive depictions and discussions of sexuality are commonplace, Nelson's novel still manages to push the boundaries; however, the rough and graphic sexuality of the book is not simply prurient or gratuitous. Masculinity, in a large part, depends highly upon how men interact with one another, and in no other situation do men interact so complexly and closely as in war. The necessary camaraderie. The close physical contact. The long hours of boredom punctuated by the short, hot minutes of sheer terror. And these warriors are almost always boys. It is no wonder that connected feelings of what it is to be a man, what do we learn from our fathers, how do we feel about women, what would the touch of another man's skin feel like, all swirl into a densely intricate psychological mélange in a wartime environment. Kurt's conquests and adventures are comic and tragic, instructional and nonsensical, erotic and distasteful, but they are never boring. What makes the character so interesting and vital is the fact that he addresses concepts that most men do not, that most men do not even have to address. The misunderstanding of masculinity represents most of what men fear and dread in their lives, how they measure up as men or do not. And the primary reason that masculinity is so misunderstood is generated from that very fear of facing it. Gay men have to face it, because it becomes a constant in their sexually constructed lives. They are defined and identified by what it means to be a man; definitions are often cruel and exacting, just as Kurt Strom can be. But as we are willing to face the problems and mysteries of masculinity in our modern culture, we also learn that definitions can be enlightening, helpful, and even loving—just as Kurt Strom can be.

❋ CHAPTER 5

One Constant Flaming Question: Men, Kinship, and Masculinity in the Fiction of Reynolds Price

> "Like many boys on the near edge of manhood, I had one constant flaming question—*What are grown men like, truly, in secret?*...I needed to study the make of men's bodies ..."
>
> —Reynolds Price, "The Enormous Door"

> "Men's language has not been sufficient to explain masculinity, but men's myths have been able to communicate the meanings of men's lives. The meaning that is lost in the words can be found in the stories."
>
> —Frank Pittman, M.D., *Man Enough: Fathers, Sons, and the Search for Masculinity*

According to literary critic James A. Schiff, "Reynolds Price is probably the finest living southern novelist and, perhaps, the most significant southern man of letters of the latter half of the twentieth century."[1] Price, a lifelong native of North Carolina and Milton professor at Duke University, has a prolific writing career which spans over forty years and most genres, including novels, short stories, plays, poetry, translations, and critical essays.[2] One of Reynolds Price's most impressive creative talents is his ability to write about common, everyday people and their equally common conflicts, yet still make an examination of these fictional lives and stories complex and important. In a review of criticism of Price's 1963 short story collection, *The Names and Faces of Heroes*, James A. Schiff points out:

> William Barrett wrote, "Out of their simplicity [Price] is able to distill a wonder and awe at the most commonplace situations in life."... Paul Pickrel in *Harper's* called

> attention to Price's "simple people"; Hicks referred to Price's "simplicity"; the reviewer in *TLS* wrote of Price's "simple, earthy themes" in a review entitled "Southern Folks"; and Barrett went on to cite Price's ability to "convey feeling so simply." Though the term *simple* was almost always laudatory—critics were greatly impressed with Price's ability to write so powerfully about seemingly unextraordinary events and people....[3]

When writing about simple southerners, Price also has the ability to transcend the often facile and traditional depictions of such characters in the hands of lesser authors. Schiff argues, "the characters themselves serve to dispel the stereotypical notion that rural southerners must be either ignorant provincials or sensational grotesques. Price never condescends to or distorts his characters but rather endows them with dignity, humor, wit, and natural intelligence." Another basic human characteristic which Price does not shy away from when creating his characters is a sense of their own sexuality. Price believes that there exists " an innate bi- or polysexuality in all creatures'; however, because our forebears thought it a crucial condition for the maintenance of a perilous balance of power in family-centered societies,' we are now faced with a population unnaturally deprived of its most benign instincts.'"[4] Out of this need to represent common southerners without neglecting their sexuality and same-sex relationships, Price has managed to construct some of the most interesting and critically important texts on homosexuality and masculinity written in the last fifty years.

Price's most ambitious work of fiction, a family trilogy collectively entitled *A Great Circle*, consists of three novels written over a twenty-year period: *The Surface of Earth* (1975), *The Source of Light* (1981), and *The Promise of Rest* (1995). The books chronicle the lives of a North Carolina family, the Mayfields, and include as other important characters married kinships, deep friendships, and African American family servants. Basically spanning the entire twentieth century, the books vary in theme, such as race, gender, sexuality, and familial attachments; they also vary greatly in length and time span. *The Surface of Earth* depicts three generations of Mayfields from early in the century until World War II; the novel's sweeping span of time and family experience, class and characters, recalls the Russian grand narrative tradition. *The Source of Light*, a more intimate and personal book, concerns one important year for the Mayfields, 1955–1956. Finally, *The Promise of Rest* is one of Price's few completely contemporary works, and deals with the death of Wade Mayfield from AIDS in the early 1990s. Though the themes of the individual novels vary, Schiff argues for an over-arching theme for the trilogy: "the grand theme of *A Great Circle* is love, though certainly not a joyful, sentimental, or romantic love. Price's brand turns out to be rather dark, obsessive, and consuming in nature."[5] Love, in Price's fiction, can be brutal and exacting, but it can also be fulfilling and worthwhile.

Reynolds Price also has to his literary credit a collection of stories and novels involving another family. The Mustian family appears in Price's first published work, the 1958 short story, "A Chain of Love," and in his first two novels, *A Long and Happy Life* (1962) and *A Generous Man* (1966). Price concludes the Mustian stories with his 1988 novel, *Good Hearts*. Though a North Carolina family, the rural Mustians differ from the Mayfields of *A Great Circle*; the Mustians represent a less educated and lower-middle-class family as opposed to the more locally worldly and traveled Mayfield clan. According to Schiff, the Mustian stories do not form the same family saga structure that is created in *A Great Circle*:

> Despite their status as independent, self-contained narratives, the Mayfield volumes are closely interconnected in regard to theme and plot, and form an organic whole. The Mustian novels, on the other hand, are far less dependent upon one another, functioning more as separate stories which just so happen to use the same characters and settings.

Schiff further notes that the Mustian stories concern one generation of the family; whereas the Mayfield novels span an entire century and six generations. As he does in the Mayfield novels, Price also examines male homoerotic relationships in the Mustian stories. Certain male characters from the Mustian stories fulfill a similar function to the homosexually constructed characters from *A Great Circle*; they represent a study of male homoerotic interaction, desire, and masculinity. "The central erotic figure in each Mustian novel is a desirable, handsome, and virile male,..." as Schiff argues, "who attracts the gaze of women and men alike." Schiff, the foremost Reynolds Price scholar and critic writing today, also expresses a very interesting point of view in the context of the Mustian novels. He believes, "each of the three novels deals with a significant ritual or moment of transformation," and "*A Generous Man* looks at the crossing of a threshold, the emergence into manhood (perhaps *the* central ritual in Price's work)."[6] It is within the pages of the latter volumes of both series of family stories, *The Source of Light*, *The Promise of Rest*, and *Good Hearts*, that this "central ritual," this "emergence into manhood," realizes its fullest development as a study of southern masculinity embedded in male homoerotic relationships. Writing about *The Source of Light*, in 1983, Constance Rooke supplies the most logical and basic reason as to why Price's later fiction deals so openly with homosexuality; in his earlier writing Price's circumspection on the subject was based on a common cultural reality of the pre-1980s in American letters. Popular and literary authors did not write about homosexuality (at least in any positive context) for fear of negative social and economic repercussions. Rooke states that "this surprising proliferation of homosexual references may be explained in part as a sign of changing times, a response to increasingly liberal attitudes toward homosexual relationships and their depiction in literature."[7] Thus, *The Source of Light* (1981) and *The Promise of Rest* (1995) from *A Great Circle*, and *Good Hearts* (1988), the final volume of the Mustian novels, provide the most fertile ground for an examination of why a critic such as James A. Schiff maintains that the emergence into manhood is perhaps the most important and central ritual represented in Price's entire body of fictional work. Schiff's comment also begs the questions as to exactly why that theme, the ritual of masculine initiation, becomes much more evident and intricate after Price feels more socially comfortable with a frank depiction of homosexual relationships in his novels.

All of Reynolds Price's fiction is fraught with the concepts of ritual and initiation, perhaps owing to his strong biblical literary influence. According to Rooke, "the masters' whom Price acknowledges are the Bible, Milton,

Tolstoy, [and] Eudora Welty'…. "[8] In several of his early short stories, Price creates what Michael Hogan calls "wonderfully textured portraits of male sexuality and intimacy, in which relationships between males are as fundamental a human need as water or oxygen…." Hogan goes on to argue that Price's stories address Eve Kosofsky Sedgwick's theory of a potentially unbroken continuum between homosocial and homosexual when he states, "what Price achieves in these stories is no less than a restoration of that continuum, a sense of balance between male social and sexual modes of being."[9] However, it is in his later, more blatantly homoerotic narratives in which rituals and initiations fall under the sole purview of manhood and masculinity. In these works, the relationships between and among men represent a close knit community of masculinity constructed of fathers and sons (and surrogate versions of both) and strong male friendships which serve to form a male kinship that precludes the participation of women.

Prominent psychiatrist Frank Pittman, in his book, *Man Enough: Fathers, Sons, and the Search for Masculinity*, outlines the complexities of how women influence male concepts of masculinity. Pittman's basic argument is that the definition of masculinity must ultimately be produced for boys by men; however, the inevitable roles that women play in that social production can range from healthy to destructive. When a young man's sense of masculinity is left to complete definition by his mother, Pittman contends, "no matter how good a job a woman does in teaching a boy how to be a man, he knows that she is not the real thing, and so he tends to exaggerate the differences between men and women that she embodies." These hypermasculine men, males with an inflated sense of their own manhood, tend to interact with women on an almost exclusively dysfunctional level. According to Pittman, "men who escape women, or seduce them, or silence them, or even beat and murder them are doing so not because they sadistically enjoy hurting a woman… but because they feel weak, burdened with a sense of imperfect masculinity."[10]

The male characters in Reynolds Price's novels addressed here do not avoid the company or companionship of women; in fact they actively pursue it. Their self-sense of masculinity, however, is defined by their relationships with other men, Pittman's definition of a healthy masculine subjectivity. Thus, the female characters in these novels are often, and incorrectly (or, at least, incompletely), viewed by literary critics as simple, plain, uninteresting, boring, or superfluous when compared to the complexities of the male homoerotic and homosocial relationships. Michael Kreyling's essay, "Men without Women: Communities of Desire and Race in *A Great Circle*," illustrates this critical stance toward Price's work. In her favorable 1981 *New York Times Book Review* review of *The Source of Light*, Joyce Carol Oates point out, "it is one of the puzzling aspects of the novel that Hutch doesn't seem to grasp what the reader so quickly grasps—that his homosexual liaisons are much more meaningful to him, because more interesting, than his laconic courtship of Ann."[11] Though critics such as Kreyling and Oates make valid points about Price's treatment of female characters at the expense of more interesting male characters, particularly the homosexual characters, they miss an important point. Women characters in the novels are not sacrificed at the expense of homoerotic characters; rather women characters exist in the background of exclusive male rites and initiations of masculinity, as they usually do in life. For an illustrative, albeit harsh, similar tale one need only look to classical mythology or Euripides' *Bacchae* to find an analogy of gender-specific initiation rituals and the consequences of interloping. Pentheus pays the ultimate price, being ripped to death and devoured, for spying on the frenzied female initiation ritual of Dionysos' all-female worshipers, the Maenads. The Bible, the source of Price's most profound literary influence, contains a similar, famous story of gender-specific initiation, that of Abraham's symbolic mock sacrifice of his son, Isaac, at God's behest. When Abraham leaves for the land of Moriah, the place God commands him to go, he leaves behind his wife, Sarah, and takes with him to help and witness the ritual "two of his young men" (Gen. 22.1–3). Price has written several critical essays on the Abraham and Isaac story. As with Charles Nelson's work, Price creates the iterability of gay masculine initiation by its constant depiction both literally and symbolically, by images and stories—tales that go back as far as recorded time.

The Source of Light

"It is impossible to please all the world and one's father."
—Jean De La Fontaine

The Source of Light (1981), the second volume of Reynolds Price's family trilogy, *A Great Circle*, is, in essence, a basic, human story, the death of a parent. North Carolina native Hutchins Mayfield, a young man in his mid-twenties and a prep school teacher in Virginia, receives a scholarship to study at Oxford. Hutch, an only child whose mother died in childbirth, has been reared by his grandmother, assorted aunts, household servants, and at times by his boyishly charming, alcoholic father, Rob. The novel, set in Virginia, North Carolina, and various locations in England, covers a rather short time period, May 1955–March 1956; it is written in several relatively short, third-person-narrated chapters and punctuated by numerous letters, dreams, poems, and telegrams. The central conflict of the novel concerns Rob's hesitancy in telling Hutch that he is dying of lung cancer, afraid it will force Hutch to cancel his plans for England and Oxford. Woven through this story are the conflicts and anxieties of a young man growing up in the South of the 1950s, trying to become a man himself, one with scant few models of success, and his initiation into a type of masculinity which is constructed of close and exclusive kinships between and among men; some are sexual, while some are purely emotional, and some intersect those two points. And, as Michael Kreyling points out about Price's family trilogy, "the simultaneity of the social and the erotic…is essential to its meaning. For Price's Mayfield men, as for Hemingway's heroes from Jake Barnes on, as with Augustine in his autobiographical *Confessions*, desire does not exist apart from the sexed, physical body in its network of social entanglement."[12] For the Mayfield men, sexual desire is a basic part of their social interaction, a kind of primary physical drive toward the emotional.

The novel begins with the symbolic enactment of a complex initiation ritual, that of baptism; however, the baptism enacted here may have Christian roots in rebirth, but it is very much also an initiation into manhood. As Schiff notes: "Price's concern is less with what ultimately happens to Hutch and more with how Rob and Hutch negotiate this crucial final ritual: the death of the father and the emergence of the son." Schiff goes on to argue that after Rob's death, "Hutch emerges from his old life, in which he was a son circling about a father, and finds himself born into his new existence as a free and independent man."[13] While helping his son move, in preparation for his trip to England, from his home in Virginia back to North Carolina, Rob and Hutch make a trip to Warm Springs, one of the many therapeutic hot springs that are still common in rural Virginia today. The first scene has Hutch undressing as he prepares to enter the spring pool and take the curative waters. Price uses the mirror image, the reflection, simultaneously objective and subjective, as a means for Hutch to consider his own body in terms of manhood. As Hutch gazes into a full length mirror in the changing room, Price writes:

> Now he studied his groin, full in the warm day, and thought how little it had caused but pleasure—a grown man's first means of work hung on him, an aging toy. But he smiled and reached a hand toward the cool glass, stroked the dim image. It bobbed in gratitude—pony, pet turtle—and Hutch laughed once, then heard his father's voice at the pool.[14]

Until this point, Hutch's penis has only caused pleasure; it has failed to achieve a "grown man's" work, begetting offspring, and without this purpose is only a "toy," a pet, that responds readily to the solitary pleasures of masturbation; however, it is also something else entirely. If Hutch's act of masturbation represents his own homosexual desire, manifested in the physical desire for a penis that only causes pleasure, that does not and cannot procreate, then Rooke believes, "the one obvious, potential disadvantage of homosexual love is that it cannot involve the creation of a child. In a novel obsessed with generation and family trees this limitation does seem to matter."[15] Flannigan-Saint-Aubin contends that Hutch's reflective examination of his penis represents a common connection to an examination of masculinity: "Masculinity, in its psychologic and cultural manifestations and implications, is assumed to be the homologue of the phallic genitality of the male with, at the very least, metaphoric connections to it—in part, aggressive, violent, penetrating, goal-directed, linear."[16] Interestingly, Hutch is interrupted from observing his penis by his father's voice, the representation of paternity and generations, though his father does not specifically call to him; Hutch only overhears a conversation. It is simply the sound of the father's voice that wakes him from his sexual introspection. Phallic imagery is common throughout the trilogy, and is best represented by a small male doll with a working penis, carved from bark by Hutch's great-grandfather and passed down to each generation of Mayfield men. Kreyling argues that the phallus and all of the common phallic imagery throughout the trilogy represent a kind of initiation marker into masculinity and homosexual order, the balance of the "unbroken continuum between homosocial and homosexual." According to Kreyling, "the phallic totem not only symbolically links the generations; it also significantly marks the progress of Mayfield desire from predatory heterosexuality to an ideal of unproblematic, pure, unsurpassable community in male sexual exclusivity."[17] The little phallus on the bark doll, its sole marker of sex and gender, represents the Mayfield men's continuing obsession with reproduction of generations, hetero sexuality, and homosexuality. As Flannigan-Saint-Aubin points out, phallic metaphors, in a phallocentric and patriarchal culture such as ours, can represent both positive and negative aspects of masculinity. To be phallic in the positive sense is "to be penetrating: inquisitive, persistent, steady, objective, courageous, discriminating, dominant. To be phallic in the negative sense is…to be intrusive: violent, unyielding, discriminatory, exploitive, domineering."[18] *The Source of Light*, with its common and prolific references to the penis, and the phallus, demonstrates this dual concept and further asserts Kreyling's argument for the dominance of a "pure" form of homosexual masculinity and relationships to displace a predatory form of heterosexuality. When the penis is viewed in a homoerotic context (which it most often is), it is almost always affirmative, replete with the positive metaphorical attributes listed above. When the penis is viewed in a heterosexual context, it is almost always harmful, replete with the negative metaphorical attributes listed above.

As father and son float in the warm water of the spring pool, a womblike environment, indicated by the fact that the water is described as "precisely the heat of a well human body," Rob, aware of his impending death, asks his son: "Were you ever baptized?" (4). When Hutch tells him no, the father commands the son to "descend," with the baptismal ritual phrase, "Father, Son— ,"and Hutch obeys, sinking to the bottom of the clear water and lying supine. Hutch's descent into the water, symbolic of baptism and the mythic drowned man, represents the coming changes in his life: his adulthood and manhood, his trip to England, his status as a lover, and (though unknown to him at the time) the death of his father. When Rob calls for the African American attendant to show him Hutch's deceptive drowning act, the man says to him: "Dead again…Looks real, don't it? He do that a lot, every time he come—like to scared his young friend to death last week" (5). Apparently, Hutch has repeated the initiation ritual many times, indicating that repetition is important in its process and completion. When Hutch dramatically breaks through to the surface of the pool, Rob greets him with the remainder of the baptismal phrase, "Holy Ghost," and the process is complete; Hutch has been initiated into manhood by the father, reborn as a sexual adult. To indicate this sexual maturity and its inherent danger to the masculinity of the Mayfield men, later, in a discussion of women, Hutch jokes that in England he plans to "make women think they've been rushed to heaven before their time." Rob asks his son: "How many would you estimate you'd rushed?…I'd like to know. It would help me to know what women mean to you, It's a danger that runs in your family, you've noticed—the Mayfield side" (7). Manhood and masculinity, for the Mayfield men, are dangerous states of hypersexuality, what Kreyling calls "predatory heterosexuality." And this state can be ameliorated and tempered by homosexual relationships. The "young friend" the attendant refers to, the one Hutch frightened with his baptism and false drowning, illustrates this point and represents another set of rituals, masculinity, and sexuality.

A likely candidate for Kreyling's proposed "unproblematic, pure…male sexual exclusivity" in the novel is introduced in the character of Strawson Stuart, a former prep school student of Hutch's. When Hutch makes a final trip to the school to pick up his mail, he encounters Straw in a way that allows Price to intricately, yet subtly, detail the relationship between the two men. Hutch finds Straw sprawled, cruciform, on the hood of his car:

> A boy—Strawson Stuart, long for his age, Hutch's pupil for two years. He lived in town; his eyes were shut. Hutch said, "I heard you had died. Monday night at Morse Mitchell's party, but I didn't know I'd get the body for disposal."
>
> Straw sat up solemn. "Well, you have." he extended his arms cruciform and held the pose. Then he smiled, the second dazzler of the day. "No, I've risen and come by to help you load …." (14)

Straw has experienced his own rebirth ritual, one that involves his entry into sexuality and manhood. We learn that Hutch and Straw have been lovers; Straw is the "young friend" the hot springs attendant spoke of, the one who was visibly frightened by Hutch's baptism/drowning. In a parenthetical aside, Hutch thinks, "he had drowned for Straw; even more than Rob, it had shaken the boy who seemed unshakeable" (15). Part of Straw's being "shaken" is represented by his introduction into manhood. After Hutch awakens Straw's sexuality, he sees himself as emotionally linked to the young man and imbues him with a type of needy worship: "Now the different place which Straw constituted, in power and need, demanded homage" (15). To extend the worship metaphor into a trope which Price will use throughout the novel to identify homosexual masculinity and desire, Hutch views Straw as a god linked to electricity, a "young god of Want and Use, no more kind or cruel than electric current" (15). Electricity, used in some way to describe or represent all of the sexually desirable men in the book, becomes, like masculinity in Price s fiction, a nebulous and almost neutral force, neither "kind or cruel," only present and needful of constant consideration, a contemplation bordering on reverence.

According to Rooke, "these males have a more electric appeal, a stronger magnetism than any females in the book."[19] The reader also learns that Straw will be visiting Hutch in England as part of his summer "tour of the continent" after graduating from prep school, a long standing Southern tradition.

Rob, Hutch's primary avatar of homoerotic electric masculinity, returns to his isolated country home in North Carolina to find the electricity out, indicative of his terminal illness. When he tries to find the fuse box, he discovers that all power has failed him: "The flashlight was also dead..." (18). Like his life of wandering and irresponsibility, Rob must fumble in the dark, trying to find his way around his own house. After he falls asleep in total darkness, all of the electricity in the house comes back on and he realizes from his bed that he is "scalded in light," as if the return of his masculine energy is too much for his failing physical body, too painful to endure (21). Interestingly, the return of electric power, and thus a brief period of vitality, prompts Rob to engage in a ritual mirror examination, a reflection, of his manhood and sexuality, almost identical to Hutch's mirror ritual which begins the novel:

> It was not till he moved toward the porch and caught himself in the mirror that he saw his dick wagging solid before him, half-gorged with the sham immunities of sleep. He stopped and turned full-face to the glass. He could hardly remember using it before.... Despite the lights and the unshaded windows by the door, he took himself in hand and stroked till he crested hard again above his curly navel—the bare head as eager as ever and sleek with the same purple blood, same hope. The belly and chest it pointed to were still lean and white, the nipples high and flat. (22)

Rob's reflective assessment of his genitals, just like Hutch's mirror study of his penis, represents a subjective consideration of his own masculinity. According to Flannigan-Saint-Aubin, "the symbolic meaning that men attach to the form and function of the male organ suggests the metaphoric connections between the experiences of the male body and psychological masculinity: In other words, the experiences of the male body constitute indices, albeit lacunary ones, of masculinity."[20] The major index of Rob's masculinity is his heterosexual conquests; his examination and introspection of his masculinity and sexuality prompt the negative, predatory heterosexual nature of phallic symbolism. Still holding his erection in his hand, he calls Min Tharrington, an old girlfriend in Raleigh, a woman he has pursued, after a fashion, for his entire life. When she asks why the late call, if there is news, Rob thinks, "he didn't want to tell her anything, only see her, touch her if she'd let him after so long" (23).

Hutch also finds a person to focus his awakened sexual thoughts upon. After Hutch's mirror examination of his penis, his next sexual thought is a positive, homoerotic one, when he meets Straw at the car, and remembers: "the sight of the stripped boy asleep in his arms last Saturday dawn stood clear in Hutch's mind. He watched it gladly with no regret" (15). Apparently, one of Flannigan-Saint-Aubin's "lacunary indices" of masculinity when represented by the phallus can be found in homosexual desire, at least in Price's fiction.

Price further extends the mirror image, self-reflection theme when Hutch and his college girlfriend, Ann, travel to New York City in preparation for his trip, by ship, to England. While seeing the sights of the city, they come upon Ripley's *Believe It Or Not Museum,* and Hutch has a novelty photograph made of himself:

> Hutch photographed alone at a baize table playing out a hand of poker, chips stacked before him. In the finished print, ten minutes later, he was shown at play with three solid partners, all wearing his face at appropriate angles—accomplished with mirrors and surprisingly good....The sight of his four faces bluffing each other had drawn a firm line to the tawdry hour. ...Hutch was gray with exhaustion and the picture's news—an unlosable game...(36)

Hutch's picture of his multiple selves, at play with one another, represents myriad concepts, including the decentered subject and a postmodern fragmented identity, continually in flux. However, it also refers back to his previous mirror encounter, the masturbatory and indulgent consideration of his nude body and all of the dynamics it contains, such as his masculinity, his sexuality, and his position as a mature adult. Interestingly, he has the picture made in the presence of his girlfriend who never knows about his homosexual encounters; the photograph displays, but does not reveal, the identity secret—

that Hutch finds sexual desire and fulfillment more with men than with women. The fact that Hutch is depicted playing poker, a game of chance, with himself is similar to Charles Nelson's character, Kurt Strom, in *The Boy Who Picked the Bullets Up*, and his attitude that homosexuality, and its commonly multiple conquests, is simply a type of game. Hutch, rather ironically, views the game in the picture as "unlosable," because he holds all of the cards. What he truly considers is that he is only playing with himself; instead of poker what Hutch plays is a game of subjectivity and identity solitaire.

Indeed, in the entire novel, Hutch never consciously considers his homosexuality, prompting Constance Rooke to believe:

> One of the novel's peculiarities is that it supplies abundant, vaguely Freudian data to "explain" Hutch's sexual interest in other men, and at the same time implicitly denies any need for explanation. We never see Hutch reflecting upon his homosexual liaisons, nor does he mention them to Ann. There are strong conflicting signals here, of perfect self-acceptance or deep repression.…Our guesses may be naïve or too labored, and there is more of this uncertainty than there needs to be: it obscures to some extent our vision of Hutch.[21]

The evidence for Hutch's homoerotic desires is hardly "vaguely Freudian." Schiff makes an exhaustive examination of the Freudian nature of Hutch's internally conflicted homosexuality, pointing out, "Hutch's early interest in young men has much to do with his desire to recover and vicariously love an image of his young father." Schiff further demonstrates that "'the normal incest wishes of infancy'…shed light on Price's fiction, particularly since Price follows Freud in suggesting there is 'an innate bi- or polysexuality in all creatures' which for social reasons is repressed."[22] Hutch's failure to address consciously his homosexuality is evidenced by this social repression, especially within the novel's time frame and historical context of mid-1950s American suppression and suspicion over homosexuality. However, Hutch does not repress his homosexuality as physical expression; he only represses any reflection upon it, which leads Rooke to her assertion that Price is presenting the polar concepts of "perfect self-acceptance or deep repression," not allowing for any middle ground. Perhaps Hutch (and Price) has his reasons for the graphic physical homosexuality and the nebulous psychic homosexuality in *The Source of Light.*

After Hutch arrives in England and begins school at Oxford, he writes a long letter to Alice Matthews, an old friend of his dead mother's, in which he tells her that his letters to her will constitute a type of casual journal, because, "I've always avoided the rapt mirror-gazing that diaries invite" (60). Hutch considers diary writing, an analogy of self-introspection and reflection, self-absorbed to the point of emotional torpidity, something to be avoided, at least on the conscious level. Emotional "mirror-gazing" does not hold Hutch's interest as much as physical "mirror-gazing," reflecting his ease with physical homosexual relationships and his absolute avoidance of ruminating upon them. Michael Kreyling argues, convincingly, that in Price's fiction he "presents sexuality as essential rather than performative, ignited by desire for beautiful forms in particular bodies rather than socially constructed under quasi-political conditioning." For support of this point, Kreyling uses David M. Halperin's concept that "unlike sex, which is a natural fact, sexuality is a cultural production; it represents the *appropriation* of the human body and of its erogenous zones by an ideological discourse."[23] Thus Hutch is unwilling to participate in a discourse that is philosophical and theoretical as to the nature of homosexuality as a political position; for him it is the love of the male body, including his own, and it need not be discussed or contemplated lest it become an overt ideological discourse, one that simply appropriates the body for its own ends.

After his brief physical relationship with Strawson Stuart, Hutch's next avatar of dashing male sexuality comes in the form of Lew Davis, a young Welshman he meets on the ship to England. Lew, an itinerant circus worker, is returning home to Wales after traveling with a circus in Canada. In a letter to Rob, Hutch writes about Lew: "I think he's a gypsy, but he swears he's not" (52). Hutch's desire for Lew to be a gypsy supports Rooke's contention that all of Hutch's male sexual partners represent the "attractive 'buccaneer,'" vagabond young men who remind Hutch of his childhood with his young and irresponsible father, Rob.[24] Hutch and Lew plan a road trip through the English countryside before Hutch's classes begin at Oxford and after Lew has visited his family in Wales. In a comic letter to Hutch to confirm the plans, Lew tacitly acknowledges their sexual attraction for one another: "I told my muvver an American poet would be paying me to give him a tour round Cornwall. She said 'You wouldn't know Cornwall from Spain and if he's a poet you'll be wanting to paint a scarey face on your arse.' So I have done that with iodine and am ready when you are. For the trip I mean" (60). As if to give Hutch paternal permission to seek out male lovers, among other advice, a letter from his father arrives a few days before he is to meet Lew.

This long letter, in which Rob tells his son for the first time of his impending death from lung cancer, is to serve Hutch as both a sort of abbreviated guide to living and a short biography of his father's life, which Rob entitles, "My Life and What It Showed Me *or* What I Think I Saw" (83). Rob writes to Hutch about how he will best remember him, the day he left Hutch in North Carolina shortly before his trip to England: "If there's memory after death,...I'll hope to remember the view I had of you in the mirror of my truck as I left you in Edom" (83). Rob wishes to reconstruct Hutch by his reflection, allowing Price again to draw upon the metaphor of men willing, and often eager, to examine the subjective image cast by a mirror, more so than the objective image before them. The subtitle of Rob's instructional letter, "What I Think I Saw," is highly indicative of Lacan's concept of the mirror stage of identity development in which a child, before the acquisition of the symbolic order of language, gazes into a mirror and creates a fictional identity, a *gestalt* of an ideal person. According to Lacan, this mis-recognition of self, this *meconnaissance*, creates a primary sense of alienation which will always cloud and obscure an individual's true self-image. Ultimately, we must always deal with the gap between how we see ourselves and how others see us; misunderstanding and confusion become the very basis for our social identity. And the Mayfield men are only too willing, or perhaps able, to consider their own masculinity and subjective natures in very real acts of "rapt mirror-gazing" which appear constantly throughout the novel. This mirror imagery also serves another important function in the novel. Rob wishes that Hutch fundamentally change the way he lives his life, vary from the destructive relationship patterns engraved upon the family by the previous generations of Mayfield men. Ironically, a mirror image achieves the opposite effect. If mirror gazing is paramount to self-image, then the only result will be a reflected life. More importantly, the mirror references also reinforce the concept of repetition of initiation into manhood. In *The Source of Light*, the majority of mirror images reflect the male body and sexuality coupled to a self-examination of one's masculine subjectivity. It is as if repetition of sexual initiation is self-contained; the male characters' own bodies carry with them the ability to repeat and reconstruct sexual experience, the prime reason that Price also utilizes continual references to masturbation.

The preface to Rob's instructional letter to Hutch concerns how he plans to structure his experiences; it also reveals much about Price's attitudes toward sexuality and masculinity. Rob writes:

> I was trying to remember happy time alone— before now, I mean. All I could come up with was the hours spent jacking off. Nobody ever told me it was dangerous or wrong, so I took to that with serious application at about age four. ... I was wrong yesterday—I've had some very nice lonely minutes but all before the age of twelve. (84)

Sexual maturity and experience alter this idea of pure, solitary joy from self-gratification, and the following section of the letter first informs the reader of how Price allows for a type of natural bisexuality in his characters, a sexuality not influenced by societal norms. Rob's letter about his early sexual experiences shows no sign of regret or remorse, only a kind of natural happiness in his memories. Rooke points out that in the book, "the protagonist has male lovers, and assorted other characters are given homosexual experiences or desires or awareness—all with very little fanfare or anxiety."[25]

Schiff argues that Price's fiction, while often considered "traditional," takes chances on this theme that are both subtle and profound:

> Though popular culture tends to be fixated on romantic heterosexual love, Price's Mayfield novels demonstrate that love is a good deal more complex and diverse than one might imagine. For instance, the line between hetero- and homosexuality, which seems so absolute in contemporary American culture, blurs in Price's work, leading the reader to question the divisions that have been created.[26]

Rob continues to write that after the age of twelve:

> However alone I was, I was always working to the close accompaniment of one or another of the many mental pictures from my gallery of hopes, little packets of girls like baseball cards. Or Con DeBerry when I was fourteen (he and I stayed steamed up after each other through that whole summer, all fumbling hands in hot barns and sheds). Nice minutes, as I said, but pretty sad memories—love thrown to the wind. (84–85)

Rob's solitary sexual fantasies and his brief homosexual infatuation with Con DeBerry represent love but a supposedly selfish love, one that is nonproductive and wasteful, "thrown to the wind." Constance Rooke notes that the images of self-gratification in the book relate directly to masculinity and appreciation of one's own masculine subjectivity: "Another sexual option, of course, is masturbation. A sane and reliable source of pleasure, it is also related to worship of the male god and to narcissism." She also argues that homosexuality, while tacitly indulged in by the characters, serves a counterpurpose to the novel's preoccupation with family.[27]

For the Mayfield men, heterosexuality is the prime factor in continuing a family line, even if that line is a continuation of past sorrows and disappointments. Homosexuality and desire for the male body in a community of men must be acknowledged as an option; however, that option's major drawback is that it is basically effete, constructing a profound irony in the novel. The male characters, as Joyce Carol Oates pointed out about Hutch's gay relationships, are the true locus of happiness and emotional fulfillment for the Mayfield men, but they must be pushed aside, displaced by women, in favor of propagation of the family line. According to Kreyling, this anxiety generated between choice and duty has a toll on the female characters in all of the *A Great Circle* trilogy: "The trilogy is shaped, for better or worse, by a tidally developing gender hierarchy that originates in historical circumstance and ends, in *The Promise of Rest*, in overt hostility.... The place for the sexual female in the Mayfield trilogy evolves only to second best, for she cannot (or does not) add to the community of love and work."[28] Perhaps this concept, more than any other, best defines what so confuses Constance Rooke in her critical work on Price and homosexuality, the silence on the subject, which for Rooke can only mean deep repression or some unattainable (thus false) sense of perfect acceptance. Perhaps the horrible irony of the situation simply hurts the characters too much for them to discuss an evident truth openly—the Mayfield men, obsessed with procreation, only find real, true sexual and emotional love with other men.

Shortly after Hutch receives this instructional letter from his father, he and Lew, the Welshman he met on the ship to England, tour the countryside before Hutch's Oxford classes begin. Lew and Hutch's relationship allows Price to examine interaction between men on several levels, and Price effectively inserts their relationship into the novel as a "road" story—two buddies, alone on the open road, no women and no pressure, getting to know one another. They are the same age, yet from very different backgrounds and cultures. Lew tells Hutch, "You've had it very easy, all you wanted—iced lollies in the sun and more on the way. I was one of six children to a drunk stonemason in a four-room cottage on the Gower Peninsula of poor old Wales" (95). However, as they discover, their attitudes about masculinity and sexuality converge at a common point. They travel to Cornwall so Hutch can see Tintagel, the traditional location for King Arthur's court at Camelot. Hutch explains his lifelong fascination with King Arthur: "Why?—Arthur had been his childhood favorite, with Pocahontas and Alexander" (89). All of Hutch's favorite childhood tales, of history or myth, involve a community of men, adventurers who, more or less, eschew the company of women, in favor of male companions, when they set off on their respective quests, even Captain John Smith and his men, the heroes of the colonial Virginia Pocahontas story. In light of Hutch's continuing interest in these stories, Constance Rooke's designation of the young men in his life as "buccaneers" now seems even more appropriate. When they visit Castle Dore, the traditional location of the court of King Mark and the famous Tristan and Isolde love story from Arthurian legends, Hutch contemplates his own personal definition of love; one that incorporates the displacement of his masturbatory and masculine worship of the male body concepts, just as Rob had considered his self-gratification and homosexual experience as "love thrown to the wind":

> What came with birth and trebled at puberty, he'd known right along. He'd always suspected himself of enjoying his body more than anyone else he'd known. Alone or with others it had simply never failed him, and he'd used it daily at least for twelve years. But had he ever known a constant need only one could fill?—from all reports, that seemed to be love. He believed he hadn't. (91)

Price's "brand" of love, complex in its definition, usually seems connected to a community of males who exercise ritual initiations into manhood and masculinity.

In 2003 Price, a respected theologian and biblical translator in his own right, published a slim volume of essays entitled *A Serious Way Of Wondering: The Ethics of Jesus Imagined*. In this work, Price supposes how Jesus would react to issues never fully addressed in the Gospels, issues such as suicide, depression, and homosexuality. Maintaining the core of Jesus' philosophy, Price creates scenarios to illustrate his points. He writes of his method, "I'll speculate in the form that comes most naturally to someone who has lived by storytelling for more than forty years. I'll invent a scene...." The scene he invents for an examination of homosexuality reflects his concept of love so intricately expressed in *The Source of Light*. Price imagines Jesus, after his crucifixion, appearing to a guilt-ridden Judas, who, as Price points out (and a fact almost always entirely ignored in Biblical study) was perhaps, even probably, a young man of around nineteen at the time. In Price's invented scene, Judas has betrayed Jesus because he was in love with him; as he says to the risen Christ, "I loved you, sir, completely." Judas' confusion over his feelings and his jealousy over Jesus' complete love for all of the disciples drives him to despair which manifests itself in the ultimate betrayal. Price depicts Jesus and his disciples as a group not unlike Arthur and his knights or Alexander and his soldiers. He states: "It's hardly possible to maintain that Jesus himself, a man who traveled in the company of vigorous young men likely deprived of regular sexual access to women, would never have encountered homosexual behavior or the moral questions which arise from it." Once again, Price constructs a community of men who predicate love on homoerotic male companionship. He asserts about men in this type of community, "a readiness on the part of many such men to satisfy one another's sexual needs in ways that range from the hygienic matter-of-fact to the adolescent-sentimental and the firmly committed." Jesus himself seems conflicted on the philosophy of love. He tells Judas:

> But this may be what I have to say, the thing I know—you need me, yes, but you also need every man, woman, child, dog, bird, snake, rock, tree and fish every moment forever. I think the hard part is all that *love*.
> ...Didn't I say it to you and the other boys at our last supper? Isn't that all I ever said—that you should love each other the way I mainly loved you?
> ...The hard part from here on out is, what can *love* mean?

Not only does Jesus appear confused about love, illustrated by the fact that he asks as many questions on the subject as he makes pronouncements, he also reestablishes love as the primary dynamic in a community of men, the disciples at the last supper. Note how Price translates the Greek term for disciples as *boys*. He does this in all of his many respected biblical translations and insists that his interpretation of the term is closest to correct, relating it to an almost Southern notion of a bunch of good old boys.[29] Love becomes the primary factor in the relationship between man and everything in creation; adult sexuality becomes just another expression of that love. Price also has Jesus conflate the traditional Western concepts of love, that defined by *eros*, passionate and physical love; *philia*, love connected to loyalty and companionship; and *agape*, spiritual and paternal love for and of the deity. Love, in a community of men, cannot be parceled out into separate spheres, pigeon-holes designed to segregate physical, spiritual, and fraternal love. Because of this conflation of love, Jesus and his disciples, just like the Mayfield men and their male companions, are all trying to love one another very hard and in a unique way. So hard that it kills Jesus and Judas. Perhaps this religiously inspired definition of love better illustrates, and confirms, Schiff's previous assertion that Price's brand of love "turns out to be rather dark, obsessive, and consuming in nature."

To extend further the dynamic of a male community fueled, in a large part, by companionship, homoeroticism, and the danger of women interlopers, while Hutch and Lew hike the wilds of Cornwall, Lew tells Hutch a story about his days in the British Army:

> I had this mate in the army—from Oxford; you should look him up: little low-built chap with deep set black eyes. He was just eighteen and pure as new cream; but soon as I saw him, I said, "Stand clear. That one's wound tight as wire. Whoever cuts *his* string had better be seated and gripping iron rails!" ...name was Gary. (92)

Lew, along with Gary and two other soldiers visit a prostitute, take turns, and all contract a venereal disease from her. Lew tells Hutch, "On schedule my knob popped a nice red blister. I went in for tests and a pint of penicillin" (92). However, After Lew informs Gary of their shared predicament, Gary refuses treatment:

> he woke with this sore at the side of his mouth; he had full lips, another good sign....But next day the thing had spread and looked hot. I said he should have it seen to at once before his looks were marred for good....(we always told him he was made for pictures). (93)

After Gary informs Lew that he performed oral sex on the prostitute, and thus the location of his "sore," Lew tells Hutch, "He'd managed it up-right in that stinking shed. Well, peace to his wounds!—a hero of love, through filth and flame" (93). Lew's tale is, of course, cautionary, but more so than a simple soldier's parable of sex and hygiene. It speaks to the complex concept of a community of men engaged in a masculine ritual of initiation, community sex with a prostitute, and the dangers inherent in that ritual, that introduction to heterosexual sexuality. Michael Kreyling argues, "Lew Davis's story about an army buddy who sprouts venereal sores around his mouth after visiting a prostitute, carries a stigmatizing of the (white) female body perilously close to misogyny."[30] However, the story really emphasizes the erotic attraction among men as opposed to complete disdain for women and their sexuality, considering that acquiring a sexually transmitted disease from a prostitute is neither odd nor unusual. Lew appreciates Gary's newness by describing him as "pure as new cream." His physical description of his fellow soldier also indicates more than a passing, casual acknowledgment of his physical beauty: his full lips, deep-set black eyes, the fact that Lew and the other military men told him that he was handsome enough to be a movie star. However, Lew's most telling remark is about Gary's burgeoning sexuality, that his innocent looks concealed a heated sexuality, one that was flawed from the first act by contact with a woman, one that could "mar" his masculine beauty. He becomes, ironically, "a hero of love," for his folly, because as Lew puts it, his sexual initiation has been "through filth and flame." Lew's story stands as an example of the intricate workings of how men interact on a social and sexual level, but it also emphasizes the appreciation for fellow men, especially comrades of some sort, as both sexual and beautiful objects of desire.

As opposed to Charles Nelson's depiction of homosexual sex as a dangerous and adventurous game in his fiction, Price allows characters to describe homosexual sex as a game, but his usage of the metaphor usually represents the more comic or derogatory, as indicated earlier when Lew's mother, after learning that Hutch was a poet, advised him to "paint a scarey face on your arse." Interestingly, the comic and derogatory comments about homosexuality are made by women characters, as if women do not, or cannot, understand the sexuality generated by a community of men. They consider homosexuality and the community of masculinity that it creates either derisively or comically. It is as if, in the opinion of the female characters, men involved in camaraderie which extends into homoeroticism, or even sexual contact, are immature; they are simply playing boyish games. While visiting Cornwall, Hutch and Lew stay at a local boarding house run by a widow, Mrs. Mason. When she learns that they have come to explore the Arthurian legend ruins in the region, she tells them of two male students from Cambridge who had recently stayed with her for the same purpose and been disappointed in their meager historical finds: "'Never mind; they recovered.'…'I heard em playing leapfrog for three nights straight!'" (96). This reference to homosexual sex as an immature children's game comes directly before one of Price's powerful representations of ritual and homosexuality, as if to contrast the two positions.

After Mrs. Mason makes her remark about the men playing leapfrog, Hutch goes to the room, and bed, that he shares with Lew only to find Lew asleep. When Hutch climbs into the bed, he feels something cold between them, an object. Hutch reaches down and realizes that it is "a knife, a dull table-knife." Lew, whom he thinks is asleep, whispers to him: "She lay down and Tristan put his naked sword between them. To their good fortune they'd kept on their clothes. So they slept divided in the heart of the wood and were found there, pure by the wretched Mark" (97). Lew has invoked the Tristan and Isolde story to maintain their platonic relationship and avoid the sexual. His "sword," the dull table knife, is meant to serve as a barrier between their bodies, a phallic representation of both masculinity and aggression used as a sexual buffer as opposed to a sexual weapon. In the Arthurian legend, the phallic sword separates a man and a woman; it becomes a dividing line in place of its more accepted role as a symbol of conjoining of bodies. For Hutch and Lew, two males, the phallic knife represents the act that could alter their friendship from the casual to the sexual, the friendly to the emotional. A penis, and all it stands for, has come between them. After Lew's recitation, Price writes, "Neither of them slept at ease all night" (97). It is, for the first time, a moment of knowledge and recognition for both men, the possibility that they both desire one another sexually and must avoid the temptation. Ironically, this very same set of circumstances, heterosexual and homosexual, informs several of the Arthurian legends that infuse the Cornwall countryside where they sleep—Tristan and Isolde, Guinevere and Lancelot, and even the brothers Balin and Balan who are joined and separated by a mystical sword destined to make its owner kill the man he most loves.

Maintaining a location factor to their relationship, the next day Hutch and Lew sail from Penzance to Tresco, one of the isolated Scilly Islands off the coast of Cornwall. There they find a young widow, Kay Gibbons, and her eight-year-old son, Archie, who let them a room for their stay. Kay's husband, a fisherman, has recently drowned. The location of the island is important in that it becomes a haven for the two young men, separated from the rest of the world. On their first walk around the rocky island they discover Kay Gibbons' garden, and Hutch thinks, "Five minutes before as they'd come through the garden, he'd thought the word *Eden*. He thought it again" (98). Later, Hutch tells Lew, "I think I may just stay here, have my trunk sent from Oxford. I suspect this is heaven" (100). To extend the Edenic/Paradise motif further, Hutch finds the hull of a wrecked fishing boat and naps in it. While he is asleep, Hutch dreams that he, Lew, and his girlfriend, Ann, are the sole inhabitants of the island and that they have entered into a new, prototypical relationship with traditional gender roles:

> In his dream, he, Ann, and Lew were together on this island in the Garden. They seemed the only people, and they didn't seem in flight from any other place. At least they had managed a calm unquestioned division of labor to fill the days—summer days but they worked against the coming cold. Hutch wandered the paths and fields and beaches, gathering stones to build a hut. Lew chased down rabbits, choked them with his bare hands, skinned and cured them over smoky fires. Ann softened the dried skins and sewed them neatly, like states on a map, into one growing cover—a broad deep quilt of tan and blue fur under which, with winter, they would sleep together. (102)

Constance Rooke believes that this location and dream basically serve to define Price's structured gender roles in the novel, women as "needy" and men as "buccaneers":

> Most of the women in the novel, including the many walk-ons, can be classified as needy, waiting types; most of the men are buccaneers. One especially striking case of this role definition occurs with Archie's parents: a woman passing time in her cottage, the man lost at sea. Price suggests an ancient history for such roles when Lew in the Garden dream hunts rabbits while Ann sews their skins into a quilt....[31]

While Rooke's contentions are correct, she fails to note the location of both Archie and his mother and Hutch's Garden dream, a faraway and isolated ideal place where old and new concepts of sexuality and gender roles can be expressed. During Hutch's nap in the ship's hull, Archie happens upon him and reinforces the idea of an isolated community, one where a healthy and innocent sense of sexuality is a component part: "He could see Hutch was chilly in the rising breeze but fast asleep. He could see in the fork of his legs that his thing was standing hard. He stayed still and silent, wondering if there was any chance in the world this man might stay here and never go" (102). Hutch's Garden dream awakens his desire for a basic community constructed of the elements most important in all of Price's fiction: love, work, and sexuality. The island represents a location, almost mystical, where all of these elements might come together, free from the social strictures of the mainland.

The sexual consummation of Hutch and Lew's relationship is intricately woven into the fabric of isolation and place, a necessarily distant community of men. After a day of exploring the island, Hutch returns to their shared room to find Lew asleep. When Lew awakens, they both realize that their time together is growing short and their sexual feeling for one another must be forgotten or addressed. Lew is the first to point out their isolated community, how it both brings them together and ultimately separates them: "You've been very nice, very Yank about it all. But notice you brought me to the end of the earth. We won't be slogging round Oxford together" (111). With this prompt, they discuss why they have traveled so far:

> "You'd be welcome any time."
> "As a tripper," Lew said, "—hot winkles and chips."
> "The Scillies were your idea. I'd never heard of them."

> Lew said "Fair enough." Then he said "Know why?"
> Hutch knew now he did. Their outward flights could cross only here, in unwatched solitude. He wanted them to and, in the last minute, that chance of intersection became all he'd wanted—or at least a seam worth gambling on to close the tear through which he felt his whole life wasting. He rolled to his left side, facing Lew, and laid his hand on the cool lean belly. (111)

Just like Hutch's first homosexual encounter, with his former student, Strawson, back in Virginia in an isolated cabin at the mountain resort of Warm Springs, the solitude becomes a complex part of sexuality, forcing the notion of a male homoerotic community to *hide*, owing more to the strict social regulations of the 1950s than shame or fear on the parts of the participants. When Hutch and Straw meet on the campus of the prep school, and Hutch remembers the night they spent together making love, he realizes that his memory has been clouded by this social order: "Though Straw had graduated and Hutch resigned, the place itself—the campus in sunlight, its order—had kept Hutch from thinking of the hours that followed their bath in the spring. Now the different place which Straw constituted, in power and need, demanded homage" (15). Notice that Hutch's consideration ofhis sexual relationship with Straw puts the young man in a location, "the different place." When Hutch and Lew do finally make love in Kay Gibbons' cottage on the rocky, distant island, Price configures their act of passion as geographical: "For more than an hour, they met one another in all ways two bodies can meet—released from time at the west edge of Europe, suspended sweating over Kay and Archie, generous and gentle, happy and used" (111). The two young men, once together, create a community of masculine desire free from time and predicated upon place, suspended over the traditional relationship, itself far from complete, represented by the truncated family asleep below them.

After they make love on the island, Hutch and Lew decide to part ways but keep in touch, and Hutch returns to Oxford. When he arrives there, a letter from Ann, his girlfriend back home, awaits him. She has taken a roommate, Linda, back in Richmond to help share expenses, and the girl's boyfriend, as described by Ann, represents another of Price's avatars of male sexuality, the electrically (and sexually) charged buccaneer. In this instance, Price moves dramatically from the purely metaphorical into an amalgamation of the figurative and the literal. The boyfriend, Bailey, is a lineman for the electric company. Ann writes to Hutch about their first meeting:

> He was electrocuted last winter, the bad sleet-storm in February. Had to go out with one other man at four in the morning to patch wires broken by ice and trees....Bailey by then was icy himself and reached out dark, brushed a bare hot wire, and took (he swears) two thousand pure volts. At that point he suddenly pulled up his shirt—in the story I mean (at that point in the story)— and proved it all. He's as brown and lean as a broad leather belt; but from neck to navel, and points south apparently, he has a white burn-scar straight as a die. Said it fried to the bone. I admired it sufficiently. He said it had taught him all he needed to know. (119)

Bailey is not only described in terms of electricity, he has absorbed electricity directly into his body. Ann's comment, that the scar travels "points south," implies that his genitals have been electrified also, giving his sexuality a literal electric charge. But most importantly, Bailey admits that being electrocuted, and electrified, has taught him some kind of complete knowledge. When Ann jokingly assumes the lesson he learned from the accident was not to trust someone helping you, he corrects her: "No ma'm—that from now on I'm free."...I've died, paid for all my sins, and am now in Heaven" (119). Bailey's electrical "freeing" bears a close resemblance to Hutch's earlier scenes of baptism, with both Rob and Straw, an initiation, a death of the old and a birth of the new in a community of homoerotic awareness; however, Bailey's is, once again, a literal baptism by fire, a radical cleansing to the bone. And, just as Hutch assumed that the isolation of the Scilly Islands made them a brand of heaven, a paradise on earth, Bailey's death and resurrection have given him the same impression of the world in general. He has become truly free, weighed, measured, and paid for his sins, and now inhabits a world, not simply an isolated corner, in which freedom is the byproduct of his electric baptism, a fact that becomes clearer later in the novel.

In Price's fiction, regardless of geographical setting, he never moves too far away from the South. To introduce southern sensibility, and masculinity, to the rather staid halls of Oxford, Hutch receives a visit from his former student and lover, Straw Stuart. Their first outing well represents Price's talent for both drawing vivid characters and infusing his writing with a distinctly southern flavor. Hutch and Straw go to Stratford to see a performance of *Macbeth* starring Laurence Olivier and Vivien Leigh. After a brief description of the actors' flawless performances in their respective roles, Hutch and Straw are invited backstage to meet the famous British icon of American Southern characters, from Scarlett O'Hara to Blanch DuBois. Already suffering from tuberculosis of the brain that will eventually prove fatal, Leigh welcomes the two in a confused but delightful manner reminiscent of a Williams character: "'And you're Southern, your note said, I'm more than an honorary Southerner myself.' For a moment her voice took on the plaintive sweetness of Scarlett and Blanche. 'The South was kind to me'" (141). Price, in that short line, a play on Blanche DuBois's emblematic lament from Tennessee Williams' *A Streetcar Named Desire*, ingeniously draws the reader back to the South from England. The fantasy of performance becomes a conduit for culture, constructed by one of that culture's most enduring popular figures, the very model of Southern womanhood, from the strong and resourceful to the needy and mad. To reinforce the concept of returning to the South and to illustrate the homoerotic nature of Hutch and Straw's relationship, Leigh says to them, "Carolina—I've seen it from trains: dark green, all pines. Will you go back there?" (141). When Hutch tells her that he hopes to return to North Carolina, she looks at them and asks, "Together?" Hutch, who suspects that Leigh has recognized the nature of his and Straw's relationship, "wondered how she meant it—Lady Macbeth, now a calm matchmaker?" (141). Leigh's tacit acknowledgment of the connection between the two men makes Hutch realize that he will have to deal with Straw now, that Straw has earned a deserved place in his life. Price uses this scene to reintroduce the South into the novel, and to set the stage for Straw's important reappearance into Hutch's emotional life. After Hutch and Straw return to

Hutch's rooms at Oxford, they catch up on news of their lives for one another. Their exchange represents a careful examination of many of Price's contentions about how gay men relate to one another, and it also delineates many of Hutch's personal concepts of youthful vigor and innocence as the prime driving forces behind male homoerotic attraction. When Hutch comments on how much Vivien Leigh liked Straw and his charm, Straw says, "Those older women do. I'm the spirit of youth" (142). His use of the phrase is axiomatic; for Hutch, Straw *is* the spirit of youth. Hutch's reply to the statement is telling and prophetic: "—For ten minutes at the rate you're going" (142). They open a bottle of Scotch, drink, and decide to open up to one another. Hutch reminds Straw that his rooms at the university are "a hermit's cell, six hundred years old" (143). Throughout the remainder of the scene, Price uses references to the age of the room, its position as a venerable witness to six centuries of such nights, men drinking together and confessing. Straw's comments on the room's age also brings up the unavoidable homoerotic:

> Straw raised up and scanned the long dark room. "Shit," he said. "Bet you young hermits were groveling on each other's butts before the plaster was dry on the wall."
> Hutch laughed. "Could be."
> Straw was still looking around. "I'm certain," he said. "Had to warm up somehow." (143)

Their environment, the ancient room, has probably born witness to most of life's conflicts and problems, so it seems an appropriate setting for the discussion that follows.

Hutch learns that the reason that Straw has been so taciturn is because over the summer he had a brief sexual affair with a much older married woman, the wife of the town doctor back in Virginia. The woman became pregnant and her husband aborted the baby before Straw even knew of the pregnancy. Just as Michael Kreyling argued about Lew Davis's story about the prostitute and his army buddy, Straw's story and Hutch's reaction to it "[carry] a stigmatizing of the (white) female body perilously close to misogyny." After Straw tells the story, Hutch's thoughts go to how the disastrous heterosexual encounter has changed Straw:

> Hutch felt a yellow surge of nausea in his throat. What he'd honored in this boy for nearly two years was the clear sight of life, a flood of cheerful animal life that had pressed Straw's body and face from within into one more mask of the thing Hutch hunted and worshiped in the world—the same strong grace that still moved pictures of Rob through his memory. Now supine on ragged cushions in a room that had seen worse surely in six hundred years, Straw seemed nonetheless filthy past cleaning. (144)

The blatant nature of Hutch's view of Straw, as a recreation and surrogate of his young father, a "mask," is evident. Schiff mentions this concept repeatedly in his critical writing on Price: "Hutch's early interest in young men has much to do with his desire to recover and vicariously love an image of his young father." And: "As we see in Price's work, homosexual desire often arises from, responds to, and acts as fulfillment of father-son desire: Hutch's desire for young men is a projection of his desire for his father."[32] However, Hutch's severe and critical thoughts about Straw's behavior also reveal a disdain for the interruption of female sexuality into the realm of the masculine, the community of men driven by homoerotic desire. Using the age of the room as a silent witness, Hutch even admits to himself that Straw's sexual transgression, though sad, was neither unusual nor particularly terrible. Straw has, in effect, corrupted one of Hutch's images of his father, his young and healthy sexuality that resulted in Hutch's birth, his very creation. Straw's sexuality has resulted in the opposite, the negation of life and generation that seems so important to Hutch (and Price), which once again raises the basic irony of the novel: Family, children, generations, and reproduction are paramount to a full and useful life. Where do gay men fit into this picture? Can, or should, a homoerotic community of men simply use women's bodies to perpetuate themselves? These questions all come "perilously close to misogyny." A search for their complex and often illusive answers lies at the heart of what propels the story forward.

To illustrate the question of homosexual sex and its status as nonreproductive, in the next scene, Straw and Hutch make love, a sexual experience that Hutch considers his most passionate ever:

> He lay facing Straw and, never quite waking, accepted for what seemed like hours the gestures of pure blind service—mouth and hands, anointment and soothing; no word of request, no feeding gaze. The pleasure was strong as any Hutch had known, maybe stronger because of the silence and dark. (147)

Earlier in the night, during their discussion of Straw's affair and the woman's subsequent abortion of their unborn child, Straw had told Hutch, "I can see I was hoping to really *make* something, the thing that matters" (146). After their intense love making, Hutch considers asking Straw, "*Have you made something now*?" (147). Both men fail to see the irony in their relationship, an irony that will continue into the next novel in the trilogy, that children, while a complex part of most heterosexual relationships, are not the essential marker of love or success between gay men. In the next section of *The Source of Light*, Hutch also struggles with the complexities of fatherhood and love, the death of Rob and his own experience with paternity.

Shortly after Straw visits Hutch in England, Hutch's girlfriend from Virginia, Ann Gatlin, meets him in Rome for a Christmas holiday. While in Rome, Hutch receives a message that his father, back in North Carolina, is dying and that he must return immediately, but not before he and Ann make love, resulting in a pregnancy which will come to light after all of the characters have reassembled back in the states. Once again, Price puts Straw into the mix of people in Hutch's life, to remind the reader that Straw represents a viable alternative for an emotional attachment, and thus can validate the notion of a homoerotic community of men. The character constantly illustrates this concept, to the point of frustration. As Joyce Carol Oates asked in her review of the novel, why is it so easy for the reader to see plainly what Hutch cannot? Hutch's denial of his homosexuality and ability to form a meaningful relationship with another man is only matched by Straw's persistence in giving him the opportunity.

Price's homoerotic imagery of men as sexually electric and giving off an interior light plays an important part in Rob's death scene, an internal view of the dying process as rebirth ritual. With Hutch present at the death bed, Rob, after he loses consciousness, discovers himself walking up to a small rural house and finding a lantern on the porch. After he lights the lantern and searches the empty house, he sees a light coming from underneath a door. It is the elemental light of birth: "from the crack at the sill, another light seeped" (210). On opening the door, Rob finds a young girl, her legs apart and giving birth, and the entire room lit bright by nothing more than a "clean lamp on a stand," and a metaphysical illumination radiating from the woman's womb. Rob finally realizes what the scene means in timeless terms, indicated by the present tense: "His mother, himself, the room he is born in. Feasible center, discovered in time, revised now and right" (210). The electricity and light generated by homosexual desire, all of the "electric young men," are ultimately overshadowed by the light of birth, the glow of the creation of generations.

To further emphasize the concepts of homoerotic "electricity," ritual, and death, shortly after Rob's funeral, Hutch travels to Richmond, Virginia, to visit Ann. When he arrives at the apartment she shares with her friend, Linda, Hutch discovers that Ann is not at home; however, Linda and her boyfriend, Bailey, the electrocuted power company lineman, are there. At their first meeting, the exchange between Hutch and Bailey illustrates how Price creates a sexually charged dynamic which runs like a sub-rosa current through the community of men who recognize it. While Linda tellingly cooks dinner in the kitchen, the traditional woman's role, the men, within earshot, discuss Bailey's electrical burn. Jokingly, Hutch tells Bailey, "I thought you were long since dead ...Ann said you'd been electrocuted" (242). Bailey's response to Hutch's comment involves an intricate interplay of ritual and homoerotic exhibition between men:

> Bailey waited, then stood in place, and pulled his shirt up to his tight dark nipples.
> Linda said, "Stop showing that thing. I hate it."
> "You don't," Bailey said but he only watched Hutch.

> Hutch's eyes traced the burn—white and satiny—the length of chest and belly to the navel, the trouser waist. "Does it go to the ground?" (242)

Linda's contention, that she hates the scar, represents female displeasure with such a lurid and obvious mark of male sexuality, almost a brand of brotherhood. When Bailey contradicts her comment, he looks only at Hutch. In response to Hutch's question about the extent of the scar, which leads seductively down Bailey's stomach in a straight line toward his penis, he says, "'it knew where to stop, took pity on Linda.' With his finger he stroked its trail to his belt and reached beneath" (242). Earlier, in her letter to Hutch, Ann wrote that the scar was like a marker, "but from neck to navel, and points south apparently, he has a white burn-scar straight as a die." She also wrote that Bailey believed the scar "had taught him all he needed to know" (119). As if to represent this knowledge, Hutch, in full view of Linda, offers up his hand to Bailey's chest in an almost supplicant act: "he put out a flat hand and pressed Bailey's chest, the height of the burn. 'We're glad you were spared.'" Linda's response to Hutch's comment, though a joke, illustrates the secretive and ritual exchange between the two men: "'Speak for *you*.' Linda said. She had turned now, grinning." As if to complete the implicit homoerotic nature of the ritual, Bailey tells her: "'He is' and leaned into the hand" (243).

Bailey's electrical scar, which runs the length of almost his entire body, is reminiscent of another famous electric scar in American literature, one that belongs to the master of an entire homoerotic community of men steeped in ritual. In Herman Melville's *Moby-Dick* (1851), the mysterious and mystical captain of the *Pequod*, Captain Ahab, is also marked by electricity. When Ishmael first sees Ahab on the deck, he describes him:

> Threading its way out from among his grey hairs, and continuing right down one side of his tawny scorched face and neck, till it disappeared in his clothing, you saw a slender rod-like mark, lividly whitish. It resembled that perpendicular seam sometimes made in the straight, lofty trunk of a great tree, when the upper lightning tearingly darts down it, and without wrenching a single twig, peels and grooves out the bark from top to bottom, ere running off into the soil, leaving the tree still greenly alive, but

> branded. Whether that mark was born with him or whether it was the scar left by some desperate wound, no one could certainly say.

Ahab's scar remains as mysterious and guarded as he does. Ishmael points out that "by some tacit consent throughout the voyage little or no allusion was made to it, especially by the mates."[33] Later, we are led to believe that the scar is indeed from a lightning bolt, perhaps called down while Ahab worshiped fire with his secretive Parsee companion and seer, Fedallah. Bailey, in his own right, is also a commander of electricity, a lineman for the county. Just like Ahab, he has played with fire, been burned and marked, and lived to tell about it. Both men claim a mystical knowledge from their ritualistic experiences; however, Bailey's scar represents more of a sexual knowledge of his own masculine power, a power manifested in his scarred yet pleasing body.

In the final section of *The Source of Light*, Hutch receives letters from both of his previous male sexual partners, letters that further develop the concepts of a community of homosexual men, replete with electric sexuality. Strawson, after having been expelled from college, is living in Hutch's old North Carolina family place with Grainger, the black caretaker, and considers joining the Navy, a traditional bastion of homoerotic male community. He writes to Hutch about his trepidation in joining the vast outside community of heterosexual masculinity: "So I think I'm not ready, and may never be, to join the great Pussy and Grain-Liquor Talking-Club that waits outside" (283). Straw considers Hutch's isolated country house a refuge from the sham outside world populated by men who mainly drink and talk, brag and ease their collective pain. Though Straw believes the outside world of male heterosexuality is flawed, he is also tempted by it. He also writes to Hutch that he has purchased a new appliance for the old house, with its antiquated electrical wiring that has already failed Rob, Hutch's dead father: "We read to each other at night and watch T.V. Hope you don't mind that, but we bought a used one to keep us in at night—me anyway. It cost thirty dollars and is as big as my knee…and it seems to do the job. I've slept by myself every night, no guests" (283). Straw has reined in his electrical sexuality, transferring it to the new, circa 1956, technology of electrical images represented by television, a simulacrum of the outside world.

The other letter, from Lew Davis, Hutch's Welsh friend, serves to remind Hutch of the electric sexuality which Lew possesses. Lew writes to Hutch that he got a job in a winery in Swansea, but ran into trouble:

> Unfortunately my electric skin drew in the owner's daughter, seventeen and all right. End of future in fortified wines. I'm thinking of getting treatments for the problem. Could they cancel my charge or reverse it or something? You're the one with training. Give a poor sod advice. (284)

Though he makes the offer jokingly, Lew is well aware of the hazards of his magnetic sexuality, represented by his "electric skin," and asks Hutch's advice for either turning off his "charge" or reversing its polarity, which seems to allude to altering his sexuality to exclusively male partners. His comment to Hutch about training refers to Hutch's homosexual experience, knowledge Lew wishes to draw upon.

As the novel concludes, the reader learns that Ann became pregnant in Rome with Hutch's child, and, like Straw's married affair, ended the pregnancy with an abortion without telling Hutch. Once again, heterosexual sexuality, with its primacy to reproduce and create successive generations in Price's fiction, has failed for the latently homosexual men. To reinforce this concept, Hutch's final interaction occurs back at Oxford, with a stonemason, James Nichols, whom he had met earlier and found sexually attractive. After they strike up a friendship, James quickly becomes another of Hutch's avatars of homoerotic desire. To add to James' complex place in Hutch's life and his desirability, the stonemason is also a single father, raising a daughter on his own, which gives him a direct connection to Rob, Hutch's dead and beloved father. While on a car trip to visit James' daughter, Nan, Hutch looks at James and thinks:

> that something in the boy seemed identical with Rob, of the same good essence. Nothing ghostly or urgent but a gentle palpable return to the oldest presence he'd known and needed—the vulnerable potent needy youth who'd stood at the rim of Hutch's own childhood and asked for help. (309)

After they part ways, James reappears in Hutch's Oxford rooms, unannounced and waiting. The scene gives Price the opportunity for his final description of male homoerotic attraction as electric and vital. Hutch observes James from the hallway, and sees him turn on a portable radio, which plays for a few seconds and then goes silent: "The radio had stopped—dead batteries?" When Hutch enters the rooms, James tells him, "your wireless is dead." When he taps the radio and it resumes playing, James says, "Hullo, I'm a healer!" His touch, his physical ministrations, have regenerated the electricity, brought it back to life like Hutch's memory of Rob, healed some breach in the homoerotic electric current.

Later, Hutch sees James in terms of light and electricity: "James's pallor was a firm luminescence in the air, stronger than the lamp and desolate. Rob again, a thousand times in memory. Moth to his own flame, dying and fed" (314). James' homoerotic charge, like Rob's, can sustain and destroy. When Hutch asks James how he got into the room, James' answer seems ominous, as if Hutch's dalliances in the world of homosexual sex may have been safe so far, but now harbor some vague, inchoate danger. Straw's youth and Lew Davis' good nature are replaced with James Nichols, a man who has just been released from prison for assaulting his ex-wife's boyfriend. He tells Hutch that he "soared in silent from the river…on me bat-leather wings" (315).

James' furtive nighttime arrival to Hutch, in the guise of a winged creature, suggests more foreboding than his previous sexual encounters. Schiff notes several examples of male sexuality in Price's fiction as representative of an incubus, a sexual demon who visits one at night and performs passionate, often violent and nonconsensual sex on a sleeping person. Schiff supplies psychoanalytic support for his assertions:

> Though the incubus traditionally suggests an evil spirit or demon in male form that desires sexual intercourse with sleeping women, the term in modern psychological usage is less demonic and more inclusive, suggesting a nightmare of a sexual nature that gives one the feeling of being burdened with a heavy weight on the chest (the Latin *incubare* means "to lie upon"). For Ernest Jones, a student of Freud and also his biographer, the incubus, which is virtually a synonym for the term *nightmare*, is "an

> expression of intense mental conflict centreing [*sic*] about some form of 'repressed' sexual desire…An expression of a mental conflict over an incestuous desire."[34]

Thus James, whom Hutch blatantly compares to his father, becomes an icon of both masculinity and paternity, further supported by his young fatherhood. Interestingly, Hutch sought out and even pursued the earlier homoerotic avatars of his father's sexuality and vitality, Hutch and Lew, and the encounters, when controlled and manipulated by Hutch, are pleasant and fulfilling, described in terms of light and playfulness. When Hutch's "father" pursues him, the encounter becomes ominous, as if a child's love for a parent is immune to the taint of the physical body, even if sexual. Suddenly, homosexual contact between two men returns to the vampiric; James seems a homosexual predator and Hutch his victim. This idea is further supported by the indistinct nature of Hutch and James' interaction in the Oxford bedroom, where they agree to "sleep" for the night, the connotation of the word left vague. As Kreyling points out, "the conclusion of *The Source of Light* leaves the issue of Hutch's sexual choices in an ambiguous condition." However, Kreyling regards Hutch's nascent, perhaps sexual, relationship with James in a more positive light, as opposed to the dark and foreboding imagery of the scene:

> Sex with the stonemason is not merely physical, for James Nichols (the mason) has a daughter and Hutch fantasizes that he and James can become de facto parents to the girl.
>
> …In Hutch's imagination, as *The Source of Light* concludes, a queer union *can* achieve the social ends of procreation—the nourishing and educating of children—even though the biological means are null.[35]

Once again, Price demonstrates how antithetical homosexual relationships and a homoerotic community of men are to the continuation of generations, especially in a work whose main thrust is the preservation of biological bloodlines. "Nourishing and educating of children," though highly important, is not the final social marker of reproduction; thus Hutch and James' fantasy relationship is fallow in terms of family for Price.

Though much more than a simple fictive interlude between two works in a trilogy, *The Source of Light* acts as a kind of generational bridge, replete with all of the conflicts and problems which drive the other two novels—a rather microcosmic tale of the entire Mayfield clan of men. Hutch, that tale's main conduit, actively, and furtively, pursues a place in the homoerotic community of men; however, his pursuit is not without consequences. These consequences form the framework of the final volume of the trilogy, *The Promise of Rest.* Schiff, writing about the conclusion of *The Source of Light*, argues for Hutch's new found freedom and promise of a new and different future: "On the verge of a new life as an artist, free at last of familial entanglements, and initiated into fulfilling erotic encounters, Hutch is alive and happy. Yet as the reader will see in *The Promise of Rest*, this state of mind cannot last forever."[36] Schiff notes that Hutch has been initiated, gone through a ritual process, into homosexuality and joined a community of men, an act perhaps facilitated by the break in familial entanglements. But as Schiff also argues, Hutch's newfound contentment cannot, and will not, last because he recreates all of the same knotty family entanglements anew, in what appears an almost desperate attempt to continue biological generations of Mayfield men, in his own dysfunctional family in the final chapter of the trilogy. His initiation into the homoerotic community of men, though not broken, is not complete, and something else comes flying in, on leather bat wings, through the dark and opened nighttime window of the Mayfield family—AIDS.

Good Hearts

"Ships are but boards, sailors but men."
—William Shakespeare, *The Merchant of Venice*

Good Hearts (1988), the third and final chapter of Reynolds Price's Mustian novels, is the culmination of the story of the family most prominent in

Price's early work, including his books, *A Long and Happy Life* (1962) and *A Generous Man* (1966). Though the stories are interrelated, they do not form the same type of collection, a true family saga trilogy, as the works that constitute *A Great Circle.* The concept of ritual runs throughout all three of the Mustian novels, though the rituals are not as necessarily homoerotically focused as those of *A Great Circle.* Schiff argues:

> Each of the three novels also deals with a significant ritual or moment of transformation: *A Long and Happy Life* offers an examination of courtship; *A Generous Man* looks at the crossing of a threshold, the emergence into manhood (perhaps *the* central ritual in Price's work); and *Good Hearts* concerns itself with separation in a long-established marriage.

Schiff's contention, that the ritual emergence into manhood may just be the central ritual in Price's *oeuvre,* speaks to the author's almost obsessive literary need to write about young men on the brink of full manhood and maturity, young men who must pass through some ritual of initiation to complete their transformation. Only in the third installment of the Mustian stories, *Good Hearts,* does Price feel comfortable with an evident examination of homosexuality and initiation, though in the earlier works, as Schiff notes, "Price seems far more interested...in male sexuality and beauty. The central erotic figure in each Mustian novel is a desirable, handsome, virile male...who attracts the gaze of women and men alike."[37] In *Good Hearts,* the reader finds that the handsome and dashing Wesley Beavers, the most erotically charged and masculine male character in all of the Mustian novels, has had his own initiation into the homoerotic community of men, and it comes to the page, interestingly enough, as a fond memory in middle age.

Good Hearts is basically the story of a marriage in the midst of middle-age doldrums. Rosacoke Mustian and Wesley Beavers, married for twenty-eight years and one grown son to their credit, have reached the point in their marriage where an all too common inertia has set in. Completely out of character, in response to his failing marriage, Wesley, a car mechanic, suddenly leaves home, drives away from Raleigh, North Carolina, and lands in Nashville,

Tennessee, in the trailer of a beautiful young lab technician named Wilson. It is while he is at work in a garage in Nashville that Wesley recounts the story of his ritual initiation into the world of homosexuality, and the memory retelling renders the story that much more potent; his fondness for the past becomes manifest in his actions of the present. While working on an expensive BMW, Wesley notices that the owner is paying his work undue attention. Price writes, "Wesley had soon figured out from his well-fit clothes and slow needy eyes that the fellow had to be queer, but that had just got Wesley interested. From his first days in the Navy in Norfolk, he had been a steady queer target—sailors in general were, back then."[38] The BMW owner's desiring gaze sends Wesley back to his youth, when he was a sailor, and how he first came to find and accept the homoerotic attraction that he generated. Wesley remembers how surprised he was to learn that sailors were often the focus of homosexual men in big port cities: "at first it shocked hell out of Wesley, even hearing the older sailors discuss it as calm as they did. He had said right off that if a man ever touched him below the waist, he believed his skin would crawl right off his bones and head for home if he didn't kill the guy first. Or both" (124). His homophobia, common for both the time and place, seems intractable until a slow night at a bar when he meets a handsome man, who quickly tells Wesley that he is gay, and who takes him back to his motel room. After some prerequisite drinking, as the man begins to undress him, "what Wesley was most conscious of was that a series of fences in his mind just silently fell down in lovely slow motion, like in a horse race movie, as the guy tried to jump them" (125). As Wesley's inhibitions fall away, he learns to experience his body in the hands of another man as opposed to all of the women who have ministered to his physical needs in the past: "the guy prowled and grazed over Wesley's body like something gentle but almost starved. Wesley estimated that he'd met the guy's every hope and need; the guy had anyhow kept saying 'Incredible. Absolutely incredible'" (126). Wesley goes on fondly to recall other homosexual encounters he had while in the Navy, most notably one with a French artist in St. Tropez and one with a teacher in Baltimore. His experiences are, in a large part, quite similar to the military homosexual adventures detailed in the works by Charles Nelson, though not as numerous or graphic.

To illustrate how his initiation into homosexual sex, as one of Price's youthful avatars of male beauty and sexuality, changed him, Wesley realizes that his encounters kept him from "joining his working mates through the years in their meaner queer jokes. There'd be no reason, in his years with Rosa, to turn back to men. The roar of his early manhood had cooled enough to let him focus fine again" (126–127). Wesley, like several of Price's characters, demonstrates an almost innate bisexuality, created in a large part by his physical beauty. Wesley is almost grudgingly and in a very masculine way aware of his own attractiveness, and Price writes, "it was a dream Wesley had made from the sight of his own good face in mirrors and the things riled women had said about his body and soul. Surely God didn't build such towers to burn? Surely they were meant to be true lighthouses, guiding others to joy—or safety at least" (62). Probably because Wesley considers his sexuality as a gift, he is able to configure his homosexual liaisons into his past in a healthy way, but it does not change the fact that after he willingly accepts an invitation home with the BMW owner, a law professor at Vanderbilt, Wesley cheerfully declines his needy invitation for physical contact. When Wesley accepts his invitation to spend the night, he even goes so far as to sleep in the same bed with the man, but he thinks, "the thought wouldn't work; he was aimed at women. And even though, years ago, his firm brown hide had not been allergic to any well-meaning earthly touch, women were the only real magic for Wesley, in the visible world" (137).

Wesley's story remains, ultimately, about the marriage to the woman he loves so dearly. Price uses Wesley's homoerotic initiation memories to construct him as a complete and complex character, to move past the predictable image of the country bumpkin car mechanic. Price is never condescending to any of his country characters, and chooses to write them as having a sophisticated internal life. Wesley's initiation into and memory of the homoerotic community of men, a community he once willingly and joyfully joined, serves to show how Price, in 1988, was becoming bolder in his depiction of his avatars of male sexuality, and that boldness would reach its climax in the concluding installment of *A Great Circle.*

❋ CHAPTER 6

The Promise of Rest

> "That it should be the questions and shape of a life, its total complexity gathered, arranged and considered, which matters in the end, not some stamp of salvation or damnation which disperses all the complexity in some unsatisfying little decision—the balancing of the scales..."
>
> —Tony Kushner, *Angels in America: Millennium Approaches*

A reader has natural, and perhaps naive, expectations from the third installment of a planned trilogy—resolution, finality, completion. However, Reynolds Price, an author whose very hallmark is the stark, realistic depiction of southern life, refuses the reader any such facile ending to such a complex body of work. In his study of Price's *A Great Circle* trilogy, Schiff maintains that the novel represents a departure for Price on several levels, among those its contemporary setting and frank examination of race. As Schiff states on the impact of the advent of AIDS in the book, "one finds the Mayfield men [in 1993] with their history of erotic hunger, suddenly living in an era in which love can kill."[1] More important though, Schiff argues that male homosexuality has finally come to the surface in Price's fiction, out of the shadows and into the light: "*Promise* more openly confronts issues of homosexuality, which becomes the dominant and preferred form of coupling in the novel."[2] This frank depiction of homosexuality in the novel allows Price's characters to philosophize upon being gay finally, and how one's sexuality influences concepts of masculinity. Once Price's gay characters confront their own homosexual natures, they seem naturally to move toward a subjective consideration of what it means to be masculine.

The Promise of Rest picks up Hutchins Mayfield's life some thirty-seven years after the end of *The Source of Light,* in 1993. Hutch, now sixty-two and a successful, well-known poet and professor at Duke University, is in the midst of serious family turmoil, including a separation from his wife of thirty-six years, Ann, the girl he fell in love with in *The Source of Light*, and the imminent death of their estranged gay son, Wade, from AIDS. As Schiff notes, several of the unresolved issues from the previous two novels remain, most notably Hutch's amorphous sexuality: "Hutch's sexuality continues to be a mystery, and one wonders whether he has deceived himself his entire life by having chosen a woman over a man."[3] Schiff also illustrates the same point made by Joyce Carol Oates in her review of *The Source of Light*, when he states, "though the possibility of marriage to Ann is distinct in *The Source of Light*, by the end of the novel it appears such a marriage is doomed because of Hutch's need both for solitude and young men—a situation the reader seemingly understands better than Hutch."[4] One of the primary reasons for this lack of self-knowledge on Hutch's part must certainly relate to his views on homosexuality, expressed intellectually in this novel for the first time; in the previous novels, homosexuality represents an emotional state, seemingly unassailable by and immune to any type of rational consideration or reflection. In *The Promise of Rest*, homosexuality becomes an issue for debate, mainly thrust into the light by Wade's relationship with his African American partner, Wyatt Bondurant, and his slow death from AIDS, which Price and all of his characters always refer to as "the plague."

As with the previous two novels in the trilogy, Price maintains the young avatars of homoerotic attraction. Strawson Stuart, though now in his fifties, still haunts Hutch's life, literally and figuratively, and is constantly depicted as being able almost magically to reconfigure himself back into the boy that Hutch loved, ameliorating his age. The role of the sexually magnetic and electrically charged young man from the earlier works is filled here by Hart Salter, one of Hutch's married English Literature graduate students at Duke. The departure from Price's usual approach to homosexuality is represented by two supporting characters: Maitland Moses, a young gay student in one of Hutch's poetry classes, and Mait's older, vaguely dangerous, yet highly sexual, boyfriend, Cam Mapleson, a former marine and AIDS hospice worker. Of course Hutch's gay son, Wade, also creates opportunity for the characters to discuss homosexuality, family, and masculinity in a distinctively Southern context, and to examine the homoerotic connections between Mayfield fathers and sons further. The homoerotic, masculine community of men, constantly present in Price's fictive world, has finally earned recognition beyond emotional acknowledgment, and when it becomes the topic for discussion, the reader learns some surprises about how and where gay men figure into Reynolds Price's fictional gay South.

When characters in the novel do finally openly discuss their homosexual feeling for one another, it becomes evident that they predicate their beliefs on a very gender-based definition of what it means to be gay and to be a man. As Hutch and Straw drive to New York City to bring Wade home to North Carolina so Hutch can care for him, they face several issues about their shared past. Straw tells Hutch, "I'd have spent my whole life bearing your weight, if you'd said the word." Hutch's reply is a complex explanation of why he does not believe that an openly, successful homosexual relationship is possible between two men:

> Finally Hutch thought of the question he'd asked himself years ago; it was still the main question for him and Straw. "But what in God's name could you and I have done—two thoroughly opposite brands of gent, trapped there in the country in a too-big house and with an old Negro man and the rest of our lives to kill while the world snickered at us at the grocery store: two old sissies, harmless as house dust."[5]

At this rather bleak, Faulknerian description, Straw immediately recognizes the question of their masculinity as a threat to any relationship they may have shared, and tells Hutch, "aside from the fact that you and I are about as sissy as Coach Knut Rockne, we'd have had everything any man and woman have" (54). Straw argues that their masculinity, never in question when compared to such a masculine icon as a rough, man's man football coach, would not have precluded a successful relationship, and both elide the concept that a gay partnership between two men who are less than their narrow definition of "masculine" can be anything but laughable. Hutch's reply to Straw relates directly back to the previous two novels in the trilogy; he tells Straw that they could never have had what is truly important in any relationship, a biological child, offspring, the Southern obsession with the continuation of generations. Then Hutch spews a venomous mock history of his idea of a homosexual relationship between two men and its inevitable conclusion, a view that feeds upon old hackneyed misconceptions and internalized homophobia:

> We'd have never had children, which is one huge lack in any arrangement that means to last; and worse, we'd have both had male-thinking minds. We'd have run out of things to talk about or to care for in common, and then we'd have just butted skulls round the clock like exceptionally dumb bull elephants. We'd have understood each other far too well before six months passed—all our big and small testosterone traits. (54)

Ironically, what Hutch has described, regardless of two "male-thinking minds," is his long and disastrous heterosexual marriage to Ann, and their biological child has failed to mitigate all of the "gay" relationship faults that Hutch lists. As he continues his diatribe against the possibility of a healthy and happy homosexual relationship between two men, Hutch once again enumerates stereotypical arguments on the subject which translate just as easily to many heterosexual relationships:

> Every mystery we'd had for each other would have worn out fast—we'd be as obvious as cheap fireworks. And that would have led to despising each other, then hate, then worse. We'd have loathed what time did to each other's bodies. And sooner or later, hot as we were, we'd have been sneaking out to cheat each other with every willing youngster in sight till we got so old we were paying for sex in motels and car seats. (54)

It becomes highly evident to the reader just why Hutch has fought his homosexuality throughout the entire trilogy. He suffers from the most destructive type of internalized homophobia that precludes him from acknowledging that he derives his only true emotional and physical pleasure from the homoerotic community of men. Straw, who recognizes this flaw in

Hutch, challenges him and will not allow him to continue with his self-denial and its sad aftermath. Straw tells him:

> We failed at our one big chance. Don't ever again, not in my presence anyhow, try to wiggle your hips and slide past the fact. The two of us together had something a whole lot better than we've had since; you chose to ignore it and here we stand, two pitiful starved-out men out of luck. (54)

It is this very attitude, conceived in his own homophobia, that truly causes almost all of Hutch Mayfield's problems, especially with his estranged wife and his dying son. To help clarify Hutch's position on homosexuality, masculinity, and happiness, Price employs a fictive technique similar to Tennessee Williams' dramatic one, that of writing about missing homosexual characters, non-masculine and unsuccessful queers safely kept "off stage."

The conduit for these missing gay characters is a young man whom Price introduces in the novel, Maitland Moses, one of Hutch's undergraduate students in a poetry writing class. Mait serves several functions; among these he represents a surrogate for Hutch's youth. In *The Source of Light*, when Hutch and Ann visit New York City and Hutch is unable to rouse Ann from a deep sleep in her hotel room, the hotel detective repeatedly, erroneously, and inextricably refers to Hutch several times as "Mr. Maitland."[6] Like Hutch, Mait is a poet obsessed with his dead father, and during a poetry reading when the class visits Hutch's home, Mait reads a poem decidedly incestuous and erotic, a paean to his own absent father who died in the Vietnam War (93). Mait, who is gay, also serves as a surrogate son for Hutch, one who is not alienated and dying from AIDS, a son who might have the chance for a successful and fulfilling life as a homosexual man. And like Wade, Hutch's biological son, Mait harbors an incestuous sexual desire for Hutch. He tells Hutch, "this endlessly prolonged initiation of mine into the sodomite tribe. You've had to put up with a lot of navel gazing—" (100). Mait considers the awakening of his homosexuality as a long initiation process into the homoerotic community of men, what he comically, and rather biblically, refers to as "the sodomite tribe." With all of his connections to Hutch, he seeks one more, as Hutch understands and asks Mait, "are you asking me if I'm queer too?" (101). Hutch's oblique answer to the question, in which he gladly confesses to having had sex with several men throughout his life, belies his true feeling toward emotional and physical relationships between men. His answer also recalls Straw's comment earlier, when he told Hutch that he would have "spent my whole life bearing your weight, if you'd said the word." Hutch tells Mait, "some how I couldn't bear another man's weight for long at a time—maybe because I bore a lovable breakable father right through my childhood" (102). Once again, one of Price's gay characters comes dangerously close to defining homosexuality in terms of a kind of misogyny, as if women are not as substantial, as subjectively weighty, as men. Homosexuality, for Hutch, is a burden that he refuses to bear consciously, but an emotional crutch that he gladly leans upon.

Hutch's views on homosexuality, masculinity, and gender come boldly to the forefront in a discussion he has with Mait about him helping care for the quickly failing Wade. Mait tells Hutch that he may have to give up his apartment for the summer and move in with the "Poufs." The reader learns that "the Poufs were an ongoing, only mildly embarrassing, pair of near-transvestites in sequins and pumps and Joan Crawford shoulder pads" (104). Interestingly, Price uses a rather obscure and antiquated British term, pouf, a derogatory designation for an effeminate homosexual man, strongly implying Hutch's equally outdated opinion of gay men and gender dynamics, further compounded by his comparison of the poufs to Joan Crawford. Mait's original use of the term "pouf" appears more playful and campy than mean; when Hutch uses the word his scorn becomes evident. Hutch tells Mait, "do yourself a favor—find an ex-convict or a nice axe-murderer, but don't stay long with those painted queens" (104). His joking comment is telling about his ideas on gender and sexuality, leaving one to believe that even criminals, if they are masculine, make better comrades than effeminate gay men. Also, Hutch's deprecating phrase, "painted queens," relates directly to his usage of "pouf," both belonging somewhere in the late nineteenth or early twentieth century, certainly not 1993. Mait complicates the issue by telling Hutch that the poufs "speak well of you."

The sad gay *creatures* that Hutch finds so reprehensible respect him, illustrating their progressive willingness to accept and even admire a closeted homosexual man, but even this fact does not deter Hutch from engaging in another mentor-type speech designed for Mait's edification on homosexuality, masculinity or the lack thereof:

> Don't narrow your choices sooner than you have to. Just because your miserable Poufs have cut themselves a path one micron wide and a millimeter deep through the whole of human feeling, please Mait, don't you. Drive off in every direction you can manage, and crash if you must—you likely won't die—but don't slim your choice down too soon. Not to feathers and lizard bags. You've got a real chance to understand the world, not just one tribe and its rhinestone blinders. (104)

In Schiff's *Understanding Reynolds Price*, he argues that in *The Promise of Rest*, "one of Price's purposes, it would appear, is to dispel myths and ignorance about homosexual behavior....Among other things, *The Promise of Rest* serves to legitimize and normalize homosexuality."[7] However, Price only attempts to legitimize and defend a very particular brand of homosexuality, one that favors the "masculine" gay man, the "good and successful" gay man who can pass for heterosexual as long as he avoids the gender traps of sequins and pumps and Joan Crawford shoulder pads. If the Pouf's social blinders are rhinestones, as Hutch notes, then his internal blinders must be made of something a bit rougher.

Michael Kreyling reads Hutch's comments about the "Poufs" in a very different light, one that speaks less of "normalizing" homosexuality and more of further marginalizing it. Kreyling notes, "Mait had approached Hutch as a role model but had won for his pains only some hackneyed pseudopaternal instruction on the distinction between 'painted queens' and Hutch's own sexual self—neither gay nor bisexual, 'no one pigeonhole.'"[8] As if to illustrate this point, that he realizes his ideas are outmoded and clichéd, after his speech about the feminine Poufs, Hutch observes Mait's reaction: "Mait's face assumed a generic expression Hutch knew too well—the universal muscular response when a student hears the teacher babbling outdated nonsense and seals himself off without saying so, least of all contradicting: the eyes go glassy and the lips beam thinly" (104). Kreyling explains why Mait's reaction to Hutch's oversimplified gender-based assessment of homosexuality is correct, when he argues that Hutch "clearly draws back from the performative parody of sex and gender carried on by the Joan Crawford-ish 'Poufs.'" Using David M. Halperin's theories of gender performance, pleasure, and sexuality for support, Kreyling contends:

> Price presents sexuality as essential rather than performative, ignited by desire for beautiful forms in particular bodies rather than socially constructed under quasi-political conditioning. Halperin argues that "Unlike sex, which is a natural fact, sexuality is a cultural production; it represents the *appropriation* of the human body and of its erogenous zones by an ideological discourse." Hutch tries to persuade Mait out of such a stance when the young man threatens fatalistically to throw himself into the either/or of outright gay or outright straight life.[9]

For Hutch, homosexuality must exist solely in what he considers a pure, non-political state; it becomes an aesthetic state predicated on primary pleasure derived from the social and physical interactions of a community of masculine males, ironically a rather complex redefinition of a homoerotic social structure based on the traditional Southern concept of the "good old boy." It seems to be a lesson the Mayfield men all learn at home—from their fathers.

The vague, nebulous homoerotic bonds between fathers and sons from the two earlier novels in Price's *The Great Circle* trilogy, Old Rob and Rob in *The Surface of Earth* and Rob and Hutch in *The Source of Light*, become more defined and overt in *The Promise of Rest*, evidenced by the interaction between Hutch, who finally admits to homosexual experiences, and Wade, who is an out gay man. Dying of AIDS, Wade wants to know his father better, and in a discussion of his father's past, Hutch tells his son, "you surely must have known for years that, before you were born, a reasonable number of my intimates were men" (112). Hutch's qualifying phrase, "before you were born," implies that after he had a son, that male became the focus of his homoerotic attraction, as illustrated by the exchange his comment generates:

> Wade's eyes were still shut. "I've estimated as much, yes sir."
> "Since when?"
> "More or less from the first, I guess, when I was maybe eight or nine—soon as I looked out and knew I was watching other bodies too."
> Hutch laughed. "Whoa here, I resisted you at every age. I've been many things but no child molester—"
> "Easy, I'm not on the vice squad yet. I *wanted* you to touch me more ways than one, but you were a gentleman round the clock always and a knockout to boot."
> "I'm a blighted cabbage leaf to what I was. You're pretty grand yourself." (112)

According to Schiff, "as we see in Price's work, homosexual desire often arises from, responds to, and acts as a fulfillment of father-son desire."[10] However, here, between Hutch and Wade, the proxies have been supplanted for the true participants; no young avatars of male homoerotic attraction need take a father or son's place. Kreyling points out that in the novel, "the bond between father and son is so intimate as to cross the realistic/biological frontier." Kreyling also demonstrates how the incestuous relationship between Hutch and Wade represents initiation into the world of the male homoerotic community, so important to Hutch's definition of masculinity, sexuality, and love:

> But the male/male, father/son bond is freighted with so much importance, in *The Promise of Rest* and the two earlier legs of the trilogy, that Price pushes it boldly. Father and son not only loved within the socially "normal" boundaries of filial affection but were honed on each other as erotically charged bodies.... Wade also remembers youthful intimations of homosexual community in the murmuring talk of Hutch and his lifetime friend Strawson Stuart on summer evenings at the Kendal farm. Eroticizing the father-son relationship risks criminalizing it, or turning it into grist for a talk show mill. But Price insists on deeper levels of love and work attainable only in male communities of desire.[11]

These "deeper levels of love" in Price's work that Kreyling writes about are expressed as both physical and emotional, and, even if vaguely incestuous, remain untainted when achieved through a ritual initiation into the homoerotic community of men. Mait's initiation into the Mayfield community of men is achieved by dint of Hutch's surrogate fatherhood. Mait's poem about his desire for his dead father, Hutch's unambiguous attraction to his buccaneer father, and Hutch's unapologetic desire for his own son all attest to Price's willingness to explore a highly taboo issue, homosexual incest, by raising it above the merely prurient to a higher level, that of true masculine community, with the extended family representing the most intimate and basic of communities.

This concept, that close ties, either by blood or familiarity, are paramount to acceptance into the homoerotic male community is best illustrated in the novel by Hutch's reaction to his surrogate son, Mait's, first boyfriend, Cam Mapleson. After Wade is hospitalized near death, Hutch frantically goes to Mait's apartment in the middle of the night for solace from the young man. It is soon evident to Hutch that he has interrupted a night of love making: "the air had a mordant smell of rut laid over the usual fug of young-male lodging—a slightly sour icebox, a mildewed shower, discarded sweatpants and the clean strong chlorine smell of cum" (167). And into this highly charged, masculine sexual environment steps one of Price's most spectacular avatars of young male beauty and sexuality, perhaps combining all of the previous and numerous examples from the entire trilogy but also raising a problem. When Cam enters the room, Hutch looks up and sees "a man as arresting in face and body as anything torn off a Roman basilica and painted again in the colors of life —black hair, dark eyes and biscuit-colored skin. He was older than Mait, he was also naked except for a towel round his hips..." (170). Cam, a former marine, instantly and inexplicably makes Hutch nervous and suspicious: "He'd begun to sense he was being lured into some narrow trap. *What does this new boy want, from Mait and me*?" (170). To illustrate his suspicion of the young man further, when Cam looks at Hutch, Hutch thinks, "*your eyes are flat as a puppet's; is there anyone in you?*" (171). Regardless of Hutch's suspicions about Cam, one final act grudgingly admits him entry into Hutch's pantheon of desirable avatars of male sexuality. Cam, clad in a towel, rises and the "towel fell to the floor round his feet. His whole body, pure white in the loins and bushed with black, flared like a phosphorous fire in the kitchen" (171). Like so many of the other men in Hutch's life, men who drew his desire—his father,

Straw, Lew, James, Bailey. Cam's nude body becomes charged, phosphorescent, giving off a crackle of sexuality. But unlike the other men who easily earn Hutch's trust and admiration, he remains highly suspicious of the former marine, Cam Mapleson. Hutch's initial question to himself, *What does this new boy want, from Mait and me?* indicates that he feels a paternal bond with Mait, one that he thinks the older man threatens. Cam's "outsider" status and even his past as a marine refuse him entry and initiation into Hutch's homoerotic community of desire, even though he is highly attractive. Cam has already gained initiation into another institution of masculinity, the Marine Corps, perhaps opting him out of the more intimate family community. Hutch's first inchoate feelings of distrust about Cam arise after he tells Hutch he was a marine, and Mait tells the old joke, "what's the difference between a marine and a queer? A six pack." (170).

Throughout the remainder of the novel, Hutch learns to accept Cam as part of Mait's life, but he never really likes him. Cam never becomes a full-fledged member of the homoerotic male community, though he is basically a likeable character, a volunteer at an AIDS hospice. Hutch's anger at Cam climaxes when he learns that Cam and Mait, while caring for the blind and near death Wade, make love in front of him and allow him to participate by feel. After Wade tells Hutch what happened, Hutch confronts Mait and Cam about the episode, what he delicately refers to as a "brief *exhibicion*," and an embarrassed Mait tries to explain the incident away by telling Hutch that they only stripped for Wade, but Cam is defiant. He tells Hutch, "we offered it to him—*I* made the offer. I'm his age. I can feel his loneliness. I had the right" (201). Cam boldly claims a right to enter this closed community of men, right by empathy; however, Hutch rebuffs his right by an almost biblical invocation of the rights of a man's house, his community: "Hutch bridled. 'The *right?* Where's your half of the deed? This is my house, Cameron, while I draw breath'" (201). Sounding like an old testament patriarch, Hutch tells himself that his anger does not stem from "puritan outrage or envy, just one more taste of bone-aching regret that once again Wade had been forced up against a human pleasure he'd never share again" (201). Hutch is the only character who considers the experience negatively. The dying Wade reveled in the experience; Mait and Cam both consider it a gift to him. Cam even tells Hutch, "I never did anything any more intimate with anyone else, male or female, than what the two of us did for Wade. I'll never forget it" (201). Hutch's rationalization of the sexual "gift" falls flat. His real displeasure in what happened is that Cam, an outsider, usurped power and skipped initiation into the Mayfield community, and for the first time, even Cam's male beauty will not mitigate his transgression in Hutch's mind—Hutch dislikes him for the rest of the story.

The most profound representation of Price's concept of initation into a homoerotic community of men comes near the end of *The Promise of Rest*, and it is the ultimate initation. During Wade's death scene, Price allows the reader into the images that he experiences, just as the reader was also given the ability to experience Rob's death in *The Source of Light.* Price writes, "the grip of Wade's mind slowly released its hold on the world," and, just like his grandfather Rob, Wade finds himself no longer sick, whole and complete again, standing in a stark room, but he is not alone:

> What he understood plainly was that this guest here was a young man, maybe twenty-five years old, in the nearly perfect body and face that made him bear strong manifestation of all Wade had hoped for, ever on Earth—an entirely admirable welcoming man, at ease in both his mind and body and eager to give both without stint.
>
> As Wade made a slight courteous bow toward the guest, the dazzling body took the first step toward him. (268)

In death, Wade has entered into a room, a location where he finds all he desired on Earth, the reward for a life well lived, and that reward is a handsome young man willing to give him everything. Rob, Hutch's father, found his reward in a similar room, by returning to the moment of his birth: "His mother, himself, the room he is born in. Feasible center, discovered in time, revised now and right" (*The Source of Light* 210). However, in *The Source of Light*, the electricity and light generated by homosexual desire, all of the "electric young men," are ultimately overshadowed by the light of birth, the glow of the creation of generations. For Wade, and ultimately the end of the trilogy, the light holds another, different final truth:

> ...when he'd arrived at the edge of the bed and held out open arms and hands, Wade felt the pouring out in his chest of unthinkable joy. By then all human names were wiped from his mind... so he never quite learned that the guest wore the ageless face of his dead grandfather Rob Mayfield, young again, a man Wade had never seen alive above ground. Wade stepped on forward into the harbor of powerful arms, and the light was blinding. (268)

Here, initiation becomes metaphysical, and Price achieves two different effects. Wade has been released from his earthly sufferings, while being "harbored" in the arms of his progenitor, the completion of one of the "great circles" of experience and generations from which the trilogy derives its title—there are others.

After Wade's death, Hutch learns that while he was living in New York, before he met Wyatt Bondurant, Wade had a brief relationship with Wyatt's sister, Ivory. Ivory, who was separated from her husband at the time of the affair with Wade, became pregnant and the identity of the father is a mystery. The boy, Raven, significantly both Hutch and Wade's middle name, travels to North Carolina with his mother for the funeral, and Hutch must face the possibility that the mixed race child might be his grandson. Unlike the characters, the reader is privileged with the knowledge that Raven is, indeed, Wade's off spring. In an effort to help complete the "great circle," Hutch gives the boy the Mayfield family wedding band that has appeared in all three novels, a circular symbol of love, failed loved, and, primarily, a continuation of the generations. In this child, Hutch sees the possibility of healing the long Mayfield family curse, a curse complexly bound up with race and sexuality; however, Hutch is also tacitly inviting the boy into the community of Mayfield men, and perhaps he can get it right. The final lines of *The Promise of Rest*, as Hutch and Raven spread Wade's ashes at the old Kendal farm, imply both an ending and a beginning: "They could hardly see to walk toward the shade and find the others to say they'd done one duty at least—one man's return to the bottomless ground; maybe even a family's end, its story told—but they looked on forward and took the first steps" (353). The Mayfield family saga ends here, with a glint of hope represented by the one element that all of the characters throughout the trilogy have so rabidly insisted is the only marker of success and happiness in any life—a child.

The Promise of Rest is a multilayered and complicated text, addressing the thorny nexus between race and sexuality. Many critics have chosen to examine the novel, along with the earlier installments, primarily in terms of race, and much work still remains to be done on that topic. However, sexuality, especially homosexuality coupled with Southern concepts of masculinity and the supremely involved dynamic of homoerotic desire among male family members, seems to be the trilogy's most difficult point of study. Schiff succinctly illustrates how this dynamic works in Price's fiction: "The older male, whether biological father or simply father figure, becomes a crucial force in the life of the younger male, particularly in regard to the younger's emerging sexual identity. Ultimately, Price's most satisfied characters are those who follow their desires...."[12] Schiff, in essence, has defined a singularly traditional and masculine rite of initiation. But Schiff also notes the pitfalls in limning such relationships:

> Price plunges into the most primitive aspects of family life and love, allowing us to observe the dangers and joys of intimacy between parents and children. Resistant to those popular tendencies that sensationalize incestuous relations, Price strives to normalize family eroticism and place it within a more natural framework, yet simultaneously he demonstrates that men and women can become paralyzed and suffer immensely because of excessive familial intimacy.[13]

The Promise of Rest is Price's most realized example of these intricate, and often taboo, relationships. Ultimately, the novel propels the entire trilogy to a point beyond the basic story of a family, while it boldly uncovers issues about masculinity, sexuality, and familial love that are oftentimes common and equally oftentimes ignored in deference to an outdated sense of decorum and propriety.

With *A Great Circle*, Reynolds Price has created an entire microcosmic world of the inter-workings of one rather common Southern family. The fact that he has managed this in a trilogy, what many modern critics consider an outdated form, further attests to his talent as a writer. According to Michael Kreyling, "trilogies produced by American novelists in this century [twentieth] can scarcely match *A Great Circle's* sweep and finesse."[14] Kreyling goes on to point out that Faulkner's *The Hamlet* stands critically far above its less admired later legs, *The Town* and *The Mansion*, and he also maintains that Dreiser's "Trilogy of Desire" suffers from "poetic inertia." But Price pulls it off, a trilogy that is readable, sustained, and highly poetic. Though the series of novels is not without their flaws, they still stand as a supreme accomplishment in American letters, and in the final analysis, *A Great Circle* is mostly about the tricky, often sad, always important relationships between the generations of fathers and sons. Simply to say that any father/son relationship, or, for that matter, any homosexual relationship, is complex is, of course, a gross understatement; however, Price does not *stop* at that basic complexity. He does not avoid such highly charged topics as homosexual incestuous desire in his fiction; instead, as Schiff states, Price plunges headlong into them. One of the fictive methods he uses to ease the reader into this fictional world of a homoerotic community of masculine desire is the concept of male initiation, with its historical importance and precedent firmly established—from the bible to Shakespeare, from *Moby-Dick* to *A Great Circle*. What Price does that is so different and new in terms of initiation and homosexuality, probably in response to a more accepting, modern society, is to push the limits, however gently and craftily, of how men relate to one another—as fathers and sons, as friends, as sexual human beings. And being Reynolds Price, he naturally pushes these limits in the codified and tradition-driven confines of the conservative American South, where history and family life allow for different, maybe even ironically radical, literary approaches to just how we live and love.

❋ Conclusion

In Martin Duberman's *Hidden from History: Reclaiming the Gay and Lesbian Past* (1989), he documents two letters written in 1826 from one Thomas Jefferson Withers to a James H. Hammond, a friend of his in law school at South Carolina College. Both young South Carolinians, in their early twenties at the time, would go on to become prominent men in the South, Withers as a judge and Hammond as a governor and senator.

The letters, playful in tone, suggest that the young men had been quite close to one another while growing up, close enough for Hammonds, the future governor, to receive this question from Withers: "I feel some inclination to learn whether you yet sleep in your Shirt-tail, and whether you yet have the extravagant delight of poking and punching a writhing Bedfellow with your long fleshed pole—the exquisite touches of which I have often had the honor of feeling?" As if there is any doubt as to what Withers is writing about, he elaborates: "Sir, you roughen the downy Slumbers of your Bedfellow—by such hostile—furious lunges as you are in the habit of making at him—when he is least prepared for defence against the crushing force of a Battering Ram." In the second letter, Withers accuses Hammond of "charging over the pine barrens of your locality, braying, like an ass, at every she-male you can discover."[1] As Duberman points out, the tone of the letters is not romantic, more homoerotic and rollicking, and speaks of a certain ease with the subject of homosexuality, a subject that modern people have been led to believe was even beyond mentioning in the early nineteenth century, much less joking and writing casually about it. Duberman, in an effort to contextualize the letters historically, recognizes the obvious problem; should they be considered "anomalous" or "representative?"[2] Duberman theorizes an answer to this question, and his conclusion, based on historical and sociological conjecture, may hold a key to why homosexuality and masculinity have had a profound influence on certain modern Southern writers. Duberman argues:

> The American South ofthe latter part ofthe eighteenth and early part ofthe nineteenth centuries was (for privileged, young, white males) one of those rare "liberal interregnums" in our history when the body could be treated as a natural source of pleasure and "wanton" sexuality viewed as the natural prerogative—the exemplification even—of "manliness."
>
> In this sense, Jeff and Jim's relaxed attitude toward sex in general, far from being anomalous, may have been close to mainstream mores.[3]

Interestingly, Duberman's assertion, "'wanton' sexuality viewed as the natural prerogative—the exemplification even—of 'manliness,'" closely resembles Michael Moon's theory of redundant gay initiation into a homoerotic masculine community, when viewed in a homosexual context. But, concerned mainly with the historical and sociological implications of the letters, Duberman makes no assumptions about how Southern literature could have been influenced by this "liberal interregnum"; however, one need only consider American literary history to realize that this period in the South directly preceded the true advent of the novel in the mid-nineteenth century. The South, and the rest of the country, were not quite ready for fictional depictions of homosexuality, especially considering the fact that they were hardly ready for portrayals of very sterilized heterosexual sex, when those works were usually punitive in tone, such as Hawthorne's *The Scarlet Letter* (1850).

Over a century later, some gay and straight men in the South began to write, tentatively and guardedly at first, about the subject of homosexuality, and these men: Tennessee Williams, Charles Nelson, and Reynolds Price, were products of that same South that produced the two South Carolina "writhing bedfellows." Of course the history of the American South had been changed significantly and forever by the horrors of the Civil War, two World Wars, and simultaneously with the careers of Williams and Price, the Civil Rights movement. However, that ideal of gay men as natural and at ease with their identities, the concept so freely expressed in the two 1826 letters, seems to have remained and survived in the background of history. Williams, writing mainly in the 1940s and 1950s, was hesitant to indulge his desire to write openly about homosexuality in his plays, probably because of the pressure brought to bear by critics and the public, pressure that denied mainstream success to any writer labeled as "gay." Nevertheless, Williams found a way, a method, for inserting gay characters into his plays. The living gay characters were broken, battered, and tortured men, men like Brick Pollitt. The dead gay characters, such as Skipper and Blanche DuBois's poet husband, who live through Williams' theater of memory, were tragic and idealized. Ironically, and perhaps purposefully, the truth lies somewhere in between. There is homoerotic pleasure and even love between men in Williams' plays, if one watches them very closely.

Charles Nelson, writing well past the "sexual revolution" of the 1960s and the Stonewall revolution of the 1970s that marked the emergence of gay pride in the United States, goes in the opposite creative direction from Tennessee Williams and decadently indulges his depiction of gay men, replete with graphic sexuality and comedy; however, in Nelson's work one can still find the Southern sensibility, the tacit approval of the "wanton" pursuit of manliness, that Duberman illustrates was common during the liberal interregnum of the late eighteenth and early nineteenth centuries in the South. With its epistolary structure, *The Boy Who Picked the Bullets Up* often reads like one of Duberman's historical letters and is a prime example of the "wanton" pursuit of manliness. Kurt Strom could certainly and easily be described as "braying, like an ass, at every she-male you can discover." Because literary criticism of Nelson's work is completely new, this examination being the first venture, several other important topics of inquiry remain to be addressed, such as the ramifications of his complex epistolary structure and the post colonial aspects of Vietnam during the brutal years of the American war; but for a study of masculinity and initiation into a homoerotic community of masculinity, Nelson's fiction represents the *ne plus ultra* texts.

Reynolds Price, highly recognizedas the current literary voice of the South, has created entire fictional families who must deal with the fact that their sexuality is primarily homoerotic and that denial is often destructive. For the Mayfield men, of Price's *A Great Circle* trilogy, the creation of and initiation into a community of desire based on homosexuality is the only place where they find true acceptance and happiness. This community, predicated in a large part on traditional concepts of masculinity, serves as a haven, a type of idyllic location, where men can genuinely relate to one another, and Price does not hesitate to go beyond the accepted boundaries of sexuality into a fictional region where incestuous relationships are no longer taboo or negative but speak to a deeper love between men, a love of generations. For Price, one of the dangers that these stories exposes is his almost misogynistic treatment of the female characters, who tend to stand on the sidelines of the male lives and represent a hindrance to the successful homoerotic community. This fictive treatment of female characters, of course, begs the question: Where do women fit into this world of homoerotic desire? In Price's fiction, perhaps unfortunately, women are necessary for the continuation of generations. Price can easily write full, well-developed, and complex female characters, as evidenced by one of his most beautifully written novels, *Kate Vaiden* (1986), told by a female first-person narrator, a feat so unusual for a writer of the opposite gender that Price dedicates an entire essay on the subject in "A Vast Common Room" (1986). Price's gay male characters always become the focus of any of his works that contain them. These gay characters, for all their masculine bravado and constant need to eschewsexual "pigeon-holing," always find their deepest, most emotional, affectionate, and fulfilling relationships with other men. It is the protection created by their closed communities of homoerotic desire that allows them to indulge and deny their homosexuality at the same time, creating most of the conflict and anxiety in Price's gay themed fiction. Price, much more so than Tennessee Williams and Charles Nelson, writes about what has been lost in the secreting away of that gay past conjured up by the two letters written between long dead young men, young men who represented a healthy love of life, sexuality, and themselves—what was one time called "lusty" before lust became a bad word.

Gay male Southern writers have had to struggle with the tension generated by a need to represent homosexuality in their works and a society that closely defines what it is to be a man. In a reference I have long since lost to time, I remember reading once that in his memoirs, a mid-nineteenth century Southern gentleman had written that to be a "successful" man, a Southerner had to do three things: build a house, have children, and write a book. How alternately wonderful and perplexing it is to have such rules—and to break them. These writers, Williams, Nelson, and Price, have taken on the challenge and shown that gay men and characters have a unique vantage point to comment on these rules. Being on the periphery of the accepted, the masculine, the heterosexual, we have to consider them all constantly. They puzzle us and fascinate us. In light of this interest, Reynolds Price's quotation from his short story, "The Enormous Door," becomes all the more telling, resonant, and appropriate: "Like many boys on the near edge of manhood, I had one constant flaming question—*What are grown men like, truly, in secret?*… I needed to study the make of men's bodies… ." Like the inquisitive boy in the short story, Reynolds Price, Tennessee Williams, and Charles Nelson have all three felt the need to "study the make of men's bodies." They have done so in drama, the novel, poetry, and other genres, and they have truly made the reader think about what it means to be Southern, to be a man, and to be gay. For the boy in the short story, the desire to know what grown men are like is a simple part of growing up, and like all boys, grown men are a secret for him to learn, a mystery. Price, Williams, and Nelson's collective work helps us see past that "near edge of manhood, "and beyond that border exists the beginning of understanding —what it means to be a man.

Notes

Notes to Introduction

1. Charles E. May, "Brick Pollitt as Homo Ludens: 'Three Players of a Summer Game' and *Cat on a Hot Tin Roof*," 282.
2. Michael Hogan, "Man to Man: Homosocial Desire in Reynolds Price's Short Fiction," 57.
3. Jefferson Humphries, "On the Inevitability of Theory in Southern Literary Study." *Southern Literature and Literary Theory,* xiii.
4. Peter Middleton, *The Inward Gaze: Masculinity and Subjectivity in Modern Culture*, 12.
5. Middleton, 11.
6. Michael S. Kimmel, *Men's Lives*. 8.
7. Michael Moon, *A Small Boy and Others: Imitation and Initiation in American Culture from Henry James to Andy Warhol*, 11.
8. Dean Shackelford, "The Truth Must Be Told: Gay Subjectivity, Homophobia, and Social History in *Cat on a Hot Tin Roof*," 103.
9. Constance Rooke, *Reynolds Price*, 12.
10. James A. Schiff, *Understanding Reynolds Price*, 14.

Notes to Chapter 1

1. See Clarence B. Hall and Clyde T. Wood, *The South*, 153.
2. See Kimball King "Tennessee Williams: A Southern Writer," 635.
3. In Seymour Kleinberg's 1978 essay, "The New Masculinity of Gay Men, and Beyond," he examines the dynamics of these same New York City sex clubs and posits a theory that aims toward Moon's conclusions: "But once one *is* there or at the Mine Shaft or any of half a dozen bars just like them, what does one use to understand this *spectacle* (my emphasis) of men?" Kleinberg concludes that, "what is different from anything else I remember, however, is the relentless pursuit of masculinity...the offense is not aesthetic; it is entirely political" (82).
4. Michael Moon, *A Small Boy and Others: Imitation and Initiation in American Culture from Henry James to Andy Warhol*, 11.
5. Judith J. Thompson, *Tennessee Williams' Plays: Memory, Myth, and Symbol*, 3.
6. King, 627.
7. James T. Nardin, "What Tennessee Williams Didn't Write," 340.
8. George McMichael, ed., *Concise Anthology of American Literature*. 2nd ed., 1843.
9. Dean Shackelford, "The Truth Must Be Told: Gay Subjectivity, Homophobia, and Social History in *Cat on a Hot Tin Roof*," 103.
10. McMichael, 1846.
11. Tennessee Williams, *A Streetcar Named Desire* (New York: Signet, 1947), 142. Hereafter cited parenthetically in the text.
12. Bert Cardullo, "Drama of Intimacy and Tragedy of Incomprehension: *A Streetcar Named Desire* Reconsidered," 80.
13. Thompson, 33.

14. Leonard Quirino, "The Cards Indicate a Voyage on *A Streetcar Named Desire*," 62.
15. Joseph N. Riddel, "*A Streetcar Named Desire*—Nietzsche Descending," 28.
16. Thompson, 34.
17. Wayne R. Dynes and Stephen Donaldson, "Introduction." *Homosexual Themes in Literary Studies*, xiv.
18. Leonard Berkman, "The Tragic Downfall of Blanche DuBois," 36.
19. Laurilyn J. Harris, "Perceptual Conflict and Perversion of Creativity in *A Streetcar Named Desire*," 92.
20. For more on male homosocial desire see: Eve Kosofsky Sedgwick, *Between Men: English Literature and Male Homosocial Desire*.
21. In Tennessee Williams' *Memoirs* (1975) he has this to say about paintings: "The work of a fine painter, committed only to vision, abstract and allusive as he pleases, is better able to create for you his moments of intensely perceptive beauty ...Van Gogh could capture for you moments of beauty, indescribable as descent into madness" (qtd. in Schvey 103).
22. Henry I. Schvey, "Madonna at the Poker Night: Pictorial Elements in Tennessee Williams's *A Streetcar Named Desire*," 104.
23. McMichael, 1846.
24. Luce Irigaray, *This Sex Which Is Not One*, 172.
25. There are repeated references throughout the play to the animal-like nature of Stanley and his friends. In scene four, Blanche tells Stella: "His poker night!—you call it—party of apes!"(72).In scene five, Blanche notes that Stanley's astrological sign is "Capricorn—the Goat!" (76).
26. Interestingly, the joke presages a common and outdated critical stance about many of Tennessee Williams' male characters. James T. Nardin maintains that "repeatedly, he [Williams] explains the real reason for the dilemmas of his characters—Brick, Chance Wayne, Val Xavier—a fear that youth and sexual vigor (their only positive attributes) are passing." Nardin goes on to note, "it is convenient to distract the audience with another problem which will gloss over the shallowness of such a dilemma" (340).
27. Peter Lyman, "The Fraternal Bond as a Joking Relationship: A Case Study of the Role of Sexist Jokes in Male Group Bonding," 145.
28. McMichael, 1845.
29. Quirino, 72.
30. Quirino, 66.
31. A study of the differences between the stage play and the 1951 Elia Kazan directed film, starring Marlon Brando and Vivien Leigh, illustrates how adept Tennessee Williams, who co-wrote the screenplay, was at implying Allan's homosexuality. Joseph Breen, the infamous Motion Picture Association of America film censor at the time, forbade any references to homosexuality or rape in the film. Williams rewrote the scene by suggesting that Allan was impotent with Blanche. Gene D. Phillips shows that "Blanche's description of Allan as unusually sensitive and tender, is enough to telegraph to a mature moviegoer that Allan is homosexual... Vivien Leigh believed, as did Kazan, that Williams rewrote the speech so cleverly that the suggestion of Allan's homosexuality was left intact" (229–230).
32. For more on Blanche DuBois as an important and iconic figure in gay culture see: Philip C. Kolin, "Reflections on/of *A Streetcar Named Desire*," *and* Ann Wilson, "The Politics of Sexual Ambiguity in *Sweet Bird of Youth*."
33. Joseph Childers and Gary Hentzi, *Columbia Dictionary of Modern Literary and Cultural Criticism*, 80.

Notes to Chapter 2

1. Tennessee Williams, *Cat on a Hot Tin Roof.* (New York: Signet, 1955), 124–125. Hereafter cited parenthetically in the text.
2. *Cat on a Hot Tin Roof* won Williams his second Pulitzer Prize for Best Play of the Year in 1955. His first was for *A Streetcar Named Desire* in 1948.
3. Marian Price, "*Cat on a Hot Tin Roof*: The Uneasy Marriage of Success and Idealism," 94.
4. There are actually *five* well-known versions of act three if one takes into consideration director Richard Brooks' 1958 screenplay for the film. Not allowed to make any references to homosexuality, Brooks' version is the most antiseptic. In it, Brick must simply grow up and accept his father's love to become heterosexually happy again—a tidy, predictable, and classic 1950s ending. How wasteful considering the cinematic perfection of casting Paul Newman as Brick and Elizabeth Taylor as Maggie the Cat.
5. Roger Boxill, "*Cat on a Hot Tin Roof*," 20–22.
6. Boxill, 21; Judith J. Thompson, apparently ignoring the fact that all of the versions of act three include the comic battle for Big Daddy's fortune, argues that "the mood of the Broadway conclusion is, rather, essentially comic: an ambience in which sudden conversions and 'miraculous' transformations of character need no justification other than the *fact* of their happening, with little regard to *how* they come about" (*Tennessee Williams' Plays: Memory, Myth, and Symbol*, 69). What Thompson fails to note is the fact that *all* of the various act threes are "essentially comic," opening the opportunity for miraculous changes that never happen.
7. Produced by The American Shakespeare Theatre, the 1974 revival of *Cat* was directed by Michael Kahn and featured Keir Dullea as Brick, Elizabeth Ashley as Maggie, and Fred Gwynne as Big Daddy. Another Broadway revival of *Cat* in 1990, directed by Howard Davies, starred Kathleen Turner as Maggie, Daniel Hugh Kelly as Brick, and Charles Durning as Big Daddy. To illustrate its continuing popularity with Broadway audiences, 2004 saw another revival of *Cat on a Hot Tin Roof* with Ashley Judd as Maggie, Jason Patric as Brick, and Ned Beatty as Big Daddy, and directed by Anthony Page.
8. Ruby Cohn, "The Garrulous Grotesques of Tennessee Williams," 55.
9. David Savran, *Communists, Cowboys, and Queers: The Politics of Masculinity in the Work of Arthur Miller and Tennessee Williams*, 99–100.
10. Mark Royden Winchell, "Come Back to the Locker Room Ag'in, Brick Honey!" 83.
11. Robert Emmet Jones, "Sexual Roles in the Works of Tennessee Williams," 549–550.
12. Harold Bloom, "Introduction." *Modern Critical Interpretations: Tennessee Williams's Cat on a Hot Tin Roof*, 3; Though Bloom greatly admires Tennessee Williams as one of the twentieth century's preeminent dramatists, he does not include *Cat on a Hot Tin Roof* among the playwright's best works. Bloom relegates it to the status of, "more a film script than an achieved drama" (3).
13. Alan Sinfield, *Cultural Politics—Queer Reading*, 53.
14. Sinfield, 47.
15. Savran, 91–92.
16. John M. Clum, "Something Cloudy, Something Clear": Homophobic Discourse in Tennessee Williams," 40.
17. Judith J. Thompson, *Tennessee Williams' Plays: Memory, Myth, and Symbol*, 76.
18. Savran, 53.
19. Boxill, 24.
20. Tennessee Williams, *The Glass Menagerie*, in George McMichael, ed., *Concise Anthology of American Literature*. 2nd ed., 1845.

21. *Cat on a Hot Tin Roof* is loosely based on a short story by Williams entitled "Three Players of a Summer Game" published in *The New Yorker* two years before he wrote the play.
22. Alice Griffin, "*Cat on a Hot Tin Roof*," 112.
23. See Michael S. Kimmel and Michael A. Messner, eds., *Men's Lives*. 2nd ed., 168.
24. Peter Middleton, *The Inward Gaze: Masculinity and Subjectivity in Modern Culture,* 20.
25. In her 2002 book, *Tennessee Williams' Plays: Memory, Myth, and Symbol*, Judith J. Thompson does a yeoman's job of connecting references in *Cat* to: Apollo, Hyacinthus, Hippolytus, Aphrodite, Artemis, Narcissus, the Phrygian Cebele, Osiris, Set, Bast, Castor and Pollux, and Saint Margaret.
26. Winchell, 88, 89.
27. Alvin B. Kernan, "Truth and Dramatic Mode in *A Streetcar Named Desire*,"18.
28. Savarn, 107.
29. Winchell, 89–90.
30. Winchell, 84.
31. See Savarn, 53.
32. Williams uses a more subtle indication of gay male sexual cruising in his very first play, *The Glass Menagerie* (1945), when the narrator, Tom Wingfield, relates his long hours spent in a dark movietheater. Williams' 1954 short story, "Hard Candy," describes in detail the homosexual sexual activity in an old movie theater, the Joy Rio. Also, Tom has become a merchant sailor who finds himself, "walking along a street at night, in some strange city, before I have found companions" (1886). To the experienced homosexual man, of any recent era, all of these activities, including Big Daddy's "bumming" around, clearly represent the underworld of secretive gay male sexual expression.
33. Clum, 38.
34. From Andre Gide to Paul Bowles, Williams also recognizes that modern North Africa has always represented a haven for ostracized Western gay men, though a complex and troubling colonial location/haven.
35. Michelangelo Signorile, *Life Outside: The Signorile Report on Gay Men: Sex, Drugs, Muscles, and the Passages of Life*, 46.
36. Pronger, 117.
37. Boxill, 21.
38. Thomas F. Van Laan, "'Shut Up!' 'Be Quiet' 'Hush!': Talk and Its Suppression in Three Plays by Tennessee Williams," 254.
39. Peter Lyman, "The Fraternal Bond as a Joking Relationship: A Case Study of the Role of Sexist Jokes in Male Group Bonding,"145
40. See Susan Bordo, *The Male Body: A New Look at Men in Public and in Private*, 81.

Notes to Chapter 3

1. The 1959 film, directed by Joseph Mankiewicz with a screenplay written by Gore Vidal and Tennessee Williams, is one of the better film versions of a Williams play. Katharine Hepburn and Elizabeth Taylor, who both received Academy Award nominations for their performances, superbly match wills as Violet and Catharine. Montgomery Clift, as the cool, detached Dr. Cukrowicz, appears somewhat lost between the strong performances of the two stars. The pop band The Motel's 1983 song, "Suddenly Last Summer," simply appropriates the play's title.
2. See S. Alan Chesler, "Tennessee Williams: Reassessment and Assessment," 870.
3. Paul J. Hurley, "*Suddenly Last Summer* as 'Morality Play,'" 393.

4. Chesler, 877.
5. Thomas F. Van Laan, "'Shut Up!' 'Be Quiet' 'Hush!': Talk and Its Suppression in Three Plays by Tennessee Williams," 257.
6. Tennessee Williams, "*Suddenly Last Summer*." *Tennessee Williams: Four Plays* (New York: Signet, 1976), 26. Hereafter cited parenthetically in the text.
7. Susan Koprince, "Tennessee Williams's Unseen Characters," 75, 80.
8. Judith J. Thompson, *Tennessee Williams' Plays: Memory, Myth, and Symbol*, 98.
9. See Chesler, 876.
10. Wilfred L. Guerin, *A Handbook of Critical Approaches to Literature*. 2nd ed., 139.
11. Thompson, 104.
12. Hurley, 393.
13. Thomas J. Richardson, "The City of Day and the City of Night: New Orleans and the Exotic Unreality of Tennessee Williams," 633, 635.
14. Richardson, 635.
15. Richardson, 636–637.
16. All of these geographical locations are still very much a part of the city of New Orleans, thanks in large part to the historical preservation society, The Vieux Carre Commission. The city still maintains much of the same atmosphere as when Williams first went there in 1938, despite the destruction caused by hurricane Katrina in August 2005. Several other writers have also used the twin natures of New Orleans, represented by the French Quarter and the Garden District, the most notable being Anne Rice.
17. Steven Bruhm, "Blackmailed by Sex: Tennessee Williams and the Economics of Desire," 529–530.
18. Alan Sinfield, *Cultural Politics—Queer Reading*, 47.
19. Bruhm, 530.
20. Thomas P. Adler, "The Search for God in the Plays of Tennessee Williams," 141.
21. Neal B. Houston, "Meaning by Analogy in *Suddenly Last Summer*," 2.
22. Thompson, 100.
23. Andrew Sofer, "Self-Consuming Artifacts: Power, Performance and the Body in Tennessee Williams' *Suddenly Last Summer*," 344.
24. Hurley, 396, 393.
25. Bruhm, 533.
26. Bruhm, 531.
27. Stofer, 341.
28. Stofer, 345.
29. Koprince, 82.

Notes to Chapter 4

1. Nelson, a mysterious and reclusive writer, seems to have written nothing else after 1989, though in 1997 he wrote, produced, and directed a stage version of both novels entitled *Grunts*. The play had a limited run at the Laughing Cup Theatre in Minneapolis, and it received marginal reviews (Skir 1).
2. There is no currently existing academic critical writing on Charles Nelson, though both novels often appear on gay fiction bibliographies and Vietnam War fiction bibliographies. The only academic acknowledgment of Nelson's work appears in the "Introduction" of Wayne Dynes' *Homosexual Themes in Literary Studies* (1992). Dynes gives Nelson the following brief mention: "Acclaimed by some critics as the best novel to come out of the

Vietnam War experience, Charles Nelson's *The Boy Who Picked the Bullets Up* depicted, with unsettling frankness, the experiences of a gay medic" (xiv).
3. Rich Grzesiak, *What Did You Do in the War, Daddy? An Interview with the Author of The Boy Who Picked the Bullets Up and Its Sequel, Panthers in the Skins of Men*, 2, 5.
4. Anne Bower, *Epistolary Responses: The Letter in 20th Century American Fiction and Criticism*, 23.
5. Grzesiak, 2.
6. Charles Nelson, *Panthers in the Skins of Men* (Secaucus, NJ: Meadowland Books, 1989), 38. Hereafter cited parenthetically in the text.
7. Maurice Charney, *Sexual Fiction*, 1, 5.
8. See Micha Ramakers, *Dirty Pictures: Tom of Finland, Masculinity, and Homosexuality*, 17.
9. David H. J. Morgan, "Theater of War: Combat, the Military, and Masculinities," 165.
10. Ramakers, 160.
11. Grzesiak, 2.
12. Michael Moon, *A Small Boy and Others: Imitation and Initiation in American Culture from Henry James to Andy Warhol*, 11.
13. Charles Nelson, *The Boy Who Picked the Bullets Up* (New York: Meadowland Books, 1981), 9. Hereafter cited parenthetically in the text.
14. See Michelangelo Signorile, *Life Outside: The Signorile Report on Gay Men: Sex, Drugs, Muscles, and the Passages of Life*, 9.
15. Steven Zeeland, *Military Trade*, 2.
16. Peter Lehman, *Running Scared: Masculinity and the Representation of the Male Body*, 155, 9.
17. Charles J. Levy, "ARVN as Faggots: Inverted Warfare in Vietnam," 183; To support the idea of homosexual as "enemy," Levy quotes a Vietnam marine on how navy corpsmen, Kurt's duty, were often treated:

> A lot of them were like prissy. I mean looked on the faggoty-type side. You could tell they were corpsmen. But I mean if that guy was in marine boot camp he'd of got bounced out. Or he'd have so many problems within the system that he fucking wouldn't be able to hack it. He'd go out of his mind. He'd be called "a faggot." (183)

In *The Boy Who Picked the Bullets Up*, Kurt writes to a friend: "Marines doubt the masculinity of corpsmen" (147).
18. Charney, 7.
19. See Ramakers, 104.
20. Laud Humphreys, "Tearoom Trade: Homosexual Behavior in Public Restrooms," 432.
21. Bob Connell, "Masculinity, Violence, and War," 181.
22. Mark Simpson, *Male Impersonators: Men Performing Masculinity*, 214.
23. Michael S. Kimmel, "Masculinity as Homophobia: Fear, Shame, and Silence in the Construction of Gender Identity," 129.
24. Morgan, 168.
25. Allan Berube, "Marching to a Different Drummer: Lesbian and Gay GIs in World War II," 383.
26. Signorile, 16.
27. John H. Driggs and Stephen E. Finn, *Intimacy Between Men*, 50.
28. Grzesiak, 1, 5.
29. Barbara Smith, "African American Lesbian and Gay History: An Exploration," 58.
30. Grzesiak, 5.
31. Driggs and Finn, 47.

32. Gregory K. Lehne, "Homophobia Among Men: Supporting and Defining the Male Role," 389, 382, 390.
33. Signorile, 38, 46, 46–47.
34. Steven Zeeland, *The Masculine Marine: Homoeroticism in the U.S. Marine Corps,* 10; Though Zeeland's statement proves a valid point about military concepts of masculinity, he inadvertently reconstructs the binary he wishes to subvert by stating that, regardless of what they do sexually, marines will "always land back on top." The comment makes a pun on male homosexual roles, "top" being the anal penetrator and "bottom" being the receptive partner; however, Zeeland's remarks play right back into notions of perceived privileged positions, with sex as a metaphor. Zeeland, himself, has failed to "see through the binarism."
35. Zeeland, *Trade*, 176.
36. Brian Pronger, *The Arena of Masculinity: Sports, Homosexuality, and the Meaning of Sex*, 137.
37. Pronger, 139.
38. Zeeland, *Marine*,10.
39. Pronger, 143.
40. Morgan, 168.
41. Randy Shilts, *Conduct Unbecoming: Gays and Lesbians in the U. S. Military*, 30, 31.
42. Ramakers, 201.
43. Lee Edelman, "Tearooms and Sympathy, or, The Epistemology of the Water Closet," 562.
44. Shilts, 670.
45. Michel Foucault, *The History of Sexuality, Volume One: An Introduction*, 86.
46. Zeeland, *Marine*, 118.
47. Susan Bordo, *The Male Body: A New Look at Men in Public and in Private*, 221–222.
48. See Shilts, 91.

Notes to Chapter 5

1. James A. Schiff, *Critical Essays on Reynolds Price*, 1.
2. Price has even written song lyrics with fellow North Carolina native and respected singer/songwriter James Taylor. Their 1991 popular song "Copperline" became a hit.
3. Schiff, *Critical Essays*, 4.
4. James A. Schiff, *Understanding Reynolds Price*, 16–17, 18.
5. Schiff, *Understanding*, 64.
6. Schiff, *Understanding*, 64, 27.
7. Constance Rooke, *Reynolds Price*, 140.
8. Rooke, 5; A well respected biblical scholar in his own right, Price has translated and critically examined several biblical stories, particularly stories from the Gospels, in works which include *A Palpable God* (1978), *Three Gospels* (1996), and *A Serious Way of Wondering* (2003).
9. Michael Hogan, "Man to Man: Homosocial Desire in Reynolds Price's Short Fiction," 56, 57.
10. Frank Pittman, *Man Enough: Fathers, Sons, and the Search for Masculinity*, 12, 11.
11. Joyce Carol Oates, "Portrait of the Artist as Son, Lover, Elegist," 30.
12. Michael Kreyling, "Men without Women: Communities of Desire and Race in *A Great Circle*,"281.
13. Schiff, *Understanding*, 93.

14. Reynolds Price, *The Source of Light* (New York: Atheneum, 1981), 3. Hereafter cited parenthetically in the text.
15. Rooke, 141.
16. Arthur Flannigan-Saint-Aubin, "The Male Body and Literary Metaphors for Masculinity," 239.
17. Kreyling, 286.
18. Flannigan-Saint-Aubin, 248.
19. Rooke, 140.
20. Flannigan-Saint-Aubin, 241.
21. Rooke, 141.
22. Schiff, *Understanding*, 66, 87–88.
23. See Kreyling, 288.
24. Rooke, 139.
25. Rooke, 140.
26. Schiff, *Understanding*, 65–66.
27. Rooke, 141.
28. Kreyling, 286.
29. Reynolds Price, *A Serious Way Of Wondering: The Ethics of Jesus Imagined*, 76–77, 82, 69, 85; In his famous essay on the history of writing, "A Single Meaning: Notes on the Origins and Life of Narrative," (1978) Price explicates a section of John 21, when the resurrected Jesus appears to the disciples while they are fishing in the Sea of Galilee:

    > Then when day broke Jesus stood on the shore though none of us knew it was Jesus.
    > He called to us "Boys, anything to eat?"
    > We said "No."
    > So he said to us "Cast the net to starboard—you'll find them."

    As Price explains his translation, he makes clear the usage of the word *boy* for the disciples: "—Jesus' call to them as 'boys' (plural of the Greek *paidion*, diminutive of *pais*, boy)." (264). In its diminutive form, the term becomes both friendly and familiar and denotes the common designation for a collection of young men, companions.
30. Kreyling, 290.
31. Rooke, 139.
32. Schiff, *Understanding*, 66; "Fathers and Sons in the Fiction of Reynolds Price: 'A Sense of Crucial Ambiguity,'" 276.
33. Herman Melville, *Moby-Dick*, 110.
34. Schiff, "Fathers and Sons," 266.
35. Kreyling, 293.
36. Schiff, *Understanding*, 103.
37. Schiff, *Understanding*, 27.
38. Reynolds Price, *Good Hearts* (New York: Atheneum, 1988), 124. Hereafter cited parenthetically in the text.

Notes to Chapter 6

1. James A. Schiff, *Understanding Reynolds Price*, 103.
2. Schiff, *Understanding*, 103–104.
3. Schiff, *Understanding*, 104–105.
4. Schiff, *Understanding*, 104.

5. Reynolds Price, *The Promise of Rest* (New York: Scribner, 1995), 53. Hereafter cited parenthetically in the text.
6. Reynolds Price, *The Source of Light* (New York: Atheneum, 1981), 35.
7. Schiff, *Understanding*, 111.
8. Michael Kreyling, "Men without Women: Communities of Desire and Race in *A Great Circle*," 284.
9. Kreyling, 288.
10. James A. Schiff, "Fathers and Sons in the Fiction of Reynolds Price: 'A Sense of Crucial Ambiguity,'" 276.
11. Kreyling, 285.
12. Schiff, "Fathers and Sons," 276.
13. Schiff, "Fathers and Sons." 277.
14. Kreyling, 300.

Notes to Conclusion

1. Martin Duberman, "'Writhing Bedfellows' in Antebellum South Carolina: Historical Interpretation and the Politics of Evidence," 155–156.
2. Duberman, 160.
3. Duberman, 161.

❋ Bibliography

Primary Sources

Nelson, Charles. *The Boy Who Picked the Bullets Up*. New York: Meadowland Books, 1981.
———. *Panthers in the Skins of Men*. Secaucus, NJ: Meadowland Books, 1989.
Price, Reynolds. *Good Hearts*. New York: Atheneum, 1988.
———. *The Promise of Rest*. New York: Scribner, 1995.
———. *The Source of Light*. New York: Atheneum, 1981.
Williams, Tennessee. *Cat on a Hot Tin Roof*. New York: Signet, 1955.
———. *A Streetcar Named Desire*. New York: Signet, 1947.
———. "*Suddenly Last Summer*." *Tennessee Williams: Four Plays*. New York: Signet, 1976. 1–93.

Secondary Critical Sources

Adler. Thomas P. "The Search for God in the Plays of Tennessee Williams." *Tennessee Williams: A Collection of Critical Essays*. Ed. Stephen S. Stanton. Englewood Cliffs: Prentice-Hall, 1977. 138–148.
Berkman, Leonard. "The Tragic Downfall of Blanche DuBois." *Modern Critical Interpretations: Tennessee Williams's A Streetcar Named Desire*. Ed. Harold Bloom. New York: Chelsea House, 1988. 33–40.
Berube, Allan. "Marching to a Different Drummer: Lesbian and Gay GIs in World War II." *Hidden From History: Reclaiming the Gay and Lesbian Past*. Eds. Martin Duberman, Martha Vicinus, and George Chauncey, Jr. New York: Meridian, 1989. 383–394.
Bloom, Harold. "Introduction." *Modern Critical Interpretations: Tennessee Williams's Cat on a Hot Tin Roof*. Ed. Harold Bloom. New York: Chelsea House, 2002. 1–3.
Bordo, Susan. *The Male Body: A New Look at Men in Public and in Private*. New York: Farrar, Straus and Giroux, 1999.
Bower, Anne. *Epistolary Responses: The Letter in 20th Century American Fiction and Criticism*. Tuscaloosa: U of Alabama P, 1997.
Boxill, Roger. "*Cat on a Hot Tin Roof*." *Modern Critical Interpretations: Tennessee Williams's Cat on a Hot Tin Roof*. Ed. Harold Bloom. New York: Chelsea House, 2002. 19–27.
Bruhm, Steven. "Blackmailed by Sex: Tennessee Williams and the Economics of Desire." *Modern Drama* 34 (1991): 528–537.
Cardullo, Bert. "Drama of Intimacy and Tragedy of Incomprehension: *A Streetcar Named Desire* Reconsidered." *Modern Critical Interpretations: Tennessee Williams's A Streetcar Named Desire*. Ed. Harold Bloom. New York: Chelsea House, 1988. 79–92.
Charney, Maurice. *Sexual Fiction*. London: Methuen, 1981.
Chesler, S. Alan. "Tennessee Williams: Reassessment and Assessment." *Tennessee Williams: A Tribute*. Ed. Jac Tharpe. Jackson: UP of Mississippi, 1977. 848–880.
Childers, Joseph, and Gary Hentzi, eds. *Columbia Dictionary of Modern Literary and Cultural Criticism*. New York: Columbia UP, 1995.
Clum, John M. "Something Cloudy, Something Clear": Homophobic Discourse in Tennessee Williams." *Modern Critical Interpretations: Tennessee Williams's Cat on a Hot Tin Roof*. Ed. Harold Bloom. New York: Chelsea House, 2002. 29–43.

Cohn, Ruby. "The Garrulous Grotesques of Tennessee Williams." *Tennessee Williams: A Collection of Critical Essays*. Ed. Stephen S. Stanton. Englewood Cliffs: Prentice-Hall, 1977. 45–60.

Connell, Bob. "Masculinity, Violence, and War." *Men's Lives*. 2nd ed. Eds. Michael S. Kimmel and Michael A. Messner. New York: Macmillan, 1992, 176–183.

Driggs, John H., and Stephen E. Finn. *Intimacy Between Men*. New York: Plume, 1991.

Duberman, Martin. " Writhing Bedfellows in Antebellum South Carolina: Historical Interpretation and the Politics of Evidence." *Hidden From History: Reclaiming the Gay and Lesbian Past*. Eds. Martin Duberman, Martha Vicinus, and George Chauncey, Jr. New York: Meridian, 1989. 153–168.

Dynes, Wayne R., and Stephen Donaldson. "Introduction." *Homosexual Themes in Literary Studies*. Eds. Wayne R. Dynes and Stephen Donaldson. New York: Garland, 1992. vii–xvii.

Edelman, Lee. "Tearooms and Sympathy, or, The Epistemology of the Water Closet." *The Lesbian and Gay Studies Reader*. Eds. Henry Abelove, Michele Aina Barale, and David M. Halperin. New York: Routledge, 1993. 553–574.

Flannigan-Saint-Aubin, Arthur. "The Male Body and Literary Metaphors for Masculinity." *Theorizing Masculinities*. Eds. Harry Brod and Michael Kaufman. Thousand Oaks, CA: Sage, 1994. 239–258.

Foucault, Michel. *The History of Sexuality, Volume One: An Introduction*. London: Penguin, 1990.

Griffin, Alice. *"Cat on a Hot Tin Roof."* *Modern Critical Interpretations: Tennessee Williams's Cat on a Hot Tin Roof.* Ed. Harold Bloom. New York: Chelsea House, 2002. 105–119.

Grzesiak, Rich. *What Did You Do in the War, Daddy?: An Interview with the Author of The Boy Who Picked the Bullets Up and Its Sequel, Panthers in the Skins of Men*. 1989. 1 March 2001 <http://members.aol.com/richg/nelson.html>.

Guerin, Wilfred L., et al. *A Handbook of Critical Approaches to Literature*. 2nd ed. New York: Harper & Row, 1979.

Hall, Clarence B., and Clyde T. Wood. *The South*. New York: Scribner, 1995.

Harris, Laurilyn J. "Perceptual Conflict and Perversion of Creativity in *A Streetcar Named Desire*." *Confronting Tennessee Williams's A Streetcar Named Desire: Essays in Critical Pluralism*. Ed. Philip C. Kolin. Westport, CT: Greenwood, 1993. 83–103.

Hogan, Michael. "Man to Man: Homosocial Desire in Reynolds Price s Short Fiction." *South Atlantic Review* 62 (1997): 56–73.

Houston, Neal B. "Meaning by Analogy in *Suddenly Last Summer*." *Notes on Modern American Literature* 4 (1980): 1–3.

Humphries, Jefferson. Introduction. "On the Inevitability of Theory in Southern Literary Study." *Southern Literature and Literary Theory*. Ed. Jefferson Humphries. Athens: U of Georgia P, 1990. vii–xvii.

Humphreys, Laud. "Tearoom Trade: Homosexual Behavior in Public Restrooms." *Constructions of Deviance: Social Power, Context, and Interaction*. Eds. Patricia A. Adler and Peter Adler. Belmont, CA: Wadsworth Publishing, 1994. 431–446.

Hurley, Paul J. "*Suddenly Last Summer* as Morality Play. " *Modern Drama* 8 (1966): 392–402.

Irigaray, Luce ."Commodities Among Themselves." *This Sex Which Is Not One*. Trans. Catherine Porter. Ithaca: Cornell UP, 1985. 192–197.

Jones, Robert Emmet. "Sexual Roles in the Works of Tennessee Williams." *Tennessee Williams: A Tribute.* Ed. Jac Tharpe. Jackson: UP of Mississippi, 1977. 545–557.

Kernan, Alvin B. "Truth and Dramatic Mode in *A Streetcar Named Desire.*" *Modern Critical Interpretations: Tennessee Williams's A Streetcar Named Desire*. Ed. Harold Bloom. New York: Chelsea House, 1988. 17–19.

Kimmel, Michael S., and Michael A. Messner, eds. *Men's Lives*. 2nd ed. New York: Macmillan, 1992.

Kimmel, Michael S. "Masculinity as Homophobia: Fear, Shame, and Silence in the Construction of Gender Identity." *Theorizing Masculinities*. Eds. Harry Brod and Michael Kaufman. Thousand Oaks, CA: Sage, 1994. 119–141.

King, Kimball. "Tennessee Williams: A Southern Writer." *Mississippi Quarterly* 48 (1995): 627–648.

Kleinberg, Seymour. "The New Masculinity of Gay Men, and Beyond." *Men's Lives*. 2nd ed. Eds. Michael S. Kimmel and Michael A. Messner. New York: Macmillan, 1992. 80–94.

Kolin, Philip C. "Reflections on/of *A Streetcar Named Desire*." *Confronting Tennessee Williams's A Streetcar Named Desire: Essays in Critical Pluralism*. Ed. Philip C. Kolin. Westport, CT: Greenwood, 1993. 1–17.

Koprince, Susan. "Tennessee Williams s Unseen Characters." *Modern Critical Interpretations: Tennessee Williams's Cat on a Hot Tin Roof*. Ed. Harold Bloom. New York: Chelsea House, 2002. 73–82.

Kreyling, Michael. "Men without Women: Communities of Desire and Race in *A Great Circle*." *Critical Essays on Reynolds Price*. Ed. James A. Schiff. New York: G.K. Hall, 1998. 279–301.

Kushner, Tony. *Angels in America: A Gay Fantasia on National Themes, Part One: Millennium Approaches*. New York: Theatre Communications Group, 1993.

Lehman, Peter. *Running Scared: Masculinity and the Representation of the Male Body*. Philadelphia: Temple UP, 1993.

Lehne, Gregory K. "Homophobia Among Men: Supporting and Defining the Male Role." *Men's Lives*. 2nd ed. Eds. Michael S. Kimmel and Michael A. Messner. New York: Macmillan, 1992. 381–394.

Levy, Charles J. "ARVN as Faggots: Inverted Warfare in Vietnam." *Men's Lives*. 2nd ed. Eds. Michael S. Kimmel and Michael A. Messner. New York: Macmillan, 1992. 183–197.

Lyman, Peter. "The Fraternal Bond as a Joking Relationship: A Case Study of the Role of Sexist Jokes in Male Group Bonding." *Men's Lives*. 2nd ed. Eds. Michael S. Kimmel and Michael A. Messner. New York: Macmillan, 1992. 143–154.

May, Charles E. "Brick Pollitt as Homo Ludens: Three Players of a Summer Game and *Cat on a Hot Tin Roof*." *Tennessee Williams: A Tribute*. Ed. Jac Tharpe. Jackson: UP of Mississippi, 1977. 277–291.

May, Herbert G., and Bruce M. Metzger, eds. *The New Oxford Annotated Bible with the Apocrypha: Revised Standard Edition*. New York: Oxford UP, 1977.

McMichael, George, ed. *Concise Anthology of American Literature*. 2nd ed. Tennessee Williams. "*The Glass Menagerie*." New York: McMillan, 1985. 1842–1886.

Melville, Herman. *Moby-Dick*. Eds. Harrison Hayford and Hershel Parker. New York: W.W. Norton, 1967.

Middleton, Peter. *The Inward Gaze: Masculinity and Subjectivity in Modern Culture*. New York: Routledge, 1992.

Moon, Michael. *A Small Boy and Others: Imitation and Initiation in American Culture from Henry James to Andy Warhol*. Durham: Duke UP, 1998.

Morgan, David H. J. "Theater of War: Combat, the Military, and Masculinities." *Theorizing Masculinities*. Eds. Harry Brod and Michael Kaufman. Thousand Oaks, CA: Sage, 1994. 165–182.

Nardin, James T. "What Tennessee Williams Didn t Write." *Essays in Honor of Esmond Linworth Marilla*. Eds. Thomas Austin Kirby and William John Olive. Baton Rouge: Louisiana State UP, 1970. 331–341.

Oates, Joyce Carol. "Portrait of the Artist as Son, Lover, Elegist." *New York Times Book Review* (26 April 1981): 30.

Philips, Gene D., S.J. "*A Streetcar Named Desire*: Play and Film." *Confronting Tennessee Williams's A Streetcar Named Desire: Essays in Critical Pluralism*. Ed. Philip C. Kolin. Westport, CT: Greenwood, 1993. 223–235.

Pittman, Frank, M.D. *Man Enough: Fathers, Sons, and the Search for Masculinity*. New York: Perigee, 1993.

Price, Marian. "*Cat on a Hot Tin Roof*: The Uneasy Marriage of Success and Idealism." *Modern Critical Interpretations: Tennessee Williams's Cat on a Hot Tin Roof*. Ed. Harold Bloom. New York: Chelsea House, 2002. 93–104.

Price, Reynolds. *A Serious Way of Wondering: The Ethics of Jesus Imagined*. New York: Scribner, 2003.

———. "A Single Meaning: Notes on the Origins and Life of Narrative." *A Common Room: Essays 1954–1987*. New York: Atheneum, 1989. 243–272.

Pronger, Brian. *The Arena of Masculinity: Sports, Homosexuality, and the Meaning of Sex*. New York: St. Martin s, 1990.

Quirino, Leonard. "The Cards Indicate a Voyage on *A Streetcar Named Desire*." *Modern Critical Interpretations: Tennessee Williams's A Streetcar Named Desire*. Ed. Harold Bloom. New York: Chelsea House, 1988. 61–77.

Ramakers, Micha. *Dirty Pictures: Tom of Finland, Masculinity, and Homosexuality*. New York: St. Martin s, 2000.

Richardson, Thomas J. "The City of Day and the City of Night: New Orleans and the Exotic Unreality of Tennessee Williams." *Tennessee Williams: A Tribute*. Ed. Jac Tharpe. Jackson: UP of Mississippi, 1977. 631–646.

Riddel, Joseph N. "*A Streetcar Named Desire*—Nietzsche Descending." *Modern Critical Interpretations: Tennessee Williams's A Streetcar Named Desire*. Ed. Harold Bloom. New York: Chelsea House, 1988. 21–31.

Rooke, Constance. *Reynolds Price*. Boston: Twayne, 1983.

Savran, David. *Communists, Cowboys, and Queers: The Politics of Masculinity in the Work of Arthur Miller and Tennessee Williams*. Minneapolis: U of Minnesota P, 1992.

Schevy, Henry I. "Madonna at the Poker Night: Pictorial Elements in Tennessee Williams s *A Streetcar Named Desire*." *Modern Critical Interpretations: Tennessee Williams's A Streetcar Named Desire*. Ed. Harold Bloom. New York: Chelsea House, 1988. 103–109.

Schiff, James A. *Understanding Reynolds Price*. Columbia: U of South Carolina P, 1996.

———. Introduction. *Critical Essays on Reynolds Price*. Ed. James A. Schiff. New York: G.K. Hall, 1998. 1–28.

———. "Fathers and Sons in the Fiction of Reynolds Price: A Sense of Crucial Ambiguity." *Critical Essays on Reynolds Price*. Ed. James A. Schiff. New York: G. K. Hall, 1998. 261–277.

Sedgwick, Eve Kosofsky. *Between Men: English Literature and Male Homosocial Desire*. New York: Columbia UP, 1985.

Shackelford, Dean. "The Truth Must Be Told: Gay Subjectivity, Homophobia, and Social History in *Cat on a Hot Tin Roof*." *Tennessee Williams Annual Review*. Murfreesboro, TN, 1998. 103–118.

Shilts, Randy. *Conduct Unbecoming: Gays and Lesbians in the U.S. Military*. New York: Fawcett Columbine, 1994.

Signorile, Michelangelo. *Life Outside: The Signorile Report on Gay Men: Sex, Drugs, Muscles, and the Passages of Life*. New York: Harper Collins, 1997.

Simpson, Mark. *Male Impersonators: Men Performing Masculinity*. London: Cassell, 1994.

Sinfield, Alan. *Cultural Politics—Queer Reading*. Philadelphia: U of Pennsylvania P, 1994.

Skir, Leo. *Grunts: A Theater Review*. 21 April 1997. 7 Sept. 2004 <http://gaytoday.badpuppy.com/garchive/entertain/042197en.htm>.

Smith, Barbara. "African American Lesbian and Gay History: An Exploration." *Queer Ideas: The David R. Kessler Lectures in Lesbian and Gay Studies*. New York: The Feminist Press at CUNY, 2003. 51–61.

Sofer, Andrew. "Self-Consuming Artifacts: Power, Performance and the Body in Tennessee Williams *Suddenly Last Summer*." *Modern Drama* 38 (1995): 336–347.

Tharpe, Jac., ed. *Tennessee Williams: A Tribute*. Jackson: UP of Mississippi, 1977.

Thompson, Judith J. *Tennessee Williams' Plays: Memory, Myth, and Symbol*. Rev. ed. New York: Peter Lang, 2002.

Van Laan, Thomas F. " Shut Up! Be Quiet Hush! : Talk and Its Suppression in Three Plays by Tennessee Williams." *Comparative Drama* 22 (1988): 244–265.

Vorlicky, Robert. *Act Like a Man: Challenging Masculinities in American Drama*. Ann Arbor: U of Michigan P, 1995.

Wilson, Ann. "The Politics of Sexual Ambiguity in *Sweet Bird of Youth*." *Tennessee Williams: A Casebook*. Ed. Robert Gross. New York: Routledge, 2002. 79–90.

Winchell, Mark Royden. "Come Back to the Locker Room Ag in, Brick Honey!" *Modern Critical Interpretations: Tennessee Williams's Cat on a Hot Tin Roof*. Ed. Harold Bloom. New York: Chelsea House, 2002. 83–92.

Zeeland, Steven. *The Masculine Marine: Homoeroticism in the U.S. Marine Corps*. New York: Harrington Park Press, 1996.

———. *Military Trade*. New York: Harrington Park Press, 1999.